Mastering Docker

Second Edition

Master this widely used containerization tool

Russ McKendrick
Scott Gallagher

BIRMINGHAM - MUMBAI

Mastering Docker

Second Edition

First published: December 2015

Second edition: July 2017

Production reference: 1200717

Published by Packt Publishing Ltd.
Livery Place
35 Livery Street
Birmingham
B3 2PB, UK.

ISBN 978-1-78728-024-3

www.packtpub.com

Credits

Authors
Russ McKendrick
Scott Gallagher

Reviewers
Srdjan Grubor
Christopher Janietz

Acquisition Editor
Prateek Bharadwaj

Content Development Editor
Sharon Raj

Technical Editor
Prashant Chaudhari

Copy Editor
Madhusudan Uchil

Project Coordinator
Virginia Dias

Proofreader
Safis Editing

Indexer
Mariammal Chettiyar

Graphics
Kirk D'Penha

Production Coordinator
Aparna Bhagat

About the Authors

Russ McKendrick is an experienced solutions architect who has been working in IT and related industries for the better part of 25 years. During his career, he has had varied responsibilities in many different sectors, ranging from looking after an entire IT infrastructure to providing first-line, second-line, and senior support in both client-facing and internal teams for small and large organizations.

Russ works almost exclusively with Linux, using open source systems and tools across both dedicated hardware and virtual machines hosted in public and private clouds at Node4 Limited, where he heads up the Open Source Solutions team.

In his spare time, he has written four books on Docker: *Monitoring Docker*, *Extending Docker*, and *Docker Bootcamp*, which are all available now from Packt, as well as contributing to *Monitoring and Management With Docker and Containers*, which was published by The New Stack.

He also buys way too many vinyl records.

I would like to thank my family and friends for their support and being so understanding about all of the time I have spent in front of the computer, writing. I would also like to thank my colleagues at Node4 and also our customers for their kind words of support and encouragement throughout the writing process.

Scott Gallagher has been fascinated with technology since he played Oregon Trail in elementary school. His love for it continued through middle school as he worked on more Apple IIe computers. In high school, he learned how to build computers and program in BASIC. His college years were all about server technologies such as Novell, Microsoft, and Red Hat. After college, he continued to work on Novell, all the while maintaining an interest in all technologies. He then moved on to manage Microsoft environments and, eventually, what he was most passionate about: Linux environments. Now, his focus is on Docker and cloud environments.

I would like to thank my family for their support not only while I worked on this book, but throughout my life and career. A special thank you goes to my wife, who is my soul mate, the love of my life, the most important person in my life, and the reason I push myself to be the best I can be each day. I would also like to thank my kids, who are the most amazing thing in this world; I truly am blessed to be able to watch them grow each day. And lastly, I want to thank my parents, who helped me become the person I am today.

About the Reviewers

Srdjan Grubor is a software engineer who has worked on projects small and big, spanning in complexity from a single-line script to two complete Linux distributions. Nowadays, among other things, he is developing a distributed PaaS system for Endless OS, based on Docker, that will provide people in remote places the full power of the internet through knowledge aggregation and asynchronous caching. He enjoys breaking things just to see how they work--tinkering and solving challenging problems. He believes that there is always room for philanthropy in technology.

Christopher Janietz is what is nowadays is called a DevOp, combining practices from the world of development and IT operations. He works for MediaMarktSaturn, Europe's largest consumer electronics retailer. Furthermore, he is a content creator for LinkedIn Germany, where he provides video training for programming as well as infrastructure automation. In his spare time, he likes to cram science papers and learn about new technologies every day.

I personally would like to thank my colleagues and friends Andreas Gero and Emanuel Kechter, two well-respected masters in the Docker universe.

www.PacktPub.com

For support files and downloads related to your book, please visit www.PacktPub.com.

Did you know that Packt offers eBook versions of every book published, with PDF and ePub files available? You can upgrade to the eBook version at www.PacktPub.com and as a print book customer, you are entitled to a discount on the eBook copy. Get in touch with us at service@packtpub.com for more details.

At www.PacktPub.com, you can also read a collection of free technical articles, sign up for a range of free newsletters and receive exclusive discounts and offers on Packt books and eBooks.

https://www.packtpub.com/mapt

Get the most in-demand software skills with Mapt. Mapt gives you full access to all Packt books and video courses, as well as industry-leading tools to help you plan your personal development and advance your career.

Why subscribe?

- Fully searchable across every book published by Packt
- Copy and paste, print, and bookmark content
- On demand and accessible via a web browser

Customer Feedback

Thanks for purchasing this Packt book. At Packt, quality is at the heart of our editorial process. To help us improve, please leave us an honest review on this book's Amazon page at http://www.amazon.in/dp/1787280241.

If you'd like to join our team of regular reviewers, you can email us at customerreviews@packtpub.com. We award our regular reviewers with free eBooks and videos in exchange for their valuable feedback. Help us be relentless in improving our products!

Table of Contents

Preface

Docker has been a game changer when it comes to how modern applications are deployed and architecture--it has now grown into a key driver of innovation beyond system administration, having an impact on the world of web development and more. However, how can you make sure you're keeping up with the innovations that it's driving? How can you be sure you're using it to its full potential?

This book shows you how; it not only demonstrates how to use Docker more effectively, it also helps you rethink and reimagine what's possible with Docker.

You will also cover basic topics, such as building, managing, and storing images, along with best practices to make you confident, before delving deeper into Docker security. You'll find everything related to extending and integrating Docker in new and innovative ways. Docker Swarm and Docker Compose will help you take control of your containers in an efficient way.

By the end of this book, you'll have a broad and detailed sense of exactly what's possible with Docker and how seamlessly it fits in with a range of other platforms and tools:

- Become fluent with the basic components and concepts of Docker
- Secure your containers and files with Docker's security features
- Extend Docker and solve architectural using first, and third-party orchestration tools, service discovery, and plugins
- Leverage the Linux container virtualization paradigm by creating highly scalable applications

What this book covers

Chapter 1, *Docker Overview*, covers the basics of Docker to give you a refresher so the following chapters don't feel so heavy.

Chapter 2, *Building Container Images*, teaches you how to create your own base image. We will cover creating an application in the image, as well as other advanced aspects of creating your own image.

Chapter 3, *Storing and Distributing Images*, discusses the places you store your images in, such as the Docker Hub and a locally hosted registry. We will also look at third-party offerings, such as Quay and the Amazon EC2 Container Registry.

Chapter 4, *Managing Containers*, teaches you how to manage your containers and the different ways you can go about doing so. This chapter will focus on the command line.

Chapter 5, *Docker Machine*, explains how to use the Docker Machine setup, new Docker hosts, and be able to have those containers created locally in places such as virtual boxes, and cloud providers, such as Amazon Web Services and DigitalOcean.

Chapter 6, *Docker Compose*, makes it incredibly easy to hand off docker environments to your developers and ensure that the configuration is exactly how you want it to be set or exactly how you have it set up on production systems to mimic.

Chapter 7, *Docker Swarm*, allows you to link Docker containers together across multiple servers. This allows for easier management as well as a better availability and interoperability between containers.

Chapter 8, *Portainer*, allows you to easily manage and control aspects of your configuration with Portainer, which is a web-based GUI for your Docker environment. You can launch containers, remove container, manage hosts that are running your containers, and get that overall view of your environment to see how it is performing.

Chapter 9, *Rancher*, allows you to launch various cluster hosts and then manage your Docker hosts and containers.

Chapter 10, *Docker Cloud*, uses a web browser to manage your Docker environment. This product is different, however, as it is a hosted service by Docker that takes some of the heavy lifting out of the setup process.

Chapter 11, *Docker Security*, focuses heavily on Docker security. After all, that's one of the most important aspects of any server, or container, in this case. We will cover the good, the not so bad, and what to look out for with regards to security. There is also a new Docker security checking configuration tool you can use to check against your containers or other containers you may use.

Chapter 12, *Docker Workflows*, brings everything you learned, which you will put to use by learning how to put Docker containers into production. It will also teach you how to monitor your containers and talk about the safeguards you can put into place to help with container recovery. We will look at how to extend to external platforms, such as Kubernetes and Amazon ECS.

Chapter 13, *Next Steps with Docker*, looks at how your applications can run better in a containerized environment by discussing discovery services. We will also look at where Docker is going, and how you can contribute to its future as well as the community.

What you need for this book

You will have to install and configure Docker 17.03 (CE) on the following platforms:

- Windows 10 Professional
- macOS Sierra
- Ubuntu 16.04 LTS desktop

Also, you should have access to a public cloud platform, such as DigitalOcean or Amazon Web Services.

Who this book is for

This book is for developers, system administrators, and engineers who want guidance on where their journey using Docker should go next. You should already have a basic understanding of Docker, even though we will be offering a quick refresher at the start of the book to bring new readers up-to-speed with the subject.

Conventions

In this book, you will find a number of text styles that distinguish between different kinds of information. Here are some examples of these styles and an explanation of their meaning. Code words in text, database table names, folder names, filenames, file extensions, pathnames, dummy URLs, user input, and Twitter handles are shown as follows: "The next lines of code read the link and assign it to the to the BeautifulSoup function." A block of code is set as follows:

```
events {
    worker_connections 1024;
}
```

When we wish to draw your attention to a particular part of a code block, the relevant lines or items are set in bold:

```
events {
  worker_connections 1024;
  }
```

Any command-line input or output is written as follows:

```
$ curl -sSL https://get.docker.com/ | sh
$ sudo systemctl start docker
```

New terms and **important words** are shown in bold. Words that you see on the screen, for example, in menus or dialog boxes, appear in the text like this: "In order to download new modules, we will go to **Files** | **Settings** | **Project Name** | **Project Interpreter**."

Warnings or important notes appear like this.

Tips and tricks appear like this.

Reader feedback

Feedback from our readers is always welcome. Let us know what you think about this book-what you liked or disliked. Reader feedback is important for us as it helps us develop titles that you will really get the most out of. To send us general feedback, simply e-mail feedback@packtpub.com, and mention the book's title in the subject of your message. If there is a topic that you have expertise in and you are interested in either writing or contributing to a book, see our author guide at www.packtpub.com/authors.

Customer support

Now that you are the proud owner of a Packt book, we have a number of things to help you to get the most from your purchase.

Downloading the example code

You can download the example code files for this book from your account at `http://www.p acktpub.com`. If you purchased this book elsewhere, you can visit `http://www.packtpub.c om/support` and register to have the files e-mailed directly to you. You can download the code files by following these steps:

1. Log in or register to our website using your e-mail address and password.
2. Hover the mouse pointer on the **SUPPORT** tab at the top.
3. Click on **Code Downloads & Errata**.
4. Enter the name of the book in the **Search** box.
5. Select the book for which you're looking to download the code files.
6. Choose from the drop-down menu where you purchased this book from.
7. Click on **Code Download**.

Once the file is downloaded, please make sure that you unzip or extract the folder using the latest version of:

- WinRAR / 7-Zip for Windows
- Zipeg / iZip / UnRarX for Mac
- 7-Zip / PeaZip for Linux

The code bundle for the book is also hosted on GitHub at `https://github.com/PacktPubl ishing/Mastering-Docker-Second-Edition`. We also have other code bundles from our rich catalog of books and videos available at `https://github.com/PacktPublishing/`. Check them out!

Downloading the color images of this book

We also provide you with a PDF file that has color images of the screenshots/diagrams used in this book. The color images will help you better understand the changes in the output. You can download this file from `https://www.packtpub.com/sites/default/files/down loads/MasteringDockerSecondEdition_ColorImages.pdf`.

Errata

Although we have taken every care to ensure the accuracy of our content, mistakes do happen. If you find a mistake in one of our books-maybe a mistake in the text or the code-we would be grateful if you could report this to us. By doing so, you can save other readers from frustration and help us improve subsequent versions of this book.

If you find any errata, please report them by visiting http://www.packtpub.com/submit-errata, selecting your book, clicking on the **Errata Submission Form** link, and entering the details of your errata. Once your errata are verified, your submission will be accepted and the errata will be uploaded to our website or added to any list of existing errata under the Errata section of that title.

To view the previously submitted errata, go to https://www.packtpub.com/books/content/support and enter the name of the book in the search field. The required information will appear under the **Errata** section.

Piracy

Piracy of copyrighted material on the Internet is an ongoing problem across all media. At Packt, we take the protection of our copyright and licenses very seriously. If you come across any illegal copies of our works in any form on the Internet, please provide us with the location address or website name immediately so that we can pursue a remedy.

Please contact us at copyright@packtpub.com with a link to the suspected pirated material. We appreciate your help in protecting our authors and our ability to bring you valuable content.

Questions

If you have a problem with any aspect of this book, you can contact us at questions@packtpub.com, and we will do our best to address the problem.

1
Docker Overview

Welcome to *Mastering Docker, Second Edition* This first chapter will cover the Docker basics that you should already have a pretty good handle on. But if you don't already have the required knowledge at this point, this chapter will help you with the basics so that subsequent chapters don't feel as heavy. By the end of the book, you should be a Docker master, able to implement Docker in your own environments, building and supporting applications on top of them.

In this chapter, we're going to review the following high-level topics:

- Understanding Docker
- Differences between Docker and typical VMs
- Docker installers/installation
- The Docker command
- The Docker ecosystem

Understanding Docker

Let's start by trying to define what Docker is. Docker's website currently sums Docker up with the following statement:

> *"Docker is the world's leading software container platform. Developers use Docker to eliminate "works on my machine" problems when collaborating on code with co-workers. Operators use Docker to run and manage apps side-by-side in isolated containers to get better compute density. Enterprises use Docker to build agile software delivery pipelines to ship new features faster, more securely and with confidence for both Linux and Windows Server apps."*

That is a pretty bold opening statement, however when you look at the figures presented by then Docker CEO *Ben Golub* during the opening of the 2017 DockerCon, which were:

- 14M Docker Hosts
- 900K Docker Apps
- 77K% Growth in Docker job listings
- 12B Images pulls
- 3300 Project Contributors

For a technology which is only three years old, I am sure you will agree that is quite impressive. To view the opening please see `https://www.slideshare.net/Docker/docker con-2017-general-session-day-1-ben-golub`.

Let's begin getting an understanding of the problems that Docker aims to solve, starting with developers.

Developers

The "works on my machine" problem is probably summed up best by the following image macro, based on the Disaster Girl meme, which started popping up in presentations, forums, and Slack channels a few years ago:

While it is funny, unfortunately it is an all-too-real problem and one I have personally been on the receiving end of.

The problem

Even in a world where DevOps best practices are followed, it is still all too easy for a developer's working environment to not match the final production environment.

For example, a developer using the macOS version of, say, PHP will probably not be running the same version as the Linux server that hosts the production code. Even if the versions match, you then have to deal with differences in the configuration and overall environment the version of PHP is running on, such as differences in the way file permissions are handled between the operating system versions, to name just one potential problem.

All of this comes to head when it is time for a developer to deploy their code to the host and it doesn't work; should the production environment be configured to match the developer's machine, or should developers only do their work in environments that match productions?

In an ideal world, everything should be consistent, from the developer's laptop all the way through to your production servers; however, traditionally this utopia has been difficult to achieve. Everyone has their own way of working and personal preferences--enforcing consistency across multiple platforms is difficult enough when it is a single engineer working on their own systems, let alone a team of engineers working with a team of potentially hundreds of developers.

The Docker solution

Using Docker for Mac or Docker for Windows, a developer can easily wrap their code in a container that they have either defined themselves or worked alongside operations to create as a Dockerfile--we will be covering this in Chapter 2, *Building Container Images*--or a Docker Compose file, which we will go into more detail about in Chapter 5, *Docker Compose*.

They can continue to use their chosen IDE and maintain their own workflows for working with the code. As we will see in the upcoming sections of this chapter, installing and using Docker is not difficult; in fact, considering how much of a chore it was to maintain consistent environments in the past, even with automation, Docker feels a little too easy, almost like cheating.

Operators

I have been working in operations for more years than I would like to admit to, and this problem has cropped regularly.

The problem

Let's say you are looking after five servers: three load-balanced web servers and two database servers that are in a master or slave configuration running Application 1. You are using a tool such as Puppet or Chef to automatically manage the software stack and the configuration across your five servers.

Everything is going great until you are told "we need to deploy Application 2 on the same servers that are running Application 1." On the face of it, no problem, you can tweak your Puppet or Chef configuration to add new users, vhosts, pull the new code down, and so on. However, you notice that Application 2 requires a higher version of the software you are running for Application 1.

To make matters worse, you already know that Application 1 flat-out refuses to work with the new software stack and that Application 2 is not backward compatible.

Traditionally, this leaves you with a few choices, all of which just add to the problem one way or another:

1. Ask for more servers? While this traditionally is probably the safest technical solution, it does not automatically mean that there will be the budget for additional resources.
2. Re-architect the solution? Taking one of the web and database servers out of the load-balancer or replication and redeploying them with the software stack for Application 2 may seem like the next easiest option from a technical point of view. However, you are introducing single points of failure for Application 2 and also reducing the redundancy for Application 1: there was probably a reason why you were running three web and two database servers.
3. Attempt to install the new software stack side by side on your servers? Well, this certainly is possible and may seem like a good short-term plan to get the project out of the door, but it could leave you with a house of cards that could come tumbling down when the first critical security patch is needed for either software stack.

The Docker solution

This is where Docker starts to come into its own. If you have Application 1 running across your three web servers in containers, you may actually be running more than three containers; in fact, you could already be running six, doubling up on the containers, allowing you to run rolling deployments of your application without reducing the availability of Application 1.

Deploying Application 2 in this environment is as easy as simply launching more containers across your three hosts and then routing to the newly deployed application using your load balancer. As you are just deploying containers, you do not need to worry about the logistics of deploying, configuring, and managing two versions of the same software stack on the same server.

We will work through an example of this exact scenario in *Chapter 6, Docker Compose*.

Enterprise

Enterprises suffer from the same problems described previously as they have both developers and operators; however, they have them on a much larger scale and also there is a lot more risk involved.

The problem

Because of this risk and that any downtime could cost sales or reputation, enterprises need to test every deployment before it is released. This means that new features and fixes are stuck in a holding pattern while:

- Test environments are spun up and configured
- Applications are deployed across the newly launched environments
- Test plans are executed and the application and configuration are tweaked until the tests pass
- Requests for change are written, submitted, and discussed to get the updated application deployed to production

This process can take anywhere from a few days to weeks or even months, depending on the complexity of the application and the risk the change introduces. While the process is required to ensure continuity and availability for the enterprise at a technology level, it does potentially introduce risk at the business level. What if you have a new feature stuck in this holding pattern and a competitor releases a similar, or worse still, the same feature ahead of you?

This scenario could be just as damaging to sales and reputation as the downtime that the process has been put in place to protect you against.

The Docker solution

Let me start by saying that Docker does not remove the need for a process such as the one just described to exist or be followed. However, as we have already touched upon, it does make things a lot easier as you are already working in a consistent way. It means that your developers have been working with the exact same container configuration that is running in production. This means that it is not much of a step for the methodology to be applied to your testing.

For example, when a developer checks in their code that they know works on their local development environment (as that is where they have been doing all of their work) your testing tool can launch the same containers to run your automated tests against. Once the containers have been used, they can be removed to free up resources for the next lot of tests. This means that all of a sudden your testing process and procedures are a lot more flexible and you can continue to reuse the same environment rather than redeploy or reimage servers for the next set of testing.

This streamlining of the process can be taken as far having your new application containers push all the way through to production.

The quicker this process can be completed, the quicker you can confidently launch new features or fixes and keep ahead of the curve.

Differences between dedicated hosts, virtual machines, and Docker

We know what problems Docker was developed to solve. We need to now discuss what exactly Docker is and does.

Docker is a container-management system that helps us easily manage **Linux Containers (LXC)** in an easier and universal fashion. This lets you create images in virtual environments on your laptop and run commands against them. The actions you perform to the containers that you run in these environments locally on your own machine will be the same commands or operations you run against them when they are running in your production environment.

This helps in not having to do things differently when you go from a development environment like the one on your local machine to a production environment on your server. Now, let's take a look at the differences between Docker containers and typical virtual machine environments.

The following illustration demonstrates the difference between a dedicated, bare-metal server and a server running virtual machines:

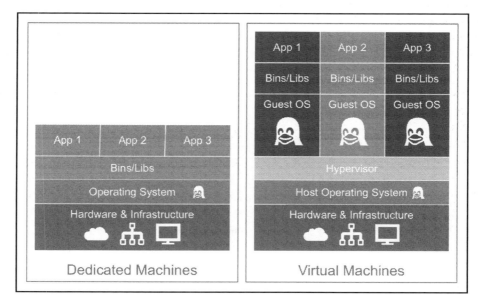

As you can see, for a dedicated machine we have three applications, all sharing the same orange software stack. Running virtual machines allow us to run three applications, running two completely different software stacks. The following illustration shows the same orange and green applications running in containers using Docker:

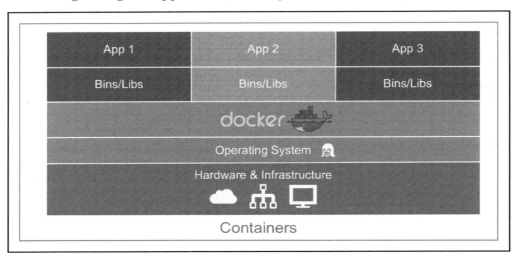

This illustration gives us a lot of insight into the biggest key benefit of Docker, that is, there is no need for a complete operating system every time we need to bring up a new container, which cuts down on the overall size of containers. Docker relies on using the host OS's Linux kernel (since almost all the versions of Linux use the standard kernel models) for the OS it was built upon, such as Red Hat, CentOS, and Ubuntu. For this reason, you can have almost any Linux OS as your host operating system and be able to layer other Linux-based operating systems on top of the host. Well, that is, your applications are led to believe a full operating system is never actually installed--just the binaries, such as a package manager and, for example, Apache/PHP and libraries needed to get just enough of an operating system for your applications to run.

For example, in the earlier illustration, we could have Red Hat running for the orange application and Debian running for the green application, but there would never be a need to actually install Red Hat or Debian on the host. Thus, another benefit of Docker is the size of images when they are created. They are built without the largest piece: the kernel or the operating system. This makes them incredibly small, compact, and easy to ship.

Docker installers/installation

Installers are one of the first pieces you need to get up and running with Docker on both your local machine as well as your server environments. Let's first take a look at what environments you can install Docker in:

- Linux (various Linux flavors)
- Apple macOS
- Windows 10 Professional

In addition, you can run them on public clouds such as Amazon Web Services, Microsoft Azure, and DigitalOcean to name a few. With the various types of installers listed earlier, there are different ways Docker actually operates on the operating system. Docker natively runs on Linux; so if you are using Linux, then it's pretty straightforward how Docker runs right on your system. However, if you are using macOS or Windows 10, then it operates a little differently since it relies on using Linux.

Let's look at quickly installing Docker on a Linux desktop running Ubuntu 16.04 and then on macOS and Windows 10.

Installing on Linux (Ubuntu 16.04)

As already mentioned, this is the most straightforward installation out of the three systems we will be looking at. To install Docker, simply run the following command from a Terminal session:

```
$ curl -sSL https://get.docker.com/ | sh
$ sudo systemctl start docker
```

These commands will download, install, and configure the latest version of Docker from Docker themselves; at the time of writing this, the Linux OS version installed by the official install script is 17.05.

Running the following command should confirm that Docker is installed and running:

```
$ docker version
```

You should see something similar to the following output:

```
russ@russ-virtual-machine: ~
russ@russ-virtual-machine:~$ docker version
Client:
 Version:      17.05.0-ce
 API version:  1.29
 Go version:   go1.7.5
 Git commit:   89658be
 Built:        Thu May  4 22:10:54 2017
 OS/Arch:      linux/amd64

Server:
 Version:      17.05.0-ce
 API version:  1.29 (minimum version 1.12)
 Go version:   go1.7.5
 Git commit:   89658be
 Built:        Thu May  4 22:10:54 2017
 OS/Arch:      linux/amd64
 Experimental: false
russ@russ-virtual-machine:~$ 
```

There are two supporting tools we are going to be using in future chapters that are installed as part of the Docker for macOS or Windows installers. To ensure that we are ready to use these tools in later chapters, we should install them now. The first tool is Docker Machine; to install this, run the following commands:

 You can check whether you are installing the latest version by visiting the releases section of the project's GitHub page at https://github.com/dock er/machine/releases/. To install a version other than v.0.11.0, simply replace the version number in the following command.

```
$ curl -L
"https://github.com/docker/machine/releases/download/v0.11.0/docker-machine
-$(uname -s)-$(uname -m)" -o /tmp/docker-machine
$ chmod +x /tmp/docker-machine
$ sudo mv /tmp/docker-machine /usr/local/bin/docker-machine
```

The download and install Docker Compose, run the following, again checking you are running the latest version by visiting the releases page at https://github.com/docker/com pose/releases/:

```
$ curl -L
"https://github.com/docker/compose/releases/download/1.13.0/docker-compose-
$(uname -s)-$(uname -m)" -o /usr/local/bin/docker-compose
$ chmod +x /tmp/docker-compose
$ sudo mv /tmp/docker-compose /usr/local/bin/docker-compose
```

Once it's installed, you should be able to run the following two commands:

```
$ docker-compose version
$ docker-machine version
```

Installing on macOS

Unlike the command-line Linux installation, Docker for Mac has a graphical installer.

 Before downloading, you should make sure that you are running Apple macOS Yosemite 10.10.3 or above. If you are running an older version, all is not lost; you can still run Docker. Refer to the other older operating systems section of this chapter.

You can download the installer from the Docker store at `https://store.docker.com/edit ions/community/docker-ce-desktop-mac/`; just click on **Get Docker**. Once it's downloaded, you should have a DMG file. Double-clicking on it will mount the image, and opening the image mounted on your desktop should present you with something like this:

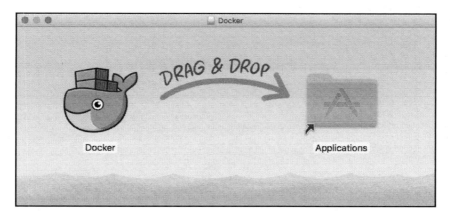

Once you have dragged the Docker icon to your `Applications` folder, double-click on it and you will be asked whether you want to open the application you have downloaded. Saying yes will open the Docker installer:

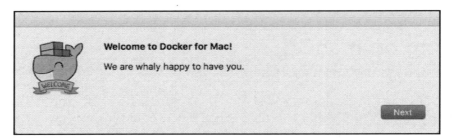

Click on **Next** and follow the on-screen instructions. Once it is installed and started, you should see a Docker icon in the top-left icon bar on your screen. Clicking on the icon and selecting **About Docker** should show you something similar to the following:

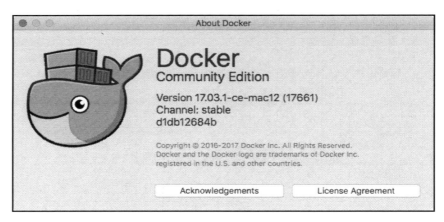

You can also open a Terminal window. Run the following command as we did on the Linux installation:

```
$ docker version
```

You should see something similar to the following Terminal output:

```
                                   1. russ (bash)
⚡ docker version
Client:
 Version:       17.03.1-ce
 API version:   1.27
 Go version:    go1.7.5
 Git commit:    c6d412e
 Built:         Tue Mar 28 00:40:02 2017
 OS/Arch:       darwin/amd64

Server:
 Version:       17.03.1-ce
 API version:   1.27 (minimum version 1.12)
 Go version:    go1.7.5
 Git commit:    c6d412e
 Built:         Fri Mar 24 00:00:50 2017
 OS/Arch:       linux/amd64
 Experimental:  true
russ in ~
⚡
```

You can also run this to check the versions of Docker Compose and Docker Machine that were installed alongside Docker Engine:

```
$ docker-compose version
$ docker-machine version
```

Installing on Windows 10 Professional

Like Docker for Mac, Docker for Windows uses a graphical installer.

Before downloading, you should make sure that you are running Microsoft Windows 10 Professional or Enterprise 64-bit. If you are running an older version or an unsupported edition of Windows 10, you can still run Docker; refer to the other older operating systems section of this chapter for more information.

Docker for Windows has this requirement due to its reliance on Hyper-V. Hyper-V is Windows' native hypervisor and allows you to run x86-64 guests on your Windows machine, be it Windows 10 Professional or Windows Server. It even forms part of the XBox One operating system.

You can download the Docker for Windows installer from the Docker Store at `https://sto re.docker.com/editions/community/docker-ce-desktop-windows/`; just click on the **Get Docker** button to download the installer. Once it's downloaded, run the MSI package and you will be greeted with the following:

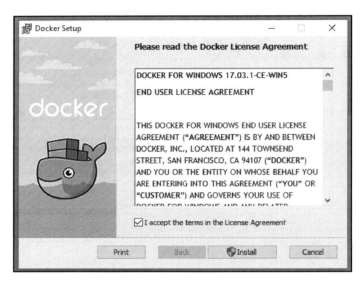

Click on **Install**, and then follow the on screen prompts, which will not only work through installing Docker, but also enabling Hyper-V if you do not have it enabled.

Once it's installed, you should see a Docker icon in the icon tray in the bottom right of your screen. Clicking on it and selecting **About Docker** from the menu will show the following:

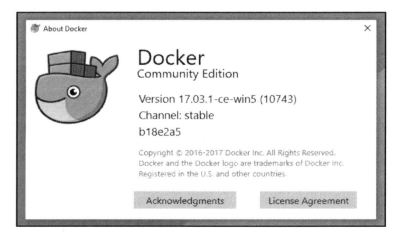

Open a PowerShell window and type the following command:

```
$ docker version
```

This should also show you similar output to the Mac and Linux versions:

```
Windows PowerShell                                                    —  □  ×
PS C:\Users\russm> docker version
Client:
 Version:        17.03.1-ce
 API version:    1.27
 Go version:     go1.7.5
 Git commit:     c6d412e
 Built:          Tue Mar 28 00:40:02 2017
 OS/Arch:        windows/amd64

Server:
 Version:        17.03.1-ce
 API version:    1.27 (minimum version 1.12)
 Go version:     go1.7.5
 Git commit:     c6d412e
 Built:          Fri Mar 24 00:00:50 2017
 OS/Arch:        linux/amd64
 Experimental:   true
PS C:\Users\russm> _
```

Again, you can also run the following:

```
$ docker-compose version
$ docker-machine version
```

Older operating systems

If you are not running a newer operating system on Mac or Windows, then you will need to use Docker Toolbox. You may have noticed that the output from running the following:

```
$ docker version
```

On all three of the installations we have performed so far, it shows two different versions, a client and server. Predictably, the Linux version shows that the architecture for the client and server are both Linux; however, you may notice that the Mac version shows the client is running on Darwin, which is Apple's Unix-like kernel, and the Windows version shows Windows. Yet both of the servers show the architecture as being Linux--what gives?

That is because both the Mac and Windows versions of Docker download and run a virtual machine in the background, and this machine is running a small lightweight operating system based on Alpine Linux. The virtual machine is running using Docker's own libraries, which connect the inbuilt hypervisor for your chosen environment. For macOS, this is the inbuilt Hypervisor Framework (`https://developer.apple.com/reference/hypervisor/`) and for Windows, Hyper-V (`https://www.microsoft.com/en-gb/cloud-platform/server-virtualization`).

To ensure that no one misses out on the Docker experience, a version of Docker that does not use these built-in hypervisors is available for older versions of macOS and unsupported Windows versions. These versions utilize VirtualBox as the hypervisor to run the Linux server for your local client to connect to.

VirtualBox is an open source x86 and AMD64/Intel64 virtualization product developed by Oracle. It runs on Windows, Linux, Macintosh, and Solaris hosts, with support for many Linux, Unix, and Windows guest operating systems. For more information on VirtualBox, see `https://www.virtualbox.org/`.

For more information on Docker Toolbox, see the project's website at `https://www.docker.com/products/docker-toolbox/`, where you can also download the macOS and Windows installers.

This book assumes you have installed the latest Docker version on Linux or have used Docker for Mac or Docker for Windows. While Docker installations using Docker Toolbox should be able to support the commands in this book, you may run into issues around file permissions and ownership when mounting data from your local machine to your containers.

The Docker command-line client

Now that we have Docker installed, let's look at some Docker commands that you should be familiar with already. We will start with some common commands and then take a peek at the commands that are used for the Docker images. We will then take a dive into the commands that are used for the containers.

Docker recently restructured their command-line client into more logical groupings of commands due to the number of features provided by Docker growing quickly and commands starting to cross over each other. Throughout this book, we will be using the new structure. For more information on the command-line client changes, read the following blog post:
https://blog.docker.com/2017/01/whats-new-in-docker-1-13/

The first command we will be taking a look at will be one of the most useful commands not only in Docker but in any command-line utility you use: the `help` command. It is run simply like this:

```
$ docker help
```

This command will give you a full list of all the Docker commands at your disposal and a brief description of what each command does. For further help with a particular command, you can run the following:

```
$ docker <COMMAND> --help
```

Next up, let's run the `hello-world` container. To do this, simply run:

```
$ docker container run hello-world
```

It doesn't matter what host you are running Docker on, the same thing will happen on Linux, macOS, and Windows. Docker will download the `hello-world` container image and then execute it, and once it's executed, the container will be stopped.

Your Terminal session should look like the following:

```
● ● ●                              1. russ (bash)
russ in ~
⚡ docker container run hello-world
Unable to find image 'hello-world:latest' locally
latest: Pulling from library/hello-world
78445dd45222: Pull complete
Digest: sha256:c5515758d4c5e1e838e9cd307f6c6a0d620b5e07e6f927b07d05f6d12a1ac8d7
Status: Downloaded newer image for hello-world:latest

Hello from Docker!
This message shows that your installation appears to be working correctly.

To generate this message, Docker took the following steps:
 1. The Docker client contacted the Docker daemon.
 2. The Docker daemon pulled the "hello-world" image from the Docker Hub.
 3. The Docker daemon created a new container from that image which runs the
    executable that produces the output you are currently reading.
 4. The Docker daemon streamed that output to the Docker client, which sent it
    to your terminal.

To try something more ambitious, you can run an Ubuntu container with:
 $ docker run -it ubuntu bash

Share images, automate workflows, and more with a free Docker ID:
 https://cloud.docker.com/

For more examples and ideas, visit:
 https://docs.docker.com/engine/userguide/

russ in ~
⚡ ▯
```

Let's try something a little more adventurous; let's download and run an NGINX container by running the following two commands:

```
$ docker image pull nginx
$ docker container run -d --name nginx-test -p 8080:80 nginx
```

The first of the two commands downloads the NGINX container image, and the second launches a container in the background called `nginx-test` using the `nginx` image we pulled. It also maps port `8080` on our host machine to port `80` on the container, making it accessible to our local browser at `http://localhost:8080/`.

As you can see from the following screenshots, the command and results are exactly the same on all three OS types. Here we have Linux:

This is macOS:

And this is how it looks on Windows:

In the following three chapters, we will look at using the Docker command-line client in more detail; for now, let's stop and remove our `nginx-test` container by running the following:

```
$ docker container stop nginx-test
$ docker container rm nginx-test
```

The Docker ecosystem

There are a lot of tools supplied and supported by Docker; some we have already mentioned, and others we will cover in later chapters. Before we finish this, our first chapter, we should get an idea of the tools we are going to be using. The most of important of them is **Docker Engine**.

This is the core of Docker, and all of the other tools we will be covering use it. We have already been using it as we installed it in the *Docker installer/installation* and Docker commands sections of this chapter. There are currently two versions of Docker Engine; there is the **Docker Enterprise Edition** (**Docker EE**) and the **Docker Community Edition** (**CE**). We will be using Docker CE throughout this book. The release cycle for Docker Engine has recently changed to become more predictable.

Docker CE and EE have stable editions that are updated once every quarter; as you may have noticed, we have been running Docker CE v17.03.x for our Docker for Mac and Docker for Windows installations. There is an also an Edge version, which introduces features at a quicker pace--every month, in fact. This version may not be suitable for production workloads; as you may have noticed, when we installed Docker on Linux, it was running the Edge version Docker CE 17.05.x.

- **Docker Compose**: A tool that allows you to define and share multi-container definitions; it is detailed in `Chapter 5`, *Docker Compose.*
- **Docker Machine**: A tool to launch Docker hosts on multiple platforms; we will cover this in `Chapter 6`, *Docker Machine.*
- **Docker Hub**: A repository for your Docker images, covered in the next three chapters.
- **Docker Store**: A storefront for official Docker images and plugins as well as licensed products. Again, we will cover this in the next three chapters.
- **Docker Swarm:** A muli-host-aware orchestration tool, covered in detail in `Chapter 7`, *Docker Swarm.*
- **Docker for Mac**: We have covered Docker for Mac in this chapter.
- **Docker Cloud**: Docker's **Container as a Service (CaaS)** offering, covered in detail in `Chapter 10`, *Docker Cloud.*
- **Docker for Windows**: We have covered Docker for Windows in this chapter.
- **Docker for Amazon Web Services:** A best-practice Docker Swarm installation that targets AWS, covered in `Chapter 10`, *Docker Cloud.*
- **Docker for Azure**: A best-practice Docker Swarm installation that targets Azure, covered in `Chapter 10`, *Docker Cloud.*

We will also be looking at some third-party services in later chapters.

Summary

In this chapter, we covered what basic information you should already know (or now know) for the chapters ahead. We went over the basics of what Docker is and how it fares compared to other host types. We went over the installers, how they operate on different operating systems, and how to control them through the command line. Be sure to remember to look at the requirements for the installers to ensure you use the correct one for your operating system.

Then, we took a small dive into the basic Docker commands to get you started. We will be looking at all the management commands in future chapters to get a more in-depth understanding of what they are as well as how and when to use them. Finally, we discussed the Docker ecosystem and the responsibilities of each of the different tools.

In the next chapters, we will be taking a look at how to build base containers, and we will also look in depth at Dockerfiles and places to store your images, as well as using environmental variables and Docker volumes.

2
Building Container Images

I am very glad you decided to flip the page and come to this chapter. Here, we will get you up and running with your own images and use custom environmental variables as well as scripts. Here is a short review of what all we will be covering in this chapter:

- The Dockerfile
- Docker build
- Building a base image using the Dockerfile
- Environmental variables
- Putting it all together

Introducing the Dockerfile

In this section, we will cover the Dockerfile in depth, along with the best practices to use. So what is a Dockerfile? A Dockerfile is simply a plain text file that contains a set of user-defined commands, which when executed by the `docker image build` command--which we will look at next--assemble a container image.

A Dockerfile looks like the following:

```
FROM alpine:latest
LABEL maintainer="Russ McKendrick <russ@mckendrick.io>"
LABEL description="This example Dockerfile installs NGINX."

RUN apk add --update nginx && \
        rm -rf /var/cache/apk/* && \
        mkdir -p /tmp/nginx/

COPY files/nginx.conf /etc/nginx/nginx.conf
COPY files/default.conf /etc/nginx/conf.d/default.conf
```

```
ADD files/html.tar.gz /usr/share/nginx/

EXPOSE 80/tcp

ENTRYPOINT ["nginx"]
CMD ["-g", "daemon off;"]
```

All of the files for this chapter are available from the following GitHub repository: `https://github.com/russmckendrick/mastering-docker/tree/master/chapter02/`

As you can see, even with no explanation, it is quite easy to get an idea of what each step of the Dockerfile is instructing the `build` command to do.

Before we move on to working our way through the previous file, we should quickly touch upon Alpine Linux.

Alpine Linux is a small, independently developed, non-commercial Linux distribution designed for security, efficiency, and ease of use. For more information on Alpine Linux, visit the project's website at `https://www.alpinelinux.org/`.

Alpine Linux, due to both its size and also how powerful it is, has become the default image base for the official container images supplied by Docker. Because of this, we will be using it throughout this book. To give you an idea of just how small the official image for Alpine Linux is, let's compare it to some of the other distributions available at the time of writing:

```
● ● ●                          2. russ (bash)
russ in ~
⚡ docker image ls
REPOSITORY        TAG           IMAGE ID         CREATED          SIZE
debian            latest        a25c1eed1c6f     2 days ago       123 MB
centos            latest        3bee3060bfc8     4 days ago       193 MB
ubuntu            latest        7b9b13f7b9c0     7 days ago       118 MB
alpine            latest        a41a7446062d     2 weeks ago      3.97 MB
fedora            latest        15895ef0b3b2     7 weeks ago      231 MB
russ in ~
⚡
```

As you can see from the Terminal output, Alpine Linux weighs in at only 3.97 MB as opposed to the biggest image, which is Fedora at 231 MB. A bare-metal installation of Alpine Linux comes in at around 130 MB, which is still almost half the size of the Fedora container image.

Reviewing the Dockerfile in depth

Let's take a look at the commands used in the Dockerfile example in the order in which they appear:

- FROM
- LABEL
- RUN
- COPY and ADD
- EXPOSE
- ENTRYPOINT and CMD
- Other Dockerfile commands

FROM

The FROM command tells Docker which base you would like to use for your image; as already mentioned, we are using Alpine Linux, so we simply have to put the name of the image and also the release tag we wish to use. In our case, to use the latest official Alpine Linux image, we simply need to add alpine:latest.

LABEL

The LABEL command can be used to add extra information to the image. This information can be anything from a version number to a description. It's also recommended that you limit the number of labels you use. A good label structure will help others who have to use our image later on. However, using too many labels can cause the image to become inefficient as well--I would recommend using the label schema detailed at http://label-schema.org/. You can view the containers' labels with the docker inspect command:

```
$ docker image inspect <IMAGE_ID>
```

Alternatively, you can use the following to filter just the labels:

```
$ docker image inspect -f {{.Config.Labels}} <IMAGE_ID>
```

For our example, we add two labels: one to identify who maintains the Dockerfile by adding maintainer="Russ McKendrick <russ@mckendrick.io>" and another, a description, description="This example Dockerfile installs NGINX.".

Generally though, it is better to define your labels when you create a container from your image rather than at build time, so it is best to keep labels down to just metadata about the image and nothing else.

RUN

The RUN command is where we interact with our image to install software and run scripts, commands, and other tasks. As you can see from our RUN command, we are actually running three commands:

```
RUN apk add --update nginx && \
        rm -rf /var/cache/apk/* && \
        mkdir -p /tmp/nginx/
```

The first of our three commands, apk add --update nginx, installs NGINX using Alpine Linux's package manager; we are using the && operator to move on to the next command if the previous command was successful. To make it more obvious which commands we are running, I am also using \ so I can split the command over multiple lines, making it easy to read. The next command in our chain is rm -rf /var/cache/apk/*; this removes any temporary files and so on to keep the size of our image to a minimum. The final command in our chain, mkdir -p /tmp/nginx/, creates a folder called /tmp/nginx/ so that NGINX starts correctly.

We could have also used the following in our Dockerfile:

```
RUN apk add --update nginx
RUN rm -rf /var/cache/apk/*
RUN mkdir -p /tmp/nginx/
```

However, like adding multiple labels, this would create an individual layer for each of the RUN commands, which for the most part we should try and avoid. There are however some valid use cases for this, which we will look at later in the chapter.

COPY and ADD

At first glance, COPY and ADD look like they are doing the same task; however, there are some important differences. The COPY command is the more straightforward of the two:

```
COPY files/nginx.conf /etc/nginx/nginx.conf
COPY files/default.conf /etc/nginx/conf.d/default.conf
```

As you have probably guessed, we are copying two files from the `files` folder on the host we are building our image on. The first file is `nginx.conf`, which contains a basic NGINX configuration file:

```
user nginx;
worker_processes 1;
error_log /var/log/nginx/error.log warn;
pid /var/run/nginx.pid;

events {
  worker_connections 1024;
}

http {
  include /etc/nginx/mime.types;
  default_type application/octet-stream;
  log_format main '$remote_addr - $remote_user
[$time_local] "$request" '
                  '$status $body_bytes_sent
"$http_referer" '
                  '"$http_user_agent"
"$http_x_forwarded_for"';
  access_log /var/log/nginx/access.log main;
  sendfile off;
  keepalive_timeout 65;
  include /etc/nginx/conf.d/*.conf;
}
```

This will overwrite the NGINX configuration that was installed as part of the APK installation in the RUN command. The next file, `default.conf`, is the most simple virtual host we can configure and has the following content:

```
server {
  location / {
    root /usr/share/nginx/html;
  }
}
```

Again, this will overwrite any existing files. So far, so good, so why use the ADD command?

```
ADD files/html.tar.gz /usr/share/nginx/
```

As you can see, we are adding a file called `html.tar.gz`, but we are not actually doing anything with the archive to uncompress it in our Dockerfile. This is because `ADD` automatically uploads, uncompresses, and puts the resulting folders and files at the path we tell it to, which in our case is `/usr/share/nginx/`, giving us our web root of `/usr/share/nginx/html/` as we defined in the virtual host block.

The `ADD` command can also be used to add content from remote sources:

```
ADD http://www.myremotesource.com/files/html.tar.gz /usr/share/nginx/
```

This, for example, would download `html.tar.gz` from `http://www.myremotesource.com/files/` and place the file in the `/usr/share/nginx/` folder on the image. Archive files from a remote source are treated as files and are not uncompressed, so you will have to take this into account when using them.

EXPOSE

The `EXPOSE` command lets Docker know that when the image is executed, then the port and protocol defined will be exposed at runtime. This command does not map the port to the host machine, but instead opens the port to allow access to the service on the container network. For example, in our Dockerfile, we are telling Docker to open port 80 every time the image runs:

```
EXPOSE 80/tcp
```

ENTRYPOINT and CMD

The benefit of using `ENTRYPOINT` over `CMD`, which we will look at next, is that you can use them in conjunction with each other. `ENTRYPOINT` can be used by itself, but remember that you would want to use `ENTRYPOINT` by itself only if you wanted to have your container be executable. For reference, if you think of some of the CLI commands you might use, you have to specify more than just the CLI command. You might have to add extra parameters you want the command to interpret. This would be the use case for using `ENTRYPOINT` only.

For example, if you want to have a default command that you want to execute inside a container, you could do something similar to the following example, but be sure to use a command that keeps the container alive.

In our case, we are using this:

```
ENTRYPOINT ["nginx"]
CMD ["-g", "daemon off;"]
```

What this means is that whenever we launch a container from our image, the `nginx` binary is executed as we have defined that as our `ENTRYPOINT`, and then whatever we have as the `CMD` is executed, giving us the equivalent of running the following command:

```
$ nginx -g daemon off;
```

Take a look at this:

```
$ docker container run -d --name nginx dockerfile-example -v
```

It would be like running the following command:

```
$ nginx -v
```

This means that the current version number of NGINX would be displayed and our container would stop as the NGINX binary would only be executed to display the version information and then the process would stop.

Other Dockerfile commands

There are some commands we have not included in our example Dockerfile. Let's take a look.

USER

The `USER` instruction lets you specify the username to be used when a command is run. The `USER` instruction can be used on the `RUN` instruction, the `CMD` instruction, or the `ENTRYPOINT` instruction in the Dockerfile. Also, the user defined in the `USER` command has to exist or your image will fail to build. Using the `USER` instruction can also introduce permission issues, not only on the container itself but also if you mount volumes.

WORKDIR

The `WORKDIR` command sets the working directory for the same set of instructions that the `USER` instruction can use (`RUN`, `CMD`, and `ENTRYPOINT`). It will allow you to use the `CMD` and `ADD` instructions as well.

ONBUILD

The ONBUILD instruction lets you stash a set of commands that will be used when the image is used again as a base image for a container. For example, if you want to give an image to developers and they all have different code they want to test, you can use the ONBUILD instruction to lay the groundwork ahead of the fact of needing the actual code. Then, the developers will simply add their code to the directory you tell them and, when they run a new docker build command, it will add their code to the running image. The ONBUILD instruction can be used in conjunction with the ADD and RUN instructions. Look at this example:

```
ONBUILD RUN apk update && apk upgrade && rm -rf /var/cache/apk/*
```

This would run an update and package upgrade every time our image is used as a base for another image.

ENV

The ENV command sets environment variables within the image both when it is built and when it is executed. These variables can be overridden when you launch your image.

Dockerfiles – best practices

Now that we have covered Dockerfile instructions, let's take a look at the best practices of writing our own Dockerfiles:

- You should try to get into the habit of using a .dockerignore file. We will cover the .dockerignore file in the next section; it will seem very familiar if you are used to using a .gitignore file. It will essentially ignore the items you have specified in the file during the build process.

- Remember to only have one Dockerfile per folder to help you organize your containers.

- Use version control for your Dockerfile; just like any other text-based document, version control will help you move forward, but only backward as necessary.

- Minimize the number of packages you need per image. One of the biggest goals you want to achieve while building your images is to keep them as small as possible. Not installing unnecessary packages will greatly help in achieving this goal.

- Execute only one application process per container. Every time you need a new application, it is best practice to use a new container to run that application in. While you can couple commands into a single container, it's best to separate them. Keep things simple; over complicating your Dockerfile will add bloat and also potentially cause you issues further down the line.

- Learn by example, Docker themselves have quite a detailed style guide for publishing the official images they host on Docker Hub, documented at `https://github.com/docker-library/official-images/`.

Building Docker images

In this section, we will cover the `docker build` command. This is where the rubber meets the road, as they say. It's time for us to build the base that we will start building our future images on. We will be looking at different ways to accomplish this goal. Consider this as a template that you may have created earlier with virtual machines. This will help save time by completing the hard work; you will just have to create the application that needs to be added to the new images.

The docker build command

Now that you have learned how to create and properly write a Dockerfile, it's time to learn how to take it from just a file to an actual image. There are a lot of switches that you can use while using the `docker build` command. So, let's use the always handy `--help` switch on the `docker build` command to view what all we can do:

```
$ docker image build --help
  Usage: docker image build [OPTIONS] PATH | URL | -
  Build an image from a Dockerfile
```

There are then a lot of flags listed that you can pass when building your image.

Build an image from a Dockerfile

Now, it may seem like a lot to digest, but out of all of these options, we only need to use `--tag` or its shorthand `-t` to name our image.

You can use the other options to limit how much CPU and memory the build process will use. In some cases, you may not want the `build` command to take as much CPU or memory as it can have. The process may run a little slower, but if you are running it on your local machine or a production server and it's a long build process, you may want to set a limit. Typically, you don't use the `--file / -f` switch as you run the `docker build` command from the same folder that the Dockerfile is in. Keeping the Dockerfile in separate folders helps sort the files and keeps the naming convention of the files the same.

It also worth mentioning that while you are able to pass additional environment variables as arguments at build time, they are used at build time and your container image does not inherit them; this is useful for passing information such as proxy settings, which may only be applicable to your initial build/test environment.

.dockerignore

The `.dockerignore` file, as we discussed earlier, is used to exclude those files or folders we don't want include in the `docker build` as by default, all files in the Dockerfile folder will be uploaded. We also discussed placing the Dockerfile in a separate folder, and the same applies for `.dockerignore`. It should go in the folder where the Dockerfile was placed. Keeping all the items you want to use in an image in the same folder will help you keep the number of items, if any, in the `.dockerignore` file to a minimum.

Building custom images using Dockerfiles

The first way we are going to look at to build your base Docker images is by creating a Dockerfile; in fact, we will be using the Dockerfile from the previous section and then executing a `docker build` command against it to get ourselves an NGINX image. So, let's start off by looking at the Dockerfile once more:

```
FROM alpine:latest
LABEL maintainer="Russ McKendrick <russ@mckendrick.io>"
LABEL description="This example Dockerfile installs NGINX."

RUN apk add --update nginx && \
        rm -rf /var/cache/apk/* && \
        mkdir -p /tmp/nginx/
```

```
COPY files/nginx.conf /etc/nginx/nginx.conf
COPY files/default.conf /etc/nginx/conf.d/default.conf
ADD files/html.tar.gz /usr/share/nginx/

EXPOSE 80/tcp

ENTRYPOINT ["nginx"]
CMD ["-g", "daemon off;"]
```

So, there are two ways we can go about building this image. The first way would be by specifying the `-f` switch when we use the `docker build` command. We will also utilize the `-t` switch to give the new image a unique name:

```
$ docker image build --file <path_to_Dockerfile> --tag <REPOSITORY>:<TAG> .
```

Now, `<REPOSITORY>` is typically the username you signed up for on Docker Hub--more on that in `Chapter 3`, *Storing and Distributing Images*; for now, we will be using `local`, and `<TAG>` is a unique container value you want to provide. Typically, this will be a version number or other descriptor:

```
$ docker image build --file /path/to/your/dockerfile --tag
local:dockerfile-example .
```

Typically, the `--file` switch isn't used, and it can be a little tricky when you have other files that need to be included with the new image. An easier way to do the build is to place the Dockerfile in a separate folder by itself along with any other file that you will be injecting into your image using the ADD or COPY instructions:

```
$ docker image build --tag local:dockerfile-example .
```

The most important thing to remember is the dot (or period) at the very end. This is to tell the `docker build` command to build in the current folder.

When you build your image, you should see something similar to the following Terminal output:

```
● ● ●                        2. dockerfile-example (bash)
⚡ docker image build --tag local:dockerfile-example .
Sending build context to Docker daemon 71.68 kB
Step 1/10 : FROM alpine:latest
latest: Pulling from library/alpine
2aecc7e1714b: Pull complete
Digest: sha256:0b94d1d1b5eb130dd0253374552445b39470653fb1a1ec2d81490948876e462c
Status: Downloaded newer image for alpine:latest
 ---> a41a7446062d
Step 2/10 : LABEL maintainer "Russ McKendrick <russ@mckendrick.io>"
 ---> Running in 48795b7150c9
 ---> b7327f3bdae9
Removing intermediate container 48795b7150c9
Step 3/10 : LABEL description "This example Dockerfile installs NGINX."
 ---> Running in f603312444da
 ---> 3ae1747eb298
Removing intermediate container f603312444da
Step 4/10 : RUN apk add --update nginx &&          rm -rf /var/cache/apk/* &&          mkdir -p /tmp/nginx/
 ---> Running in ff33a9a9ed1b
fetch http://dl-cdn.alpinelinux.org/alpine/v3.6/main/x86_64/APKINDEX.tar.gz
fetch http://dl-cdn.alpinelinux.org/alpine/v3.6/community/x86_64/APKINDEX.tar.gz
(1/2) Installing pcre (8.40-r2)
(2/2) Installing nginx (1.12.0-r2)
Executing nginx-1.12.0-r2.pre-install
Executing busybox-1.26.2-r4.trigger
OK: 5 MiB in 13 packages
 ---> 6f3e3c0ebb7e
Removing intermediate container ff33a9a9ed1b
Step 5/10 : COPY files/nginx.conf /etc/nginx/nginx.conf
 ---> 07ef10644d1e
Removing intermediate container cfb98a62593c
Step 6/10 : COPY files/default.conf /etc/nginx/conf.d/default.conf
 ---> a9784630ef94
Removing intermediate container 79a473c03afb
Step 7/10 : ADD files/html.tar.gz /usr/share/nginx/
 ---> c4580e80db6f
Removing intermediate container 2b8fd3daab87
Step 8/10 : EXPOSE 80/tcp
 ---> Running in 92d6c187cb4c
 ---> 35668e5da79a
Removing intermediate container 92d6c187cb4c
Step 9/10 : ENTRYPOINT nginx
 ---> Running in 34810588b3ff
 ---> 32970921ec29
Removing intermediate container 34810588b3ff
Step 10/10 : CMD -g daemon off;
 ---> Running in 8115aa4b0485
 ---> c64e6e3c31d5
Removing intermediate container 8115aa4b0485
Successfully built c64e6e3c31d5
russ in ~/Desktop/dockerfile-example
⚡ ▯
```

Once it's built, you should be able to run the following command to check whether the image is available and also the size of your image:

```
$ docker image ls
```

As you can see from the following Terminal output, my image size is 5.49 MB:

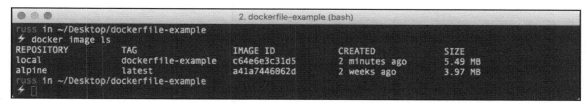

Using an existing container

The easiest way to build a base image is to start off by using one of the official images from the Docker Hub. Docker also keeps the Dockerfile for these official builds in their GitHub repositories. So there are at least two choices you have for using existing images that others have already created. By using the Dockerfile, you can see exactly what is included in the build and add what you need. You can then version control that Dockerfile for it if you want to change it later.

There is another way of achieving this; however, it is not recommended or considered to be good practice, and I would strong discourage you from using it--I would really only do this during a prototyping phase to check that the commands I am running work as expected in an interactive shell before putting them in a Dockerfile.

First, we should download the image we want to use as our base; as before, we will be using Alpine Linux:

```
$ docker image pull alpine:latest
```

Then, we would run the container in the foreground so that we can add packages to it:

```
$ docker container run -it --name alpine-test alpine /bin/sh
```

Once the container runs, you can add the packages as necessary using the `apk` command in this case, or whatever the package management commands are for your Linux flavor.

For example, the following commands would install NGINX:

```
$ apk update
$ apk upgrade
$ apk add --update nginx
$ rm -rf /var/cache/apk/*
$ mkdir -p /tmp/nginx/
$ exit
```

After you have installed the packages you require, you need to save the container. The `exit` command at the end of the preceding set of commands will stop the running container since the shell process we are detaching ourselves from just happens to be the process keeping the container running.

> It is here that you should really stop; I do not recommend you use the preceding commands to create and distribute images, apart from the one use case we will cover in the next part of the section.

So, to save our stopped container as an image, you need to do something similar to the following:

```
$ docker container commit <container_name> <REPOSITORY>:<TAG>
```

For example, I ran the following command to save a copy of the container we launched and customized:

```
$ docker container commit alpine-test local:broken-container
```

Notice how I called my image `broken-container`? I did that as one of the use cases for taking this approach is that if for some reason you have a problem with a container, it is extremely useful to save the failed container as an image or even export it as a TAR file to share with others if you need some assistance in getting to the root of a problem.

To save the image file, simply run the following command:

```
$ docker image save -o <name_of_file.tar> <REPOSITORY>:<TAG>
```

For our example, I ran this:

```
$ docker image save -o broken-container.tar local:broken-container
```

This gave me a 6.4 MB file called `broken-container.tar`. While we have this file, you can uncompress it and have a look around, as you can see from the following structure:

```
● ● ●                           1. broken-container (bash)
russ in ~/Desktop/broken-container
⚡ tree

├── 2a640dea2e1165b63947335c22f1f70163730f21a70e5c121681f8da0c75d935.json
├── a90a4db4af2a27c91da87db576184e7876798970b138cb3f91c484d947fd3456
│   ├── VERSION
│   ├── json
│   └── layer.tar
├── aa49f0f463a3618c10e90c3bf737207b8b1181432d7bd634d4e297b4af0fcba3
│   ├── VERSION
│   ├── json
│   └── layer.tar
├── manifest.json
└── repositories

2 directories, 9 files
russ in ~/Desktop/broken-container
⚡ []
```

The image is made up of a collection of JSON files, folders, and other TAR files. All images follow this structure, so you may be thinking to yourself *why is this method so bad?*

The biggest reason is trust: as already mentioned, your end user will not be able to easily see what is in the image they are running. Would you randomly download a prepackaged image from an unknown source to run your workload without checking how the image was built? Who knows how it was configured and what packages have been installed.

Another reason is that it is difficult for you to build in a good set of defaults; for example, if you were to build your image this way, then you would not really be able to take advantage of features such as `ENTRYPOINT` and `CMD` or even the most basic commands, such as `EXPOSE`. Instead, the user would have to define everything required during their `docker container run` command.

In the early days of Docker, distributing images that have been prepared in this way was common practice; in fact, I was guilty of it myself as coming from an operations background, it made perfect sense to launch a "machine," bootstrap it, and then create a gold master. Luckily, over the last few years, Docker has extended the build functionality to the point where this option is not even a consideration anymore.

Building from scratch

So far, we have been using prepared images from the Docker Hub as our base image; it is possible to avoid this altogether (sort of) and roll your own image from scratch.

Now, when you usually hear the term *scratch*, it literally means that you start from nothing. That's what we have here—you get absolutely nothing and have to build upon it. Now, this can be a benefit because it will keep the image size very small; but it can also be detrimental if you are fairly new to Docker, as it can get complicated.

Docker has done some of the hard work for us already and created an empty TAR file on the Docker Hub named scratch; you can use it in the FROM section of your Dockerfile. You can base your entire Docker build on this then and add parts as needed.

Again, let's look at using Alpine Linux as our base operating system for the image. One of the reasons why we would want to do this is that it is not only distributed as an ISO, Docker image, and various virtual machine images, but the entire operating system is available as a TAR file; you can find the download in the repository or on the Alpine Linux download page. Just select the appropriate download--the one I used was x86_64--from the **MINI ROOT FILESYSTEM** at the following URL: https://www.alpinelinux.org/downloads/.

Once it's downloaded, you need to create a Dockerfile that uses scratch and then add the TAR file, like this, for example:

```
FROM scratch
ADD files/alpine-minirootfs-3.6.1-x86_64.tar /
CMD ["/bin/sh"]
```

Now that you have your Dockerfile and operating system in a TAR file, you can build your image as you would any other Docker image by running the following:

```
$ docker image build --tag local:fromscratch .
```

Once it's built, you can test the image by running this command:

```
$ docker container run -it --name alpine-test local:fromscratch /bin/sh
```

This should launch into a shell on the Alpine Linux image; you can check this by running:

```
$ cat /etc/*release
```

This will display information on the release the container is running. To get an idea of what this entire process looks like, see the following Terminal output:

```
● ● ●                          1. scratch-example (bash)
russ in ~/Documents/Code/mastering-docker/chapter02/scratch-example on master*
⚡ docker image build --tag local:fromscratch .
Sending build context to Docker daemon 4.247 MB
Step 1/3 : FROM scratch
 --->
Step 2/3 : ADD files/alpine-minirootfs-3.6.1-x86_64.tar /
 ---> 5e6c6f57c024
Removing intermediate container 60625a681db3
Step 3/3 : CMD /bin/sh
 ---> Running in 68c002ec78b7
 ---> 53b9359df2dc
Removing intermediate container 68c002ec78b7
Successfully built 53b9359df2dc
russ in ~/Documents/Code/mastering-docker/chapter02/scratch-example on master*
⚡ docker container run -it --name alpine-test local:fromscratch /bin/sh
/ # cat /etc/*release
3.6.1
NAME="Alpine Linux"
ID=alpine
VERSION_ID=3.6.1
PRETTY_NAME="Alpine Linux v3.6"
HOME_URL="http://alpinelinux.org"
BUG_REPORT_URL="http://bugs.alpinelinux.org"
/ # exit
russ in ~/Documents/Code/mastering-docker/chapter02/scratch-example on master*
⚡ □
```

Now everything seems straightforward, and thanks to the way Alpine Linux packages their operating system, it is. However, not everything is that straightforward.

There are several tools that can be used to generate a bundle of an operating system:

- **Debootstrap**: https://wiki.debian.org/Debootstrap/
- **Yumbootstrap**: https://github.com/dozzie/yumbootstrap/
- **Rinse**: http://collab-maint.alioth.debian.org/rinse/
- **Docker contrib scripts**: https://github.com/moby/moby/tree/master/contrib/

We are not going to go into any detail on how to use any of these scripts here because if you have to consider this approach, then you probably have some pretty specific requirements.

So what could those requirements be? For most people, it will be legacy applications; for example, what happens if you have an application that requires an operating system that is no longer supported or available from Docker Hub, but you need a more modern platform to support the application on? Well, you should be able to spin your image and install the application there, allowing you host on your old legacy application on a modern, supportable operating system/architecture.

Environmental variables

In this section, we will cover the very powerful environmental variables or ENVs, as you will be seeing a lot of them. You can use environmental variables for a lot of things in your Dockerfile. If you are familiar with coding, these will probably come as secondhand to you.

For others like myself, at first they may seem intimidating, but don't get discouraged. They will be your best resource once you get the hang of them. They can be used to set information when running the container; this means that you don't have to go and update lots of the commands in your Dockerfile or scripts you run on the server.

Using environmental variables in your Dockerfile

To use environmental variables in your Dockerfile, you can use the ENV instruction. The structure of the ENV instruction is as follows:

```
ENV <key> <value>
ENV username admin
```

Alternatively, you can always use an equals sign between the two:

```
ENV <key>=<value>
ENV username=admin
```

Now, the question is why do they have two and what are the differences? With the first example, you can only set one ENV per line. With the second ENV example, you can set multiple environmental variables on the same line:

```
ENV username=admin database=db1 tableprefix=pr2_
```

You can view what environmental variables are set on an image using the Docker inspect command:

```
$ docker image inspect <IMAGE_ID>
```

Now that we know how they need to be set in our Dockerfile, let's take a look at them in action.

Putting it all together

So far we have been using a Dockerfile to build a simple image which just NGINX installed. Let's look at building something a little more dynamic. Using Alpine Linux, we will do the following:

- Set an environment variable to define which version of PHP we would like to install
- Install Apache2 and our chosen PHP version
- Set up the image so Apache2 starts without issue
- Remove the default `index.html` and add an `index.php` file that displays the results of the `phpinfo` command
- Expose port `80` on the container
- Set Apache so it is the default process

Our Dockerfile looks like the following:

```
FROM alpine:latest
LABEL maintainer="Russ McKendrick <russ@mckendrick.io>"
LABEL description="This example Dockerfile installs Apache & PHP."

ENV PHPVERSION 7

RUN apk add --update apache2 php${PHPVERSION}-apache2 php${PHPVERSION} && \
    rm -rf /var/cache/apk/* && \
    mkdir /run/apache2/ && \
    rm -rf /var/www/localhost/htdocs/index.html && \
    echo "<?php phpinfo(); ?>" > /var/www/localhost/htdocs/index.php && \
    chmod 755 /var/www/localhost/htdocs/index.php

EXPOSE 80/tcp

ENTRYPOINT ["httpd"]
CMD ["-D", "FOREGROUND"]
```

As you can see, we have chosen to install PHP7; we can build the image by running:

```
$ docker build --tag local/apache-php:7 .
```

Notice how we have changed the command slightly: this time, we are calling the image `local/apache-php` and tagging the version as 7.

```
● ● ●                           2. env-example (bash)
russ in ~/Documents/Code/mastering-docker/chapter02/env-example on master*
⚡ docker image build --tag local/apache-php:7 .
Sending build context to Docker daemon 9.728 kB
Step 1/8 : FROM alpine:latest
 ---> a41a7446062d
Step 2/8 : LABEL maintainer "Russ McKendrick <russ@mckendrick.io>"
 ---> Running in 8e84ecc4fdca
 ---> 3df4b9f2f1f7
Removing intermediate container 8e84ecc4fdca
Step 3/8 : LABEL description "This example Dockerfile installs Apache & PHP."
 ---> Running in f3f77b619bbb
 ---> 470f6dc4faf0
Removing intermediate container f3f77b619bbb
Step 4/8 : ENV PHPVERSION 7
 ---> Running in 7ef24725f815
 ---> 07f84c331c91
Removing intermediate container 7ef24725f815
Step 5/8 : RUN apk add --update apache2 php${PHPVERSION}-apache2 php${PHPVERSION} &&        rm -rf
/var/cache/apk/* &&        mkdir /run/apache2/ &&        rm -rf /var/www/localhost/htdocs/index.ht
ml &&        echo "<?php phpinfo(); ?>" > /var/www/localhost/htdocs/index.php &&        chmod 755
/var/www/localhost/htdocs/index.php
 ---> Running in 70ae843f6080
fetch http://dl-cdn.alpinelinux.org/alpine/v3.6/main/x86_64/APKINDEX.tar.gz
fetch http://dl-cdn.alpinelinux.org/alpine/v3.6/community/x86_64/APKINDEX.tar.gz
(1/14) Installing libuuid (2.28.2-r2)
(2/14) Installing apr (1.5.2-r1)
(3/14) Installing expat (2.2.0-r0)
(4/14) Installing apr-util (1.5.4-r3)
(5/14) Installing pcre (8.40-r2)
(6/14) Installing apache2 (2.4.25-r1)
Executing apache2-2.4.25-r1.pre-install
(7/14) Installing php7-common (7.1.5-r0)
(8/14) Installing ncurses-terminfo-base (6.0-r7)
(9/14) Installing ncurses-terminfo (6.0-r7)
(10/14) Installing ncurses-libs (6.0-r7)
(11/14) Installing libedit (20170329.3.1-r2)
(12/14) Installing libxml2 (2.9.4-r3)
(13/14) Installing php7 (7.1.5-r0)
(14/14) Installing php7-apache2 (7.1.5-r0)
Executing busybox-1.26.2-r4.trigger
OK: 25 MiB in 25 packages
 ---> 7c9f70a2f3c0
Removing intermediate container 70ae843f6080
Step 6/8 : EXPOSE 80/tcp
 ---> Running in c1b35bb930e6
 ---> 2e89703343e5
Removing intermediate container c1b35bb930e6
Step 7/8 : ENTRYPOINT httpd
 ---> Running in 0e385a6f78ff
 ---> 21793a9ee3d3
Removing intermediate container 0e385a6f78ff
Step 8/8 : CMD -D FOREGROUND
 ---> Running in bc5d6dbaf86c
 ---> b15a887563e2
Removing intermediate container bc5d6dbaf86c
Successfully built b15a887563e2
russ in ~/Documents/Code/mastering-docker/chapter02/env-example on master*
⚡ □
```

We can check whether everything ran as expected by running the following command to launch a container using the image:

```
$ docker container run -d -p 8080:80 --name apache-php7 local/apache-php:7
```

Once it's launched, open a browser and go to `http://localhost:8080/` and you should see a page showing that PHP7 is being used:

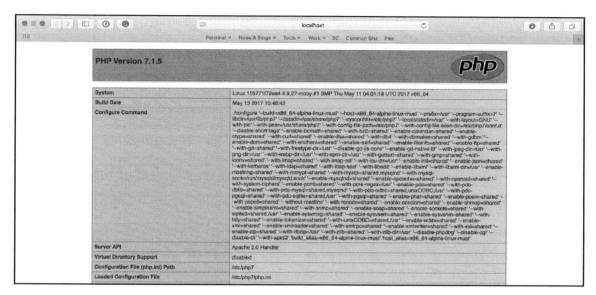

 Don't be confused by the next part; there is no PHP6. For an explanation of why not, go to `https://wiki.php.net/rfc/php6`.

Now, in your Dockerfile, change `PHPVERSION` from 7 to 5 and then run the following command to build a new image:

```
$ docker image build --tag local/apache-php:5 .
```

As you can see from the following Terminal output, the majority of the output is the same apart from the packages that are being installed:

```
● ● ●                              2. env-example (bash)
russ in ~/Documents/Code/mastering-docker/chapter02/env-example on master*
⚡ docker image build --tag local/apache-php:5 .
Sending build context to Docker daemon 9.728 kB
Step 1/8 : FROM alpine:latest
 ---> a41a7446062d
Step 2/8 : LABEL maintainer "Russ McKendrick <russ@mckendrick.io>"
 ---> Using cache
 ---> 3df4b9f2f1f7
Step 3/8 : LABEL description "This example Dockerfile installs Apache & PHP."
 ---> Using cache
 ---> 470f6dc4faf0
Step 4/8 : ENV PHPVERSION 5
 ---> Running in c7c42e66da7a
 ---> a4737a66f066
Removing intermediate container c7c42e66da7a
Step 5/8 : RUN apk add --update apache2 php${PHPVERSION}-apache2 php${PHPVERSION} &&        rm -rf
/var/cache/apk/* &&        mkdir /run/apache2/ &&        rm -rf /var/www/localhost/htdocs/index.ht
ml &&        echo "<?php phpinfo(); ?>" > /var/www/localhost/htdocs/index.php &&        chmod 755
/var/www/localhost/htdocs/index.php
 ---> Running in 54a1e94aff3a
fetch http://dl-cdn.alpinelinux.org/alpine/v3.6/main/x86_64/APKINDEX.tar.gz
fetch http://dl-cdn.alpinelinux.org/alpine/v3.6/community/x86_64/APKINDEX.tar.gz
(1/15) Installing libuuid (2.28.2-r2)
(2/15) Installing apr (1.5.2-r1)
(3/15) Installing expat (2.2.0-r0)
(4/15) Installing apr-util (1.5.4-r3)
(5/15) Installing pcre (8.40-r2)
(6/15) Installing apache2 (2.4.25-r1)
Executing apache2-2.4.25-r1.pre-install
(7/15) Installing php5-common (5.6.30-r3)
(8/15) Installing ncurses-terminfo-base (6.0-r7)
(9/15) Installing ncurses-terminfo (6.0-r7)
(10/15) Installing ncurses-libs (6.0-r7)
(11/15) Installing readline (6.3.008-r5)
(12/15) Installing libxml2 (2.9.4-r3)
(13/15) Installing php5-cli (5.6.30-r3)
(14/15) Installing php5 (5.6.30-r3)
(15/15) Installing php5-apache2 (5.6.30-r3)
Executing busybox-1.26.2-r4.trigger
OK: 47 MiB in 26 packages
 ---> 1c9a61cd8cc9
Removing intermediate container 54a1e94aff3a
Step 6/8 : EXPOSE 80/tcp
 ---> Running in 19a04ae4ae0b
 ---> ee3ade94f8bb
Removing intermediate container 19a04ae4ae0b
Step 7/8 : ENTRYPOINT httpd
 ---> Running in e548f0c014f9
 ---> 740a40fea8aa
Removing intermediate container e548f0c014f9
Step 8/8 : CMD -D FOREGROUND
 ---> Running in 0ae212140bd0
 ---> de3cbc1c775b
Removing intermediate container 0ae212140bd0
Successfully built de3cbc1c775b
russ in ~/Documents/Code/mastering-docker/chapter02/env-example on master*
⚡ 
```

We can launch a container, this time on port 9090, by running:

```
$ docker container run -d -p 9090:80 --name apache-php5 local/apache-php:5
```

Opening your browser again, but this time going to http://localhost:9090/ should show that we are running PHP5:

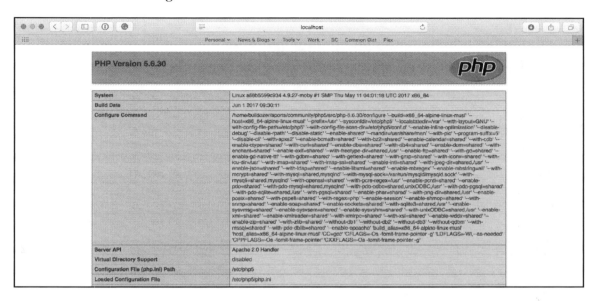

Finally, you can compare the size of the images by running:

```
$ docker image ls
```

You can see the following Terminal output:

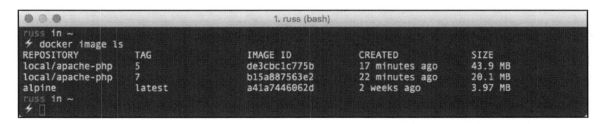

As you can see, the PHP7 image is a lot smaller than the PHP5 one. Let's see what actually happened.

So what happened? Well, when Docker launched the Alpine Linux image to create our image, the first thing it did was set the environment variables we defined, making them available to the all of the shells within the container.

Luckily for us, the naming scheme for PHP in Alpine Linux simply substitutes the version number and maintains the same name for the packages we need to install, meaning that we run the following command:

```
RUN apk add --update apache2 php${PHPVERSION}-apache2 php${PHPVERSION}
```

But it is actually interpreted as follows:

```
RUN apk add --update apache2 php7-apache2 php7
```

Or it is interpreted as this for PHP5:

```
RUN apk add --update apache2 php5-apache2 php5
```

This means that we do not have to go through all of the Dockerfile, manually substituting version numbers. This approach is especially useful when installing packages from remote URLs, such as software release pages. What follows is an example Dockerfile that installs and configures Consul by HashiCorp; we will be looking at Consul in more detail in our final chapter, and we use environment variables to define the version numbers and the SHA256 hash of the two files we downloaded:

```
FROM alpine:latest
LABEL maintainer="Russ McKendrick <russ@mckendrick.io>"
LABEL description="An image with the latest version on Consul."

ENV CONSUL_VERSION 0.8.4
ENV CONSUL_SHA256
c8859a0a34c50115cdff147f998b2b63226f5f052e50f342209142420d1c2668
ENV CONSUL_UI_SHA256
7a49924a872205002b2bf72af8c82d5560d4a7f4a58b2f65ee284dd254ebd063

RUN apk add --update ca-certificates wget && \
    wget -O consul.zip
https://releases.hashicorp.com/consul/${CONSUL_VERSION}/consul_${CONSUL_VER
SION}_linux_amd64.zip && \
    echo "$CONSUL_SHA256 *consul.zip" | sha256sum -c - && \
    unzip consul.zip && \
    mv consul /bin/ && \
    rm -rf consul.zip && \
    cd /tmp && \
    wget -O ui.zip
https://releases.hashicorp.com/consul/${CONSUL_VERSION}/consul_${CONSUL_VER
SION}_web_ui.zip && \
```

```
echo "$CONSUL_UI_SHA256 *ui.zip" | sha256sum -c - && \
unzip ui.zip && \
mkdir -p /ui && \
mv * /ui && \
rm -rf /tmp/* /var/cache/apk/*

EXPOSE 8300 8301 8301/udp 8302 8302/udp 8400 8500 8600 8600/udp

VOLUME [ "/data" ]

ENTRYPOINT [ "/bin/consul" ]
CMD [ "agent", "-data-dir", "/data", "-server", "-bootstrap-expect", "1",
"-ui-dir", "/ui", "-client=0.0.0.0"]
```

As you can see, Dockerfiles can get quite complex, and using environment variables can help with the maintenance: whenever a new version of Consul is released, I simply need to update the three ENV lines commit it to GitHub, which will trigger the building of a new image--well it would do if we had configured it to; we will be looking at this in the next chapter.

You might have also noticed we are using a command within the Dockerfile we have not covered. Don't worry, we will look at the VOLUME command in Chapter 4, *Managing Containers*.

Summary

In this chapter, we looked at an in-depth view of Dockerfiles and the best practices to write them, the `docker image build` command, and the various ways we can build containers in. We also learned about the environmental variables that you can use to pass from your Dockerfile to the various items inside your containers.

In the next chapter, now that we know how to build images using Dockerfiles, we will be taking a look at the Docker Hub and all of the advantages using a registry service brings. We will also look at the Docker registry, which is is open sourced, so you can roll your own place to store images without the fees of Docker Enterprise Cloud as well as third-party registry services.

3
Storing and Distributing Images

In this chapter, we will cover several services which allow you to store your images, such as Docker Hub and also Docker Registry, which you can use to run your local storage for Docker containers. We will review the differences between them services and when and how to use each of them. The chapter will also cover how to set up automated builds using web hooks as well as all the pieces that are required to set them up. Let's take a quick look at the topics we will be covering in this chapter:

- Docker Hub
- Docker Store
- Docker Registry
- Third-party registries
- Microbadger

Docker Hub

While we have been introduced to Docker Hub in the previous two chapters, we haven't interacted with it much other than when using the `docker image pull` command to download remote images. In this section, we will focus on Docker Hub, which has both a freely available option where you can only host publically accessible images and also a subscription option which allows you to host your own private images. We will focus on the web aspect of Docker Hub and the management you can do there.

The home page, which you can get to at `https://hub.docker.com/`, is like the one shown in the following screenshot:

As you can see, you are presented with a **Sign Up** form or in the top-right an option to **Sign in**. The odds are that if you have been dabbling with Docker, then you already have a Docker ID. If you don't, use the **Sign Up** form on the home page to create one. If you already have a Docker ID, then simply **Sign in.**

 Docker Hub is free to use and if you do not need to upload or manage your own images you do not need an account to search for pull images.

Dashboard

After logging in to Docker Hub, you will be taken to the following landing page. This page is known as the **Dashboard** of Docker Hub.

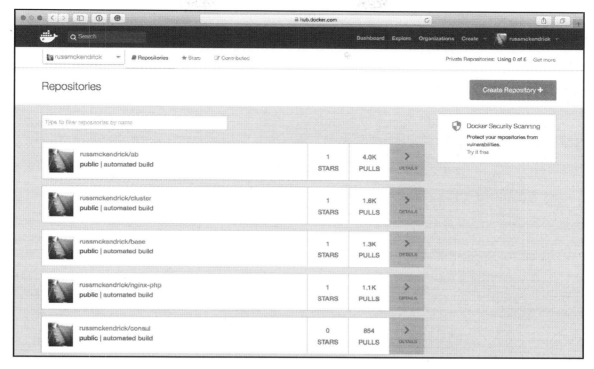

From here, you can get to all the other sub-pages of Docker Hub. However, before we look at those sections, we should talk a little about the dashboard. From here, you can view all of your images, both public and private ones. They are ordered first by the number of stars and then by the number of pulls; this order (at the time of writing) cannot be changed.

In the upcoming sections, we will go through everything you see on the dashboard, starting with the dark blue bar you have on the top.

Explore

The **Explore** option takes you to a list of the official Docker images; like your **Dashboard**, they are ordered by stars and then pulls. As you can see from the following screen, each of the official images has had over 10 million pulls:

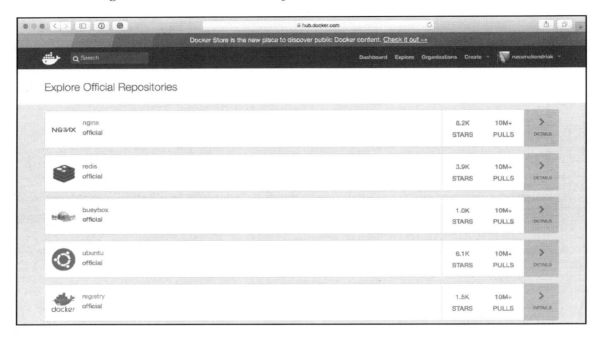

You will also notice that at the very top of the page, there is a banner asking you to check out the Docker Store. As we will be looking at this in more detail later in the chapter, we won't go into any more detail here.

Organizations

Organizations are those that you have either created or have been added to. Organizations allow you to layer on control for, say, a project that multiple people are collaborating on. The organization gets its own settings, such as whether to store repositories as public or private by default or changing plans that will allow different numbers of private repositories and separate repositories altogether from the ones you or others have.

You can also access or switch between accounts or organizations from the **Dashboard** just below the Docker logo, where you will typically see your username when you log in:

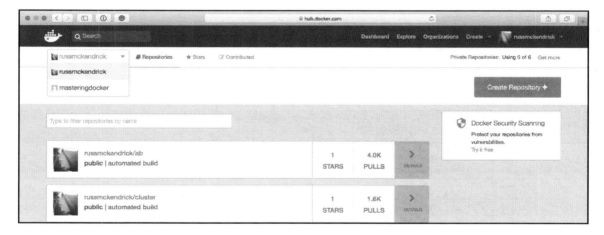

Create

We will go into more detail about creating a repository and an automated build in a later section, so I will not go into any details here other than to say that the **Create** menu gives you three options:

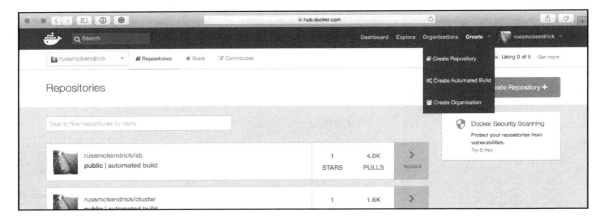

Profile and settings

The final option in the top menu are about managing **My Profile** and **Settings**:

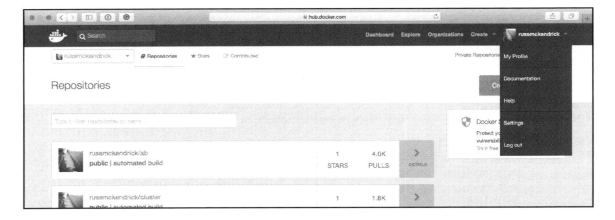

The settings page allows you to set up your public profile:

- Change your password
- See what organization you belong to
- See what subscriptions for email updates you have
- Set specific notifications you would like to receive
- Set which authorized services have access to your information
- See linked accounts (such as your GitHub or Bitbucket accounts)
- View your enterprise licenses, billing, and global settings

The only global setting as of now is the choice between having your repositories default to public or private upon creation. The default is to create them as public repositories:

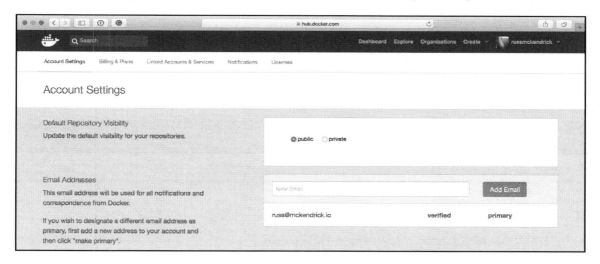

The **My Profile** menu item takes you to your public profile page; mine can be found at `http
s://hub.docker.com/u/russmckendrick/` and currently looks like:

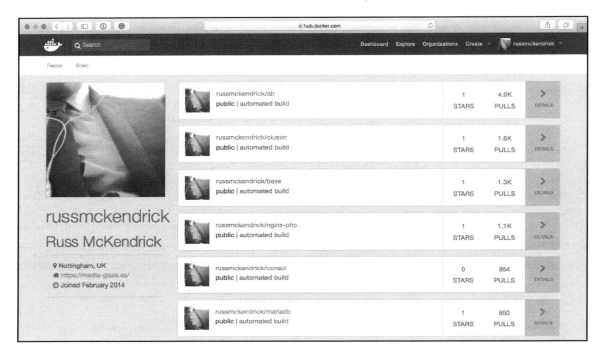

The Stars page

Below the dark blue bar at the top of the **Dashboard** page are two more areas that we
haven't yet covered. The first, the **Stars** page, allows you to see which repositories you
yourself have starred:

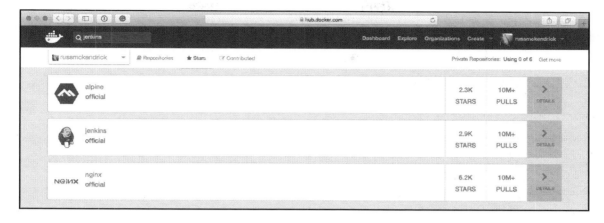

This is very useful if you come across some repositories that you prefer to use and want to access them to see whether they have been updated recently or whether any other changes have occurred on these repositories.

The second is a new setting, **Contributed**. In this section, there will be a list of repositories you have contributed to outside of the ones within your **Repositories** list.

Creating an automated build

In this section, we will look at automated builds. Automated builds are those that you can link to your GitHub or Bitbucket account(s), and as you update the code in your code repository, you can have the image automatically built on Docker Hub. We will look at all the pieces required to do so, and by the end, you'll be able to automate all your builds.

Setting up your code

The first step to creating an automated build is to set up your GitHub or Bitbucket repository. These are the two options you have while selecting where to store your code. For our example, I will be using GitHub, but the setup will be the same for GitHub and Bitbucket. In fact, I will be using the repository for this book, which you can find at `https ://github.com/russmckendrick/mastering-docker/`.

As the repository is publicly available, you could fork it and follow along using your own GitHub account:

In Chapter 2, *Building Container Images*, we worked through a Dockerfile. We will be using that as the base for our automated build. If you remember, we installed ngnix and added a simple page with the message **Hello world! This is being served from Docker**.

Setting up Docker Hub

In Docker Hub, we are going to use the **Create** drop-down menu and select **Create Automated Build**. After selecting it, we will be taken to a screen that will show you the accounts you have linked to either GitHub or Bitbucket:

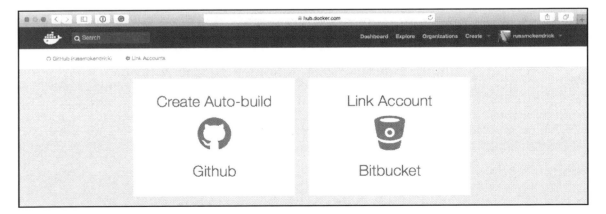

You then need to search and select the repository from either of the locations you want to create the automated build from. This will essentially create a webhook that instructs that when a commit is done on a selected code repository, a new build will be created on Docker Hub.

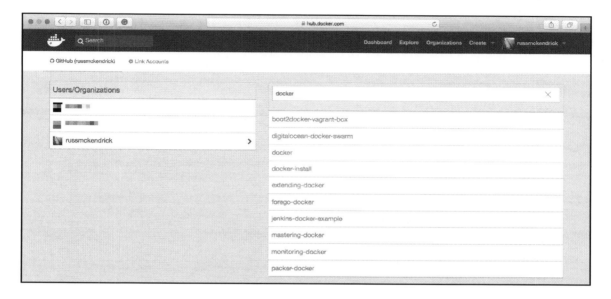

Here, I selected **mastering-docker** and visited the settings page for the automated build. From here, we can choose which Docker Hub profile the image is attached to, name the image, change it from a publicly to privately available image, describe the build, and customize it by clicking on **Click here to customize**. We can let Docker Hub know the location of our Dockerfile.

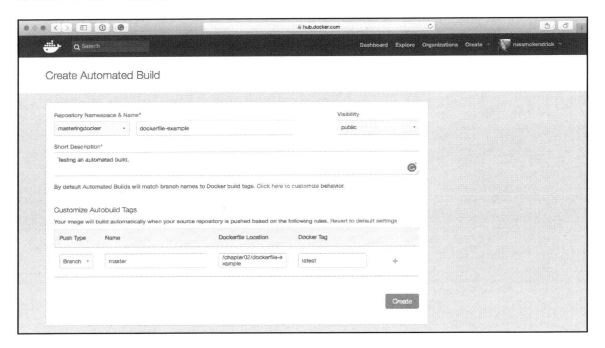

If you are following along, I entered the following information:

- **Repository Namespace & Name**: dockerfile-example
- **Visibility**: public
- **Short Description**: Testing an automated build
- **Push Type**: Branch
- **Name**: Master
- **Dockerfile Location**: /chapter02/dockerfile-example/
- **Docker Tag**: latest

Upon clicking on **Create**, you will be taken to a screen similar to the next screenshot:

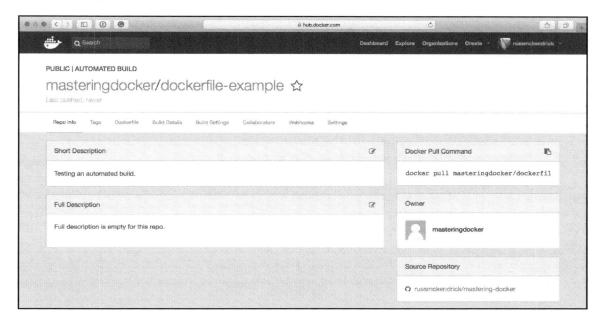

Now that we have our build defined, we can add some additional configuration: click on **Build Settings**. As we are using the official Alpine Linux image, we can link that to our own build. To do that, enter `alpine` in the **Repository Links** section and then click on **Add Repository Link.** This will kick off an unattended build each time a new version of the official Alpine Linux image is published.

Linking your images to the official images or your own base image is strongly recommend to keep your container image up-to-date and patched.

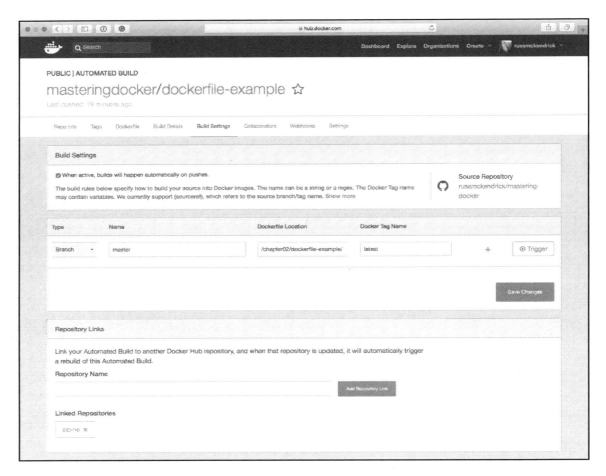

So now our image will automatically be rebuilt and published whenever we update the GitHub repository or when a new official image is published. As neither of these is likely to happen immediately, click on the **Trigger** button to manually kick off a build.

Clicking on **Build Details** will bring up a list of all of the builds for the image, both successful and failed ones. You should see a build underway; clicking on it will bring up the logs for the build:

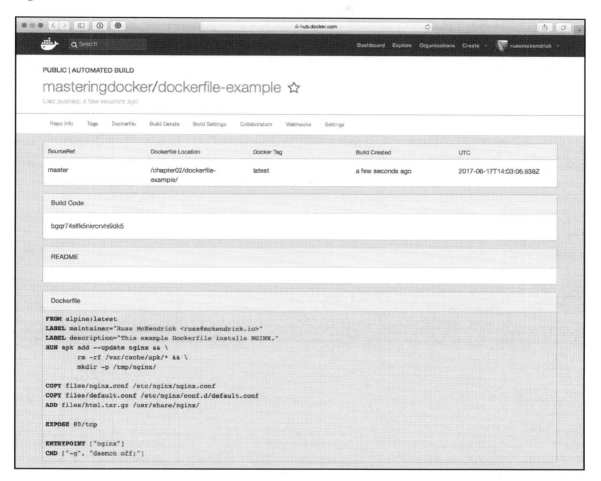

Once built, you should then able to move to your local Docker installation by running the following commands, making sure to pull your own image if you have been following along:

```
$ docker pull masteringdocker/dockerfile-example
$ docker image ls
```

The commands are shown in the following screenshot:

```
● ● ●                              1. russ (bash)
russ in ~
⚡ docker pull masteringdocker/dockerfile-example
Using default tag: latest
latest: Pulling from masteringdocker/dockerfile-example
2aecc7e1714b: Pull complete
059b1489b0a1: Pull complete
6e4602f97fc3: Pull complete
ee5e31fa6ddd: Pull complete
4b30bc355ec2: Pull complete
Digest: sha256:a656ed03b14f726510e3a62cb072cdcc7e4cfeddb9f8e52ee694c93612a42bea
Status: Downloaded newer image for masteringdocker/dockerfile-example:latest
russ in ~
⚡ docker image ls
REPOSITORY                          TAG          IMAGE ID        CREATED         SIZE
masteringdocker/dockerfile-example  latest       077956f5adfe    3 minutes ago   5.49 MB
russ in ~
⚡ 
```

You can also run the image created by Docker Hub using the following command, again making sure to use your own image if you have one:

```
$ docker container run -d -p8080:80 masteringdocker/dockerfile-example
```

Pushing your own image

In `Chapter 2`, *Building Container Images,* we discussed creating an image without using a Dockerfile. While it is still not a good idea and should only be used when you really need to, you can push your own images to Docker Hub.

 When pushing images to Docker Hub in this way, ensure that you do not include any code, files, or environment variables you would not want to be publicly accessible.

To do this, we first need to link our local Docker client to Docker Hub by running the following command:

```
$ docker login
```

You will then be prompted for your Docker ID and password:

```
● ● ●                          1. russ (bash)
russ in ~
⚡ docker login
Login with your Docker ID to push and pull images from Docker Hub. If you don't have a Docker ID, head ove
r to https://hub.docker.com to create one.
Username: russmckendrick
Password:
Login Succeeded
russ in ~
⚡ ▯
```

Now that our client is authorized to interact with Docker Hub, we need an image to build. Let's look at pushing the scratch image we built in Chapter 2, *Building Container Images*. First, we need to build the image:

```
$ docker build --tag masteringdocker/scratch-example:latest .
```

The following screenshot shows the output:

```
● ● ●                          1. scratch-example (bash)
russ in ~/Documents/Code/mastering-docker/chapter02/scratch-example on master*
⚡ docker build --tag masteringdocker/scratch-example:latest .
Sending build context to Docker daemon 4.247 MB
Step 1/3 : FROM scratch
 --->
Step 2/3 : ADD files/alpine-minirootfs-3.6.1-x86_64.tar /
 ---> ceaf29dcf11d
Removing intermediate container 218ba6dde4b4
Step 3/3 : CMD /bin/sh
 ---> Running in 782c61a2f01f
 ---> 06f66706e5eb
Removing intermediate container 782c61a2f01f
Successfully built 06f66706e5eb
```

Once the image has been built, we can push it to Docker Hub by running the following command:

```
$ docker image push masteringdocker/scratch-example:latest
```

The following screenshot shows the output:

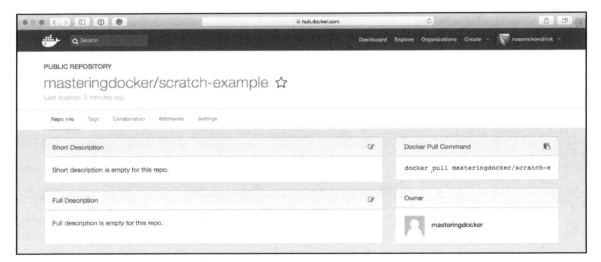

As you can see, because we defined `masteringdocker/scratch-example:latest` when we built the image, Docker automatically uploaded the image to that location, which in turn added a new image to the *Mastering Docker* organization:

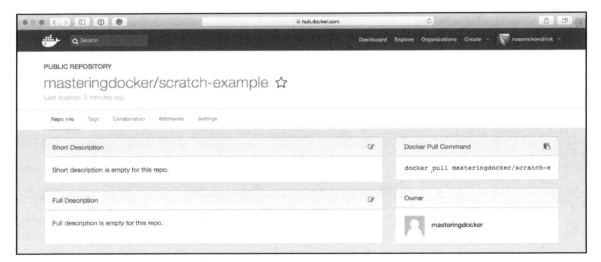

You will notice that there is not much you can do with the build in Docker Hub; this is because the image was not built by Docker Hub and therefore it does not really have any idea what has gone into building the image.

Docker Store

You may remember that in Chapter 1, *Docker Overview*, we downloaded Docker for macOS and Docker for Windows from the Docker Store. As well as acting as a single location for downloading both **Docker CE** and **Docker EE** for various platforms, it is now also the preferred location for finding both Docker images and Docker **Plugins**.

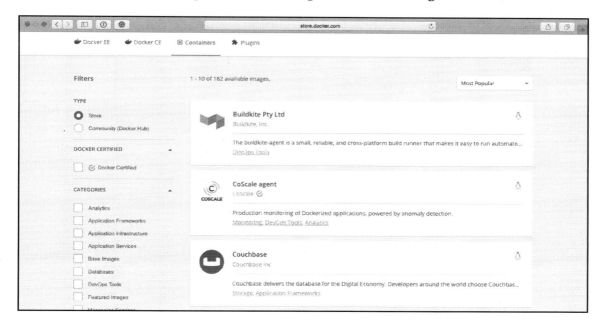

While you will only find official and certified images in the Docker Store, there is an option to use the Docker Store interface to search through Docker Hub. Also, you can download images that are not available from Docker Hub, such as the Citrix NetScaler CPX Express image (`https://store.docker.com/images/netscaler-cpx-express/`):

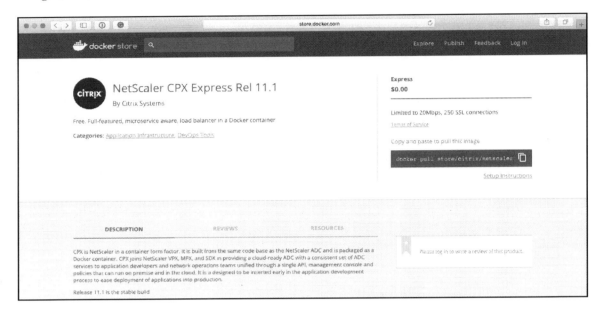

If you notice, the image has a price attached to it (the **Express** version is **$0.00**) meaning that you can buy commercial software through the Docker Store as it has payments and licensing built in. If you are a software publisher and wish to distribute your software through the Docker Store, then you can find out more details and apply to publish at the following address `https://store.docker.com/publisher/signup/`.

We will be looking at the Docker Store in a little more detail in later chapters, when we cover Docker plugins.

Docker Registry

In this section, we will be looking at Docker Registry. Docker Registry is an open source application that you can run anywhere you please and store your Docker image in. We will look at the comparison between Docker Registry and Docker Hub and how to choose between the two. By the end of the section, you will learn how to run your own Docker Registry and see whether it's a proper fit for you.

An overview of Docker Registry

Docker Registry, as stated earlier, is an open source application that you can utilize to store your Docker images on a platform of your choice. This allows you to keep them 100% private if you wish or share them as needed. The registry can be found at `https://docs.docker.com/registry/`.

This will run you through the setup and the steps to follow while pushing images to Docker Registry compared to Docker Hub. Docker Registry makes a lot of sense if you want to deploy your own registry without having to pay for all the private features of Docker Hub. Next, let's take a look at some comparisons between Docker Hub and Docker Registry, so you can make an educated decision as to which platform to choose to store your images.

Docker Registry has the following features:

- Host and manage your own registry, from which you can serve all the repositories as private, public, or a mix between the two
- Scale the registry as needed based on how many images you host or how many pull requests you are serving out
- Everything is command-line-based

With Docker Hub, you will:

- Get a GUI-based interface that you can use to manage your images
- Have a location already set up in the cloud that is ready to handle public and/or private images
- Have the peace of mind of not having to manage a server that is hosting all your images

Deploying your own registry

As you may have already guessed, Docker Registry is distributed, which makes deploying it as easy as running the following commands:

```
$ docker image pull registry:2
$ docker container run -d -p 5000:5000 --name registry registry:2
```

These commands will give you the most basic installation of Docker Registry. Let's take a quick look at how we can push and pull an image to it. To start off with, we need an image, so let's grab the Alpine image (again):

```
$ docker image pull alpine
```

Now that we have a copy of the Alpine Linux image, we need to push it to our local Docker Registry, which is available at `localhost:5000`. To do this, we need to tag the Alpine Linux image with the URL of our local Docker Registry and also a different image name:

```
$ docker image tag alpine localhost:5000/localalpine
```

Now that we have our image tagged, we can push it to our locally hosted Docker Registry by running the following command:

```
$ docker image push localhost:5000/localalpine
```

The following screenshot shows the output of the preceding command:

Try running the following command:

```
$ docker image ls
```

It should show you that you have two images with the same IMAGE ID:

```
russ in ~
 ⚡ docker image ls
REPOSITORY                     TAG       IMAGE ID        CREATED        SIZE
alpine                         latest    a41a7446062d    3 weeks ago    3.97 MB
localhost:5000/localalpine     latest    a41a7446062d    3 weeks ago    3.97 MB
registry                       2         9d0c4eabab4d    5 weeks ago    33.2 MB
russ in ~
 ⚡ 
```

Before we pull the image back down from our local Docker Registry, we should remove the two local copies of the image: we need to use the REPOSITORY name to do this rather than the IMAGE ID as we have two images from two locations with the same ID, and Docker will throw an error:

```
$ docker image rm alpine localhost:5000/localalpine
```

Now that the original and tagged images have been removed, we can pull the image from our local Docker Registry by running the following:

```
$ docker image pull localhost:5000/localalpine
$ docker image ls
```

As you can see, we now have a copy of our image that has been pulled from the Docker Registry running at `localhost:5000`:

You can stop and remove the Docker Registry by running the following:

```
$ docker container stop registry
$ docker container rm -v registry
```

Now, there are a lot of options and considerations when it comes to launching a Docker Registry. As you can imagine, the most important are around storage. Given that a registry's sole purpose is storing and distributing images, it is important that you use some level of persistent OS storage. Docker Registry currently supports the following:

- **Filesystem**: This is exactly what it says; all images are stored on the filesystem at the path you define. The default is `/var/lib/registry`.
- **Azure**: This uses Microsoft Azure storage, `https://azure.microsoft.com/en-g b/services/storage/`.
- **GCS**: This uses Google Cloud storage, `https://cloud.google.com/storage/`.
- **S3**: This uses **Amazon Simple Storage Service (Amazon S3)**, `https://aws.amazo n.com/s3/`.
- **Swift**: This uses OpenStack Swift, `https://wiki.openstack.org/wiki/Swift/`.

As you can see, other than the filesystem, all of the storage engines supported are all highly available, distributed object-level storage. For more information on how to configure these storage backends, see the official documentation at `https://docs.docker.com/registry/configuration/`.

Docker Trusted Registry

One of the components that ships with the commercial Docker Datacenter is **Docker Trusted Registry (DTR)**. Think of it as a version of Docker Hub that you can host in your own infrastructure. DTR adds the following features on top of the ones provided by the free Docker Hub and Docker Registry:

- Integrated into your authentication services such as Active Directory or LDAP
- Deployed on your own infrastructure (or cloud) behind your firewall
- Image signing to ensure your images are trusted
- Built in security scanning
- Access to prioritized support directly from Docker

More information on Docker Trusted Registry can be found at `https://docs.docker.com/datacenter/dtr/2.2/guides/`.

Third-party registries

It is not only Docker that offers image registry services; companies such as Red Hat offer their own registry. You can find the Red Hat Container Catalog at `https://access.redhat.com/containers/`. Here, you will find containerized versions of all of Red Hat's product offerings, along with containers to support its OpenShift (`https://www.openshift.com/`) offering. Services such as Artifactory by JFrog (`https://www.jfrog.com/artifactory/`) offer a private Docker registry as part of their build services.

There are also Registry as a Service offerings; we are going to take a look at two of them.

Quay

Quay is a commercial service from CoreOS; it offers both a cloud-based version (which we will be looking at here) or an Enterprise version, which you can run on premises behind your own firewall.

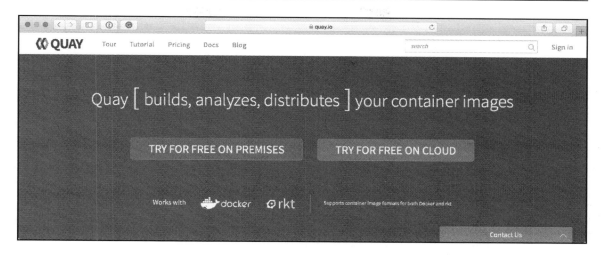

You can sign up for a free 30-day trial at `https://quay.io/`. Signing up is as simple as clicking on **Sign in** and then using your GitHub account to create an account. Once you have created your account, you will be greeted with a screen that looks like the following:

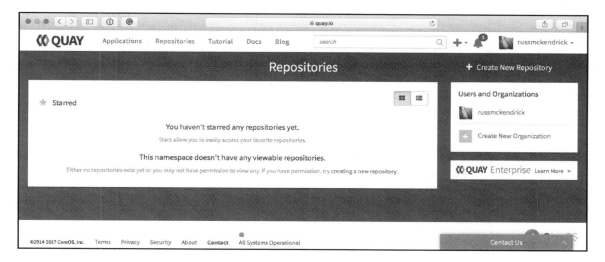

To create an image repository, like we did for the automated build for Docker Hub, click on **Create New Repository.**

This will take you to a page where you are asked to name your repository and also where it should get the image from; you have several options here:

- Empty repository

- Initialize from a Dockerfile
- Link to a GitHub repository push
- Link to a Bitbucket repository push
- Link to a GitLab repository push
- Link to a custom Git repository push

As before, we are going to link to a GitHub account, so select this. Once selected, click on **Create Public Repository** and you will then be taken to a page where you need to give Quay permission to access your GitHub account. Once you have granted permission by following the on-screen prompts, you will be asked which GitHub repository your Dockerfile is stored in:

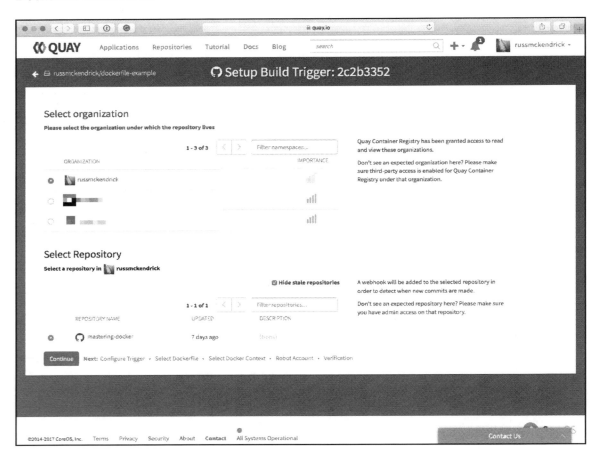

Click on **Continue** to then select the path to your Dockerfile, the build context (all of the files that go to build up your container image), and so on. Once you select and verify, the repository will be created and you will be given an option to manually trigger a build. Once it is built, you should see something similar to the following:

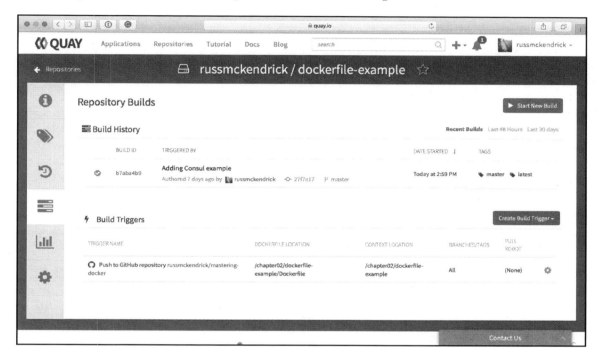

You will now be able to pull your image. For example, mine can be pulled by running the following command:

```
$ docker image pull quay.io/russmckendrick/dockerfile-example
```

The following screenshot shows the output of the preceding command:

```
● ● ●                            1. russ (bash)
russ in ~
⚡ docker image pull quay.io/russmckendrick/dockerfile-example
Using default tag: latest
latest: Pulling from russmckendrick/dockerfile-example
1f02c775bd9a: Pull complete
a3ed95caeb02: Pull complete
5e6712963917: Pull complete
34dc12b354cb: Pull complete
eda8ac5608ea: Pull complete
482a1e9a40e4: Pull complete
Digest: sha256:84290eae41b2386a775dc8837265dbfa024e5aeaf587d11c27f73ab5e7982d16
Status: Downloaded newer image for quay.io/russmckendrick/dockerfile-example:latest
russ in ~
⚡ docker image ls
REPOSITORY                                  TAG           IMAGE ID            CREATED             SIZE
quay.io/russmckendrick/dockerfile-example   latest        b86d85361a4c        9 minutes ago       5.49 MB
```

As you can see, the process is very similar to that of Docker Hub. Each time your GitHub repository is updated, an updated image will be built. Should there be any problems, you will receive an email notification. You get other options such as being able to download squashed versions of your automatically built images. For more information on Quay, go to the site at `https://quay.io/`.

Amazon EC2 Container Registry

The next registry service we are going to look at is the one from Amazon, which supports its own **Amazon EC2 Container Service** (**ECS**), which we will be looking at in more detail in a later chapter. The registry service is called **Amazon EC2 Container Registry** (**ECR**) and works a little different to Docker Hub and Quay.

The service can be found by entering ECS in the search box, which appears when you click on **Services** in the top left. Once the page loads, click on **Repositories**, and you will be asked to name your repository:

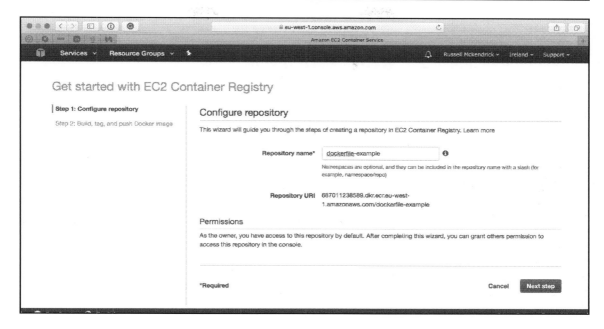

You might be thinking that after clicking on **Next step**, you will need to enter details of a GitHub, Bitbucket, or even Amazon S3 bucket that hosts your Dockerfile, but you would be mistaken. Instead, you are given instructions on how to build, tag, and push your image. For me, the instructions were as follows:

```
$ aws ecr get-login --no-include-email --region eu-west-1
```

This generates a command to log you in; for me, it looked something like the following (I have truncated the password; it is over 1,500 characters long):

```
docker login -u AWS -p
eyJwYXlsb2FkIjoiUEg5dmZZORVlKb2RRSjRBaEdtOUpXQWkydURVaGFFZ3JYRXIrQllVQi8yejN
3VXpxWjg3YUdCeng0VjBiR0F1L2ZNM0tHQWSJ9
https://687011138589.dkr.ecr.eu-west-1.amazonaws.com
```

Once logged in, you can build and tag your image with the instructions given. For example, I used the following commands:

```
$ docker image build -t dockerfile-example .
$ docker image tag dockerfile-example:latest 687011238589.dkr.ecr.eu-
west-1.amazonaws.com/dockerfile-example:latest
$ docker image push 687011238589.dkr.ecr.eu-
west-1.amazonaws.com/dockerfile-example:latest
```

After pushing, the image was visible in the AWS console:

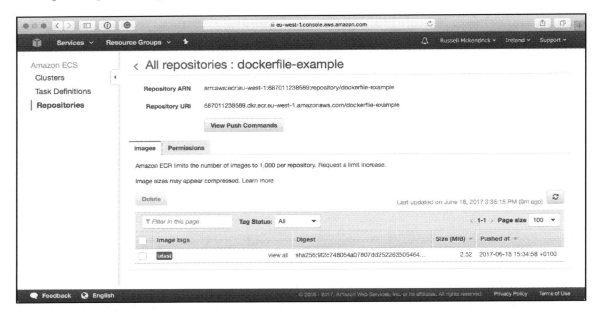

Also, after tweaking the permissions to allow anyone to pull the image, my image was available to anyone who runs the following:

```
$ docker image pull 687011238589.dkr.ecr.eu-
west-1.amazonaws.com/dockerfile-example
```

As you can see, this is more purely a registry service that allows you to push and pull images; there are no automated builds out-of-the-box; however, you should be able to build your own pipeline using the commands needed to log in, build, and push.

As already mentioned, we will be looking more at the container services offering by Amazon in later chapters. For now, if you would like more information on Amazon EC2 Container Registry, refer to the services page at http://aws.amazon.com/ecr/.

Microbadger

Microbadger is a great tool when you are looking at shipping your containers or images around. It will take into account everything that is going on in every single layer of a particular Docker image and give you the output of how much weight it has in terms of actual size or what amount of disk space it will take up.

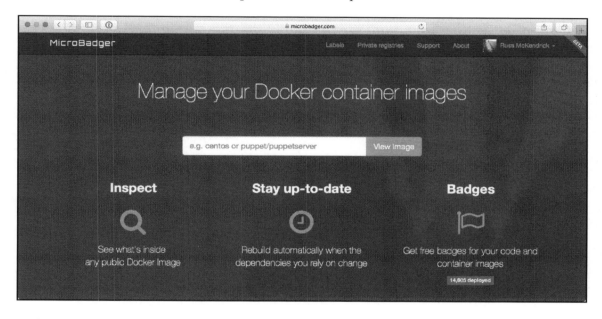

This page is what you will be presented with when navigating to the Microbadger website, `https://microbadger.com/`.

You can search for images that are on Docker Hub to have Microbadger provide information about that image back to you, or you can load up a sample image set if you are looking to provide some sample sets or to see some more complex setups.

In this example, we are going to search for our cluster application image and select the **latest tag**. As you can see from the following screenshot, Docker Hub is automatically searched with results returned in real time as you type:

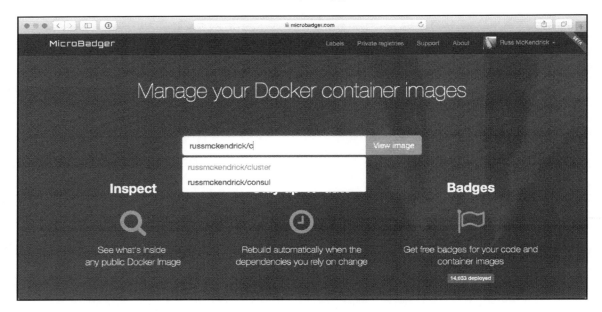

By default, it will always load the latest tag, but you also have the option of changing the tag you are viewing by selecting your desired tag from the **Versions** drop-down. This could be useful if you have, for example, a staging tag and are thinking of pushing this new image to your latest tag but want to see what impact it will have on the size of the image.

As you can see from the following screenshot, Microbadger presents information on how many layers your image contains:

As well as the size of each layer and the Dockerfile command executed during the image build, this is extremely useful when it comes to reducing the size of your images since you can see at which stage during the build image bloat is added.

Another great feature is that Microbadger gives you the option of embedding basic statistics about your images in your Git repository or Docker Hub; for example, the following screen shows the Docker Hub page for `https://hub.docker.com/r/russmckendrick/cluster/`:

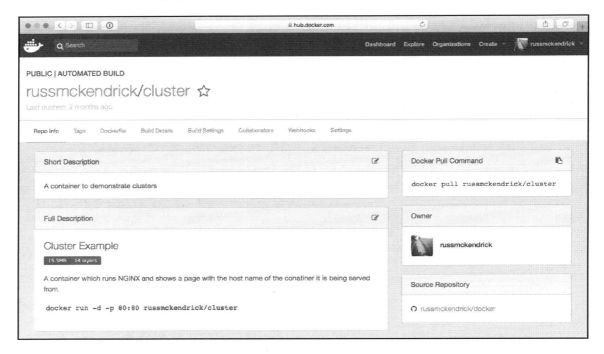

As you can see, Microbadger is displaying the overall size of the image as well as the total number of layers the image is made up of.

The Microbadger service is still in beta and new functions are being added all the time. I recommend that you keep an eye on it.

Summary

In this chapter, we looked at several ways in which you can both manually and automatically build container images using services such as Docker Hub, Quay, and Amazon ECR. We discussed various registries you can use as well as Docker Hub, such as the Docker Store and Red Hat's container catalog.

We also looked at deploying our own local Docker Registry and touched upon the considerations we need to make around storage when deploying one. Finally, we looked at Microbadger, a service that allows you to display information about your remotely hosted container images.

In the next chapter, we are going to look at how we can manage our containers from the command line.

4
Managing Containers

So far we have been concentrating on how to build, store, and distribute our Docker images. Now we are going to look at how we can launch containers and also how we can use the Docker command line client to manage and interact with them.

We will be revisiting the commands we used in the first chapter and going into a lot more detail before delving deeper into the commands that are available. Once we are familiar with the `container` commands, we will look at Docker networks and Docker volumes.

We will cover the following topics:

- Docker container commands

    - The basics
    - Interacting with your containers
    - Logs and process information
    - Resource limits
    - Container states and miscellaneous commands
    - Removing containers

- Docker networking and volume

Docker container commands

Before we look at some of the more complex Docker commands, let's review and go into a little more detail into the commands we have used in previous chapters.

The basics

In `Chapter 1`, *Docker Overview*, we launched the most basic container of all, the `hello-world` one:

```
$ docker container run hello-world
```

The output of the command is given here:

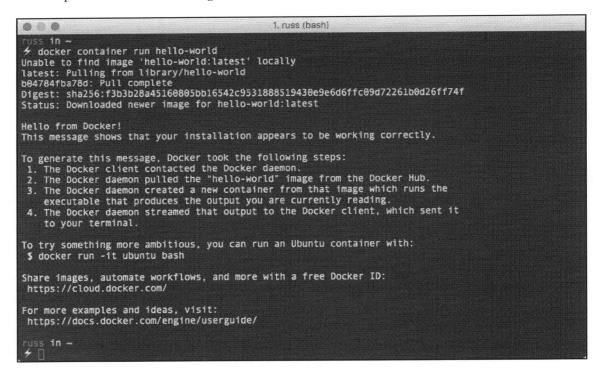

This command pulls a 1.84 KB image from the Docker Hub. You can find the Docker Store page for the image at `https://store.docker.com/images/hello-world/`, and as per the following Dockerfile, it runs an executable called `hello`:

```
FROM scratch
COPY hello /
CMD ["/hello"]
```

The `hello` executable prints the `"Hello from Docker!"` text to the Terminal and then the process exits. As the process exits, our container also stops; this can be seen by running the following:

```
$ docker container ls -a
```

The output of the command is given here:

You may notice in the following Terminal output that I ran the `docker container ls` with and without the `-a` flag, which is shorthand for `-all`, as running it without the flag does not show any exited containers.

We didn't have to name our container as it wasn't around long enough for us to care what it was called. Docker automatically assigns names for containers, and in my case, you can see that it was called `infallible_davinci`.

You will notice throughout your use of Docker that it comes up with some really interesting names for your containers if you choose to let it generate them for you. Although this is slightly off topic, the code to generate the names can be found at `https://github.com/moby/moby/blob/master/pkg/namesgenerator/names-generator.go`. As you can see, right at the end, it has the following `if` statement:

```
if name == "boring_wozniak" /*
Steve Wozniak is not boring */ {
  goto begin
}
```

Meaning there will never be a container called `boring_wozniak` (and quite rightly, too).

 Steve Wozniak is an inventor, electronics engineer, programmer, and entrepreneur who cofounded Apple Inc with Steve Jobs. He is known as a pioneer of the personal computer revolution of the 70s and 80s, and is definitely not boring!

We can remove the container with an exited status by running the following:

```
$ docker container rm infallible_davinci
```

Also, at the end of `Chapter 1`, *Docker Overview*, we launched a container using the official nginx image, which can be found at `https://store.docker.com/images/nginx/`, using the following command:

```
$ docker container run -d --name nginx-test -p 8080:80 nginx
```

As you may remember, this downloads the image and runs it, mapping port 8080 on our host machine to port 80 on the container, and calls it `nginx-test`:

```
● ● ●                              2. russ (bash)
⚡ docker container run -d --name nginx-test -p 8080:80 nginx
Unable to find image 'nginx:latest' locally
latest: Pulling from library/nginx
ff3d52d8f55f: Pull complete
226f4ec56ba3: Pull complete
53d7dd52b97d: Pull complete
Digest: sha256:41ad9967ea448d7c2b203c699b429abe1ed5af331cd92533900c6d77490e0268
Status: Downloaded newer image for nginx:latest
8cb5bdacd0acb562e92dcaa9a856534586a24557d0889c38b8f6e1ab0ded4e4d
russ in ~
⚡ docker image ls
REPOSITORY          TAG            IMAGE ID           CREATED          SIZE
hello-world         latest         1815c82652c0       9 days ago       1.84 kB
nginx               latest         958a7ae9e569       3 weeks ago      109 MB
russ in ~
⚡ ▯
```

As you can see, running `docker image ls` shows us that we now have two images downloaded and also running.

```
$ docker container ls
```

The previous command shows that we have a running container. The following Terminal output shows that mine had been up for 20 seconds when I ran the command:

As you can see from our `docker container run` command, we introduced three flags. One of them was `-d`, which is shorthand for `--detach`. If we hadn't added this flag, then our container would have executed in the foreground, which means that our terminal would have been frozen until we passed the process an escape command by pressing *Ctrl* + *C*.

We can see this in action by running the following command to launch a second nginx container:

```
$ docker container run --name nginx-foreground -p 9090:80 nginx
```

Once launched, open a browser and go to `http://localhost:9090/`. As you load the page, you will notice that your page visit is printed to the screen; hitting refresh in your browser will display more hits until you press *Ctrl* + *C* back in the terminal.

```
 docker container run --name nginx-foregound -p 9090:80 nginx
172.17.0.1 - - [24/Jun/2017:10:34:09 +0000] "GET / HTTP/1.1" 200 612 "-" "Mozilla/5.0 (Macintosh; In
tel Mac OS X 10_12_5) AppleWebKit/603.2.4 (KHTML, like Gecko) Version/10.1.1 Safari/603.2.4" "-"
172.17.0.1 - - [24/Jun/2017:10:34:10 +0000] "GET / HTTP/1.1" 200 612 "-" "Mozilla/5.0 (Macintosh; In
tel Mac OS X 10_12_5) AppleWebKit/603.2.4 (KHTML, like Gecko) Version/10.1.1 Safari/603.2.4" "-"
172.17.0.1 - - [24/Jun/2017:10:34:10 +0000] "GET / HTTP/1.1" 200 612 "-" "Mozilla/5.0 (Macintosh; In
tel Mac OS X 10_12_5) AppleWebKit/603.2.4 (KHTML, like Gecko) Version/10.1.1 Safari/603.2.4" "-"
172.17.0.1 - - [24/Jun/2017:10:34:11 +0000] "GET / HTTP/1.1" 200 612 "-" "Mozilla/5.0 (Macintosh; In
tel Mac OS X 10_12_5) AppleWebKit/603.2.4 (KHTML, like Gecko) Version/10.1.1 Safari/603.2.4" "-"
172.17.0.1 - - [24/Jun/2017:10:34:14 +0000] "GET / HTTP/1.1" 200 612 "-" "Mozilla/5.0 (Macintosh; In
tel Mac OS X 10_12_5) AppleWebKit/603.2.4 (KHTML, like Gecko) Version/10.1.1 Safari/603.2.4" "-"
172.17.0.1 - - [24/Jun/2017:10:34:14 +0000] "GET / HTTP/1.1" 200 612 "-" "Mozilla/5.0 (Macintosh; In
tel Mac OS X 10_12_5) AppleWebKit/603.2.4 (KHTML, like Gecko) Version/10.1.1 Safari/603.2.4" "-"
172.17.0.1 - - [24/Jun/2017:10:34:15 +0000] "GET / HTTP/1.1" 200 612 "-" "Mozilla/5.0 (Macintosh; In
tel Mac OS X 10_12_5) AppleWebKit/603.2.4 (KHTML, like Gecko) Version/10.1.1 Safari/603.2.4" "-"
172.17.0.1 - - [24/Jun/2017:10:34:15 +0000] "GET / HTTP/1.1" 200 612 "-" "Mozilla/5.0 (Macintosh; In
tel Mac OS X 10_12_5) AppleWebKit/603.2.4 (KHTML, like Gecko) Version/10.1.1 Safari/603.2.4" "-"
172.17.0.1 - - [24/Jun/2017:10:34:15 +0000] "GET / HTTP/1.1" 200 612 "-" "Mozilla/5.0 (Macintosh; In
tel Mac OS X 10_12_5) AppleWebKit/603.2.4 (KHTML, like Gecko) Version/10.1.1 Safari/603.2.4" "-"
^Cruss in ~
```

Running `docker container ls -a` shows that you have two containers, one of which has exited:

So what happened? When we removed the detach flag, Docker connected us to the nginx process directly within the container, meaning that we had visibility of `stdin`, `stdout`, and `stderr` for that process. When we used *Ctrl + C*, we actually sent an instruction to the NGINX process to terminate it; as that was the process that was keeping our container running, the container exited immediately as there was no longer a running process.

Standard input (stdin) is the handle that our process reads to get information from the end user.
Standard output (`stdout`) is where the process writes normal information to.
Standard error (`stderr`) is where the process writes error messages to.

Another thing you may have noticed when we launched the `"nginx-foreground"` container is that we gave it a different name using the `--name` flag.

This is because you cannot have two containers with the same name since Docker gives you the option of interacting with your containers using both the CONTAINER ID or NAME. This is the reason the name generator function exists: to assign a random name to containers you do not wish to name yourself--and also to ensure that we never call Steve Wozniak boring.

The final thing to mention is that when we launched `"nginx-foreground"`, we asked Docker to map port `9090` to port `80` on the container. This was because we cannot assign more than one process to a port on a host machine, so if we attempted to launch our second container with the same port as the first, we would have received an error message:

```
docker: Error response from daemon: driver failed programming external
connectivity on endpoint nginx-foregound
(c338635413d3aeae574e79a8eb89ede6a80a3ea4702de4800da89d0438a90be5): Bind
for 0.0.0.0:8080 failed: port is already allocated.
```

Also, since we were running the container in the foreground, we should receive an error from the nginx process as it failed to start:

```
ERRO[0003] error getting events from daemon: net/http: request cancelled
```

However, you may also notice that we are mapping to port 80 on the container--why no error there? Well, as explained in `Chapter 1`, *Docker Overview*, the containers themselves are isolated resources, which means that we can launch as many containers as we like with port 80 remapped, and they will never clash with other containers; we only run into problems when we want to route to the exposed container port from our Docker host. Let's keep our nginx container running for the next section.

Interacting with your containers

So far, our containers have been running a single process. Docker provides you with a few tools that enable you to both fork additional processes as well as interact with them.

Attach

The first way of interacting with your running container is to `attach` to the running process. We still have our `nginx-test` container running, so let's connect to that by running this command:

```
$ docker container attach nginx-test
```

Opening your browser and going to `http://localhost:8080/` will print the nginx access logs to screen in the same way when we launched the `nginx-foreground` container. Pressing *Ctrl + C* will terminate the process and return your Terminal to normal; however, as before, we would have terminated the process that was keeping the container running:

```
                             1. russ (bash)
russ in ~
⚡ docker container attach nginx-test
172.17.0.1 - - [24/Jun/2017:13:03:53 +0000] "GET / HTTP/1.1" 200 612 "-" "Mozilla/5.0 (Macintosh; In
tel Mac OS X 10_12_5) AppleWebKit/603.2.4 (KHTML, like Gecko) Version/10.1.1 Safari/603.2.4" "-"
172.17.0.1 - - [24/Jun/2017:13:03:54 +0000] "GET / HTTP/1.1" 200 612 "-" "Mozilla/5.0 (Macintosh; In
tel Mac OS X 10_12_5) AppleWebKit/603.2.4 (KHTML, like Gecko) Version/10.1.1 Safari/603.2.4" "-"
172.17.0.1 - - [24/Jun/2017:13:03:54 +0000] "GET / HTTP/1.1" 200 612 "-" "Mozilla/5.0 (Macintosh; In
tel Mac OS X 10_12_5) AppleWebKit/603.2.4 (KHTML, like Gecko) Version/10.1.1 Safari/603.2.4" "-"
^Cruss in ~
⚡ ▯
```

We can start our container back up by running the following:

```
$ docker container start nginx-test
```

This will start the container back up in the detached state, meaning that it is running in the background again. Going to `http://localhost:8080/` will show you the nginx welcome page again.

Let's reattach to our process, but this time pass an additional option:

```
$ docker container attach --sig-proxy=false nginx-test
```

Hitting the container's URL a few times and then pressing *Ctrl + C* will detach us from the process, but this time, rather than terminating the nginx process, it will just return us to our Terminal, leaving the container in a detached state--which can be seen by running `docker container ls`:

```
russ in ~
⚡ docker container attach --sig-proxy=false nginx-test
172.17.0.1 - - [24/Jun/2017:13:11:50 +0000] "GET / HTTP/1.1" 200 612 "-" "Mozilla/5.0 (Macintosh; In
tel Mac OS X 10_12_5) AppleWebKit/603.2.4 (KHTML, like Gecko) Version/10.1.1 Safari/603.2.4" "-"
172.17.0.1 - - [24/Jun/2017:13:11:51 +0000] "GET / HTTP/1.1" 200 612 "-" "Mozilla/5.0 (Macintosh; In
tel Mac OS X 10_12_5) AppleWebKit/603.2.4 (KHTML, like Gecko) Version/10.1.1 Safari/603.2.4" "-"
172.17.0.1 - - [24/Jun/2017:13:11:51 +0000] "GET / HTTP/1.1" 200 612 "-" "Mozilla/5.0 (Macintosh; In
tel Mac OS X 10_12_5) AppleWebKit/603.2.4 (KHTML, like Gecko) Version/10.1.1 Safari/603.2.4" "-"
^C
russ in ~
⚡ docker container ls
CONTAINER ID        IMAGE               COMMAND             CREATED             STATUS
       PORTS               NAMES
8cb5bdacd0ac        nginx               "nginx -g 'daemon ..."   2 hours ago         Up 2 minutes
       0.0.0.0:8080->80/tcp   nginx-test
russ in ~
⚡ 
```

exec

The `attach` command is useful if you need to connect to the process your container is running, but what if you need something a little more interactive? You can use the `exec` command; this spawns a second process within the container that you can interact with.

For example, to see the contents of the file `/etc/debian_version`, we can run the following command:

```
$ docker container exec nginx-test cat /etc/debian_version
```

This will spawn a second process, the `cat` command in this case, which prints the contents of `/etc/debian_version` to `stdout`. The second process will then terminate, leaving our container as it was before the `exec` command was executed:

```
● ● ●                          1. russ (bash)
⚡ docker container exec nginx-test cat /etc/debian_version
9.0
russ in ~
⚡ 
```

We can take this one step further by running the following command:

```
$ docker container exec -i -t nginx-test /bin/bash
```

This time, we are forking a bash process and using the `-i` and `-t` flags to keep open console access to our container. The `-i` flag is shorthand for `--interactive`, which instructs Docker to keep `stdin` open so that we can send commands to the process. The `-t` flag is short for `--tty` and allocates a `pseudo-TTY` to the session.

 Early user terminals connected to computers were called teletypewriters. While these devices are no longer used today, the acronym TTY has continued to be used to described text-only consoles in modern computing.

What this means is that you will be able to interact with your container as if you had a remote Terminal session, like SSH:

```
● ● ●                          1. russ (bash)
russ in ~
⚡ docker container exec -i -t nginx-test /bin/bash
root@8cb5bdacd0ac:/# whoami
root
root@8cb5bdacd0ac:/# ls -lhat /usr/share/nginx/html/
total 16K
drwxr-xr-x 2 root root 4.0K May 30 17:08 .
drwxr-xr-x 3 root root 4.0K May 30 17:08 ..
-rw-r--r-- 1 root root  537 May 30 13:03 50x.html
-rw-r--r-- 1 root root  612 May 30 13:03 index.html
root@8cb5bdacd0ac:/# exit
exit
russ in ~
⚡ 
```

While it is extremely useful as you can interact with the container as if it were a virtual machine, I do not recommend making any changes to your containers as they are running using the pseudo-TTY. It is more than likely that those changes will not persist and will be lost when your container is removed. We will go into the thinking behind this in more detail in Chapter 12, *Docker Workflows*.

Logs and process information

So far, we have been attaching to either the process in our container or the container itself to view information. Docker provides a few commands to allow you to view information about your containers without having to use either the attach or exec commands.

logs

The logs commands is pretty self explanatory; it allows you to interact with the stdout stream of your containers, which Docker is keeping track of in the background. For example, to view the last entries written to stdout for our nginx-test container, I just need to use the following command:

```
$ docker container logs --tail 5 nginx-test
```

The output of the command is shown here:

```
1. russ (bash)
⚡ docker container logs --tail 5 nginx-test
172.17.0.1 - - [24/Jun/2017:13:03:54 +0000] "GET / HTTP/1.1" 200 612 "-" "Mozilla/5.0 (Macintosh; Intel M
ac OS X 10_12_5) AppleWebKit/603.2.4 (KHTML, like Gecko) Version/10.1.1 Safari/603.2.4" "-"
172.17.0.1 - - [24/Jun/2017:13:11:50 +0000] "GET / HTTP/1.1" 200 612 "-" "Mozilla/5.0 (Macintosh; Intel M
ac OS X 10_12_5) AppleWebKit/603.2.4 (KHTML, like Gecko) Version/10.1.1 Safari/603.2.4" "-"
172.17.0.1 - - [24/Jun/2017:13:11:51 +0000] "GET / HTTP/1.1" 200 612 "-" "Mozilla/5.0 (Macintosh; Intel M
ac OS X 10_12_5) AppleWebKit/603.2.4 (KHTML, like Gecko) Version/10.1.1 Safari/603.2.4" "-"
172.17.0.1 - - [24/Jun/2017:13:11:51 +0000] "GET / HTTP/1.1" 200 612 "-" "Mozilla/5.0 (Macintosh; Intel M
ac OS X 10_12_5) AppleWebKit/603.2.4 (KHTML, like Gecko) Version/10.1.1 Safari/603.2.4" "-"
172.17.0.1 - - [24/Jun/2017:13:31:27 +0000] "GET / HTTP/1.1" 200 612 "-" "Mozilla/5.0 (Macintosh; Intel M
ac OS X 10_12_5) AppleWebKit/603.2.4 (KHTML, like Gecko) Version/10.1.1 Safari/603.2.4" "-"
russ in ~
⚡ 
```

To view the logs in real time, I simply need to run the following:

```
$ docker container logs -f nginx-test
```

The -f flag is shorthand for --follow. I can also, say, view everything that has been logged since 15:00 today by running the following:

```
$ docker container logs --since 2017-06-24T15:00 nginx-test
```

The output of the command is shown here:

```
1. russ (bash)
russ in ~
⚡ docker container logs --since 2017-06-24T15:00 nginx-test
172.17.0.1 - - [24/Jun/2017:14:34:04 +0000] "GET / HTTP/1.1" 200 612 "-" "Mozilla/5.0 (Macintosh; Intel M
ac OS X 10_12_5) AppleWebKit/603.2.4 (KHTML, like Gecko) Version/10.1.1 Safari/603.2.4" "-"
172.17.0.1 - - [24/Jun/2017:14:34:04 +0000] "GET / HTTP/1.1" 200 612 "-" "Mozilla/5.0 (Macintosh; Intel M
ac OS X 10_12_5) AppleWebKit/603.2.4 (KHTML, like Gecko) Version/10.1.1 Safari/603.2.4" "-"
russ in ~
⚡
```

You might notice in the preceding output that the timestamp in the access log is 14:34, which is before 15:00. Why is that?

The logs command shows the timestamps of stdout recorded by Docker and not the time within the container. You can see this from when I run the following commands:

```
$ date
$ docker container exec nginx-test date
```

The output is shown here:

```
1. russ (bash)
russ in ~
⚡ date
Sat 24 Jun 2017 15:38:43 BST
russ in ~
⚡ docker container exec nginx-test date
Sat Jun 24 14:38:46 UTC 2017
russ in ~
⚡
```

There is an hour's time difference between my host machine and the container due to British Summer Time (BST) being in effect on my host.

Luckily, to save confusion--or add to it, depending on how you look at it--you can add -t to your logs commands:

```
$ docker container logs --since 2017-06-24T15:00 -t nginx-test
```

The -t flag is short for --timestamp; this option prepends the time the output was captured by Docker:

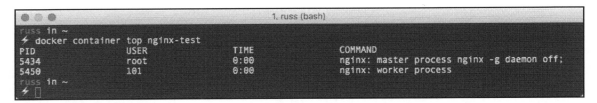

top

The top command is quite a simple one; it lists the processes running within the container you specify:

```
$ docker container top nginx-test
```

The output of the command is shown here:

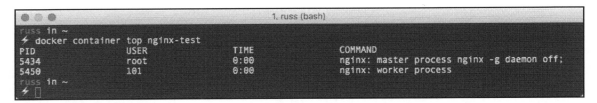

As you can see from the following Terminal output, we have two processes running, both of which are nginx, which is to be expected.

stats

The stats command provides real-time information on either the specified container or, if you don't pass a container name or ID, all running containers:

```
$ docker container stats nginx-test
```

As you can see from the following Terminal output, we are given information on the CPU, RAM, NETWORK, and DISK IO for the specified container:

We can also pass the -a flag; this is short for --all and displays all containers, running or not:

However, as you can see from the preceding output, if the container isn't running, there aren't any resources being utilized, so it doesn't really add any value other than giving you a visual representation of how many containers you have running and where the resources are being used.

It is also worth pointing out that the information displayed by the stats command is real-time only; Docker does not record the resource utilization and make it available in the same way that the logs command does.

Resource limits

The last command we ran showed us the resource utilization of our containers; by default, a container when launched will be allowed to consume all the available resources on the host machine if it requires it. We can put caps on the resources our containers can consume; let's start by updating the resource allowances of our nginx-test container.

Typically, we would have set the limits when we launched our container using the run command; for example, to halve the CPU priority and set a memory limit of 128M, we would have used the following command:

```
$ docker container run -d --name nginx-test --cpu-shares 512 --memory 128M
-p 8080:80 nginx
```

However, we didn't need to update our already running container; to do this, we can use the update command. Now you must have thought that this should entail just running the following command:

```
$ docker container update --cpu-shares 512 --memory 128M nginx-test
```

Running the preceding command will actually produce an error:

```
Error response from daemon: Cannot update container
e6ac3ce1418d520233a68f71a1e5cb38b1ab0aafab5fa00d6e0220975706b246: Memory
limit should be smaller than already set memoryswap limit, update the
memoryswap at the same time
```

So what is the memoryswap limit currently set to? To find this out, we can use the inspect command to display all of the configuration data for our running container; just run the following:

```
$ docker container inspect nginx-test
```

As you can see, there is a lot of configuration data. When I ran the command, a 199-line JSON array was returned. Let's use the grep command to filter out just the lines that contain the word memory:

```
$ docker container inspect nginx-test | grep -i memory
```

This returns the following configuration data:

```
"Memory": 0,
"KernelMemory": 0,
"MemoryReservation": 0,
"MemorySwap": 0,
"MemorySwappiness": -1,
```

Everything is set to 0: how can 128M be smaller than 0? In the context of the configuration of the resources, 0 is actually the default value and means that there are no limits--notice the lack of M at the end. This means that our update command should actually read the following:

```
$ docker container update --cpu-shares 512 --memory 128M --memory-swap 256M
nginx-test
```

> Paging is a memory-management scheme in which the kernel stores and retrieves, or swaps, data from secondary storage for use in main memory. This allows processes to exceed the size of available physical memory.

By default, when you set `--memory` as part of the `run` command, Docker will set the `--memory-swap` size to be twice of that of `--memory`.

If you run `docker container stats nginx-test` now, you should see our limits in place:

Also, rerunning `docker container inspect nginx-test | grep -i memory` will show the changes:

```
"Memory": 134217728,
"KernelMemory": 0,
"MemoryReservation": 0,
"MemorySwap": 268435456,
"MemorySwappiness": -1,
```

The values when running `docker container inspect` are all shown in bytes.

Container states and miscellaneous commands

For the final part of this section, we are going to look at the various states your containers could be in and the few remaining commands we have yet to cover as part of the `docker container` command.

Running `docker container ls -a` should show something similar to the following Terminal output:

As you can see, we have two containers; one is Up and the other has Exited. Before we continue, let's launch five more containers. To do this quickly, run the following command:

```
$ for i in {1..5}; do docker container run -d --name nginx$(printf "$i")
nginx; done
```

When running `docker container ls -a`, you should see your five new containers, named nginx1 through to nginx5:

Pause and unpause

Let's look at pausing nginx1. To do this, simply run the following:

```
$ docker container pause nginx1
```

Running `docker container ls` will show that the container has a status of Up, but Paused:

Note that we didn't have to use the -a flag to see information about the container as the process has not been terminated; instead, it has been suspended using the cgroups freezer. With the cgroups freezer, the process is unaware it has been suspended, meaning that it can be resumed.

 For more information on the cgroups freezer function, read the official kernel documentation at https://www.kernel.org/doc/Documentation /cgroup-v1/freezer-subsystem.txt.

As you will have probably already guessed, you can resume a paused container using the unpause command:

```
$ docker container unpause nginx1
```

This command is useful if you need to freeze the state of a container; maybe one of your containers is going haywire and you need to do some investigation later but don't want it to have a negative impact on your other running containers.

Stop, start, restart, and kill

Next up, we have the stop, start, restart, and kill commands. We have already used the start command to resume a container with a status of Exited. The stop command works in exactly the same way as when we used *Ctrl + C* to detach from your container running in the foreground. Run the following:

```
$ docker container stop nginx2
```

With this, a request is sent to the process for it to terminate, called a SIGTERM. If the process has not terminated itself within a grace period, then a kill signal, called a SIGKILL, is sent. This will immediately terminate the process, not giving it anytime to finish whatever is causing the delay, for example, committing the results of a database query to disk.

Because this could be bad, Docker has given you the option of overriding the default grace period, which is 10 seconds, by using the -t flag; this is short for --time. For example, running the following command will wait up to 60 seconds before sending a SIGKILL, should it need to be sent to kill the process:

```
$ docker container stop -t 60 nginx3
```

The start command, as we have already experienced, will start the process back up; however, unlike the pause and unpause commands, the process in this case starts from scratch rather than starting from where it left off.

```
$ docker container start nginx2 nginx3
```

The restart command is a combination of the following two commands; it stops and then starts the container ID or name you pass it. Also, like stop, you can pass the -t flag:

```
$ docker container restart -t 60 nginx4
```

Finally, you also have the option sending a SIGKILL immediately to the container by running the kill command:

```
$ docker container kill nginx5
```

Removing containers

Let's check the containers we have running using the docker container ls -a command. When I run the command, I can see that I have two containers with an Exited status and all of the others are running:

To remove the two exited containers, I can simply run the prune command:

```
$ docker container prune
```

When doing so, a warning pops up and you are asked to confirm whether you are really sure:

You can choose which container you want to remove using the rm command; like this, for example:

```
$ docker container rm nginx4
```

However, attempting to remove a running container will result in an error:

```
Error response from daemon: You cannot remove a running container
5bbc78af29c871200539e7534725e12691aa7df6facd616e91acbe41f204b734. Stop the
container before attempting removal or use -f
```

As you can see from the preceding output, the error very kindly suggests that using the -f flag will forcibly remove the container by stopping it and then removing it, requiring the following command:

```
$ docker container rm -f nginx4
```

Another alternative would be to string the stop and rm commands together:

```
$ docker container stop nginx3 && docker container rm nginx3
```

However, given that you can use the prune command now, this is probably way too much effect, especially as you are trying to remove the containers and probably don't care too much how gracefully the process is terminated.

Feel free to remove the remainder of your containers using whichever method you like.

Miscellaneous commands

For the final part of this section, we are going to look at a few commands that you probably won't use too much during your day-to-day Docker use. The first of these is create. The create command is pretty similar to the run command, except that it does not start the container, but instead prepares and configures one:

```
$ docker container create --name nginx-test -p 8080:80 nginx
```

You can check the status of your created container by running docker container ls -a and then start the container with docker container run nginx-test before checking the status again:

The next command we are going to quickly look at is the `port` command; this displays the port along with any port mappings for the container:

```
$ docker container port nginx-test
```

It should return the following:

```
80/tcp -> 0.0.0.0:8080
```

We already know this as it is what we configured, and also the ports are listed in the `docker container ls` output.

The final command we are going to quickly look at is the `diff` command. This command prints a list of all of the files that have been added or changed since the container started to run--so basically, a list of the differences on the filesystem between the image we used to launch the container and now.

Before we run the command, let's create a blank file within the `nginx-test` container using the `exec` command:

```
$ docker container exec nginx-test touch /tmp/testing
```

Now that we have a file called `testing` in `/tmp`, we can view the differences between the original image and the running container using the following:

```
$ docker container diff nginx-test
```

This will return a list of files; as you can see from the following list, there is our testing file along with the files that were created when nginx started:

```
C /run
A /run/nginx.pid
C /tmp
A /tmp/testing
C /var/cache/nginx
A /var/cache/nginx/client_temp
A /var/cache/nginx/fastcgi_temp
A /var/cache/nginx/proxy_temp
A /var/cache/nginx/scgi_temp
A /var/cache/nginx/uwsgi_temp
```

It is worth pointing out that once we stop and remove the container, these files will be lost. In the next section of this chapter, we will look at Docker volumes and learn how we can persist data.

Again, if you are following along, you should remove any running containers launched during this section using the command of your choice.

Docker networking and volumes

Before we finish off this chapter, we are going to take a look at the basics of Docker networking and Docker volumes using the default drivers. Let's take a look at networking first.

Docker networking

So far, we have been launching our containers on a single flat shared network. Although we have not talked about it yet, this means the containers we have been launching would have been able to communicate with each other without having to use any of the host networking.

Rather than going into detail now, let's work through an example. We are going to be running a two-container application; the first container will be running Redis and the second our application, which uses the Redis container to store a system state.

 Redis is an in-memory data structure store that can be used as a database, cache, or message broker. It supports different levels of on-disk persistence. For more information, refer to `https://redis.io/`.

Before we launch our application, let's download the container images we will be using and also create the network:

```
$ docker image pull redis:alpine
$ docker image pull russmckendrick/moby-counter
$ docker network create moby-counter
```

You should see something similar to the following Terminal output:

```
● ● ●                      1. moby-counter (bash)
russ in ~/Documents/Code/docker/moby-counter on master*
⚡ docker image pull redis:alpine
alpine: Pulling from library/redis
43d680a959df: Pull complete
4371af8a8c8e: Pull complete
99ed756029db: Pull complete
653720cb4fd4: Pull complete
a65f285e1862: Pull complete
f0d06b31f9ca: Pull complete
Digest: sha256:abd220f66aac9f530096d5c4d382eb1483dc4e3bac5dd6a56b67746cd86d0e5b
Status: Downloaded newer image for redis:alpine
russ in ~/Documents/Code/docker/moby-counter on master*
⚡ docker image pull russmckendrick/moby-counter
Using default tag: latest
latest: Pulling from russmckendrick/moby-counter
cfc728c1c558: Pull complete
21552fe8e0cd: Pull complete
3025e3fe6722: Pull complete
5c51b5fc92b9: Pull complete
da1cc31641fc: Pull complete
0477dda24b67: Pull complete
Digest: sha256:69dd4b4ae6ef09d6e87cc7bd1b0f3a71d083b844f60d20ddbdefba9872dcef80
Status: Downloaded newer image for russmckendrick/moby-counter:latest
russ in ~/Documents/Code/docker/moby-counter on master*
⚡ docker network create moby-counter
adfd04f86ceb0e0138b3c46c5ffac98810a572895583af0a5fce644378ce16c8
russ in ~/Documents/Code/docker/moby-counter on master*
⚡ []
```

Now that we have our images pulled and our network created, we can launch our containers, starting with the Redis one:

```
$ docker container run -d --name redis --network moby-counter redis:alpine
```

As you can see, we have used the `--network` flag to define which network our container was launched in. Now that the Redis container is launched, we can launch the application container by running the following:

```
$ docker container run -d --name moby-counter --network moby-counter -p
8080:80 russmckendrick/moby-counter
```

Again, we have launched the container into the `moby-counter` network; this time, we have mapped port `8080` to port `80` on the container. Notice that we did not need to worry about exposing any ports of the Redis container. That is because the Redis image comes with some defaults, which expose the default port (which is `6379`) for us. This can be seen by running `docker container ls`:

All that remains now is to access the application; to do this, open your browser and go to `http://localhost:8080/`. You should be greeted by a mostly blank page with the message **Click to add logos**:

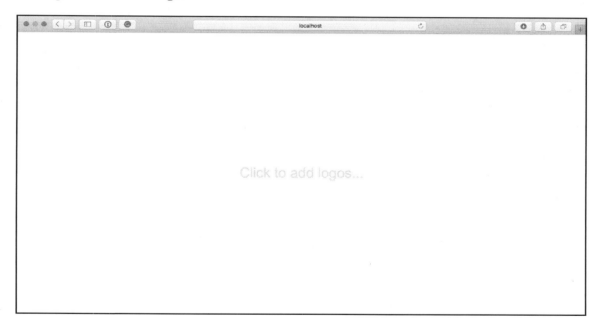

Clicking anywhere on the page will add Docker logos, so click away:

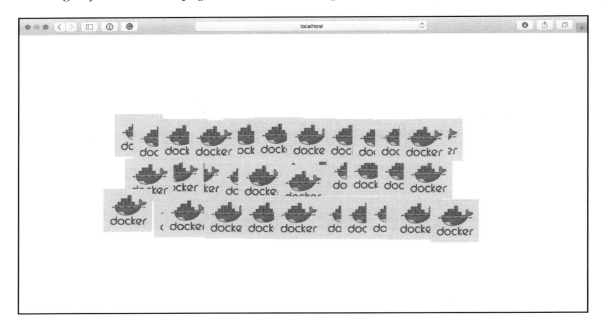

So what is happening? The application that is being served from the `moby-counter` container is making a connection to the `redis` container and using the Redis service to store the on-screen coordinates of each of the logos you are placing on the screen by clicking.

How is the `moby-counter` application connecting to the `redis` container? Well, in the `server.js` file, the following default values are being set:

```
var port = opts.redis_port || process.env.USE_REDIS_PORT || 6379
var host = opts.redis_host || process.env.USE_REDIS_HOST || 'redis'
```

This means that the `moby-counter` application is looking to connect to the host called `redis` on port `6379`. Let's try using the `exec` command to ping the `redis` container from the `moby-counter` application and see what we get:

```
$ docker container exec moby-counter ping -c 3 redis
```

You should see something similar to the following output:

```
PING redis (172.18.0.2): 56 data bytes
64 bytes from 172.18.0.2: seq=0 ttl=64 time=0.057 ms
64 bytes from 172.18.0.2: seq=1 ttl=64 time=0.087 ms
64 bytes from 172.18.0.2: seq=2 ttl=64 time=0.085 ms

--- redis ping statistics ---
3 packets transmitted, 3 packets received, 0% packet loss
round-trip min/avg/max = 0.057/0.076/0.087 ms
```

As you can see, the `moby-container` container resolves `redis` to the IP address of the Redis container, which is `172.18.0.2`. You may be thinking that the application's host file contains an entry for the `redis` container; let's take a look using the following command:

```
$ docker container exec moby-counter cat /etc/hosts
```

This returns the contents of `/etc/hosts`, which for me look like the following:

```
127.0.0.1 localhost
::1 localhost ip6-localhost ip6-loopback
fe00::0 ip6-localnet
ff00::0 ip6-mcastprefix
ff02::1 ip6-allnodes
ff02::2 ip6-allrouters
172.18.0.3 8ed5183eded1
```

Other than the entry at the end, which is actually the IP address resolving to the hostname of the local container, 8ed5183eded1 is the ID of the container; there is no sign of an entry for `redis`. Next, let's check `/etc/resolv.conf` by running the following:

```
$ docker container exec moby-counter cat /etc/resolv.conf
```

This returns what we are looking for; as you can see, we are using a local `nameserver`:

```
nameserver 127.0.0.11
options ndots:0
```

Let's perform a DNS lookup on `redis` against `127.0.0.11` using the following command:

```
$ docker container exec moby-counter nslookup redis 127.0.0.11
```

This returns the IP address of the `redis` container:

```
Server: 127.0.0.11
Address 1: 127.0.0.11

Name: redis.moby-counter
Address 1: 172.18.0.2 redis.moby-counter
```

Let's create a second network and launch another application container:

```
$ docker network create moby-counter2
$ docker run -itd --name moby-counter2 --network moby-counter2 -p 9090:80
russmckendrick/moby-counter
```

Now that we have the second application container up and running, let's try pinging the `redis` container from it:

```
$ docker container exec moby-counter2 ping -c 3 redis
```

In my case, I get a response, but it is not the one I am expecting:

```
PING redis (92.242.132.15): 56 data bytes
64 bytes from 92.242.132.15: seq=0 ttl=37 time=0.314 ms
64 bytes from 92.242.132.15: seq=1 ttl=37 time=0.211 ms
64 bytes from 92.242.132.15: seq=2 ttl=37 time=0.233 ms

--- redis ping statistics ---
3 packets transmitted, 3 packets received, 0% packet loss
round-trip min/avg/max = 0.211/0.252/0.314 ms
```

Checking the `resolv.conf` file shows that the same `nameserver` is being used:

```
$ docker container exec moby-counter2 cat /etc/resolv.conf

nameserver 127.0.0.11
options ndots:0
```

However, when performing a lookup, we cannot resolve `redis` and instead, it is falling back to my ISP's default `nameservers`, which are basically returning an error:

```
$ docker container exec moby-counter2 nslookup redis 127.0.0.11
Server: 127.0.0.11
Address 1: 127.0.0.11

Name: redis
Address 1: 92.242.132.15 unallocated.barefruit.co.uk
```

Let's look at launching a second Redis server in our second network; as we have already discussed, we cannot have two containers with the same name, so let's creatively name it redis2.

As our application is configured to connect to a container that resolves to redis, does this mean we will have to make changes to our application container? No, Docker has you covered.

While you cannot have two containers with the same names, as we have already discovered, our second network is running completely isolated from our first network, meaning that we can still use the DNS name of redis; to do this, we need to add the --network-alias flag:

```
$ docker container run -d --name redis2 --network moby-counter2 --network-alias redis redis:alpine
```

As you can see, we have named the container redis2 but set the --network-alias to be redis; this means that when we perform the lookup, we see the correct IP address returned:

```
$ docker container exec moby-counter2 nslookup redis 127.0.0.11
Server:  127.0.0.11
Address 1:  127.0.0.11

Name:  redis
Address 1:  172.19.0.3 redis2.moby-counter2
```

As you can see, redis is actually an alias for redis2.moby-counter2, which then resolves to 172.19.0.3.

Now we should have two applications running side by side in their own isolated networks on your local Docker host, accessible at http://localhost:8080/ and http://localhost:9090/. Running docker network ls will display all of the networks configured on your Docker host, including the default networks:

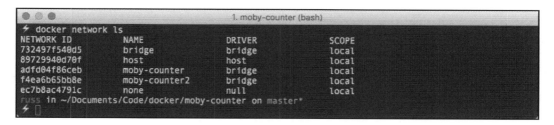

You can find out more information about the configuration of the networks by running the `inspect` command:

```
$ docker network inspect moby-counter
```

It returns the following JSON array:

```
[
    {
        "Name": "moby-counter",
        "Id":
"adfd04f86ceb0e0138b3c46c5ffac98810a572895583af0a5fce644378ce16c8",
        "Created": "2017-06-24T21:45:59.109846671Z",
        "Scope": "local",
        "Driver": "bridge",
        "EnableIPv6": false,
        "IPAM": {
            "Driver": "default",
            "Options": {},
            "Config": [
                {
                    "Subnet": "172.18.0.0/16",
                    "Gateway": "172.18.0.1"
                }
            ]
        },
        "Internal": false,
        "Attachable": false,
        "Containers": {
        "1bece530450ab46450d185be2def
9d7820ba3da36948cb77f5b51a931bb58738": {
                "Name": "redis",
                "EndpointID":
"6f5199ec31cd852f7eff961fa9afd9
4810c602af69d5a870f6209bbaed087b56",
                "MacAddress": "02:42:ac:12:00:02",
                "IPv4Address": "172.18.0.2/16",
                "IPv6Address": ""
            },
            "8ed5183eded1c904b86c279ab15
ac44ffe15c2a57f1fb2287170f221dc320633": {
                "Name": "moby-counter",
                "EndpointID":
"fcad0cbb7249b355bead29d424919f65
49c111a3a0364116d2d6e1d02b217411",
                "MacAddress": "02:42:ac:12:00:03",
                "IPv4Address": "172.18.0.3/16",
                "IPv6Address": ""
```

```
            }
        },
        "Options": {},
        "Labels": {}
    }
]
```

As you can see, it contains information on the network addressing being used in the IPAM section, and also details on each of the two containers running in the network.

 IP address management (IPAM) is a means of planning, tracking, and managing IP addresses within the network. IPAM has both DNS and DHCP services so that each service is notified of changes in the other; for example, DHCP assigns an address to `container2`. The DNS service is updated to return the IP address assigned by DHCP whenever a lookup is made against `container2`.

Before we progress to the next section, we should remove one of the applications and associated networks. To do this, run the following commands:

```
$ docker container stop moby-counter2 redis2
$ docker container prune
$ docker network prune
```

This will remove the containers and network:

As mentioned at the start of this section, this is only the default network driver, meaning that we are restricted to our networks only being available on a single Docker host. In later chapters, we will look at how we can expand our Docker network across multiple hosts and even providers.

Docker volumes

If you have been following along with the network example from the previous section, you should have two containers running:

When you go to the application in a browser (at `http://localhost:8080/`), you will probably see that there already are Docker logos on screen. Let's stop and remove the Redis container and see what happens. To do this, run the following:

```
$ docker container stop redis
$ docker container rm redis
```

If you have your browser open, you may notice that the Docker icons have faded into the background and there is an animated loader in the center of the screen; this is basically to show that the application is waiting for the connection to the Redis container to be reestablished:

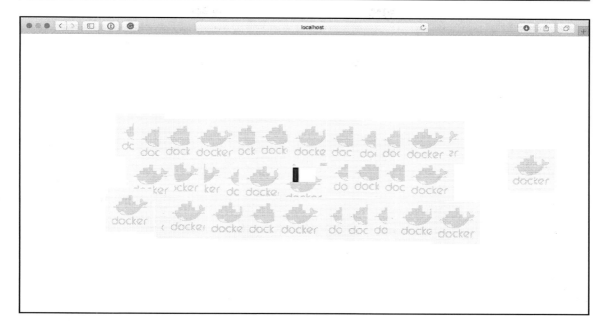

Relaunch the Redis container using the following command:

```
$ docker container run -d --name redis --network moby-counter redis:alpine
```

This restores the connectivity; however, when you start to interact with the application, your previous icons disappear and you are left with a clean slate. Quickly add some more logos to the screen, this time placed in a different pattern like I have done here:

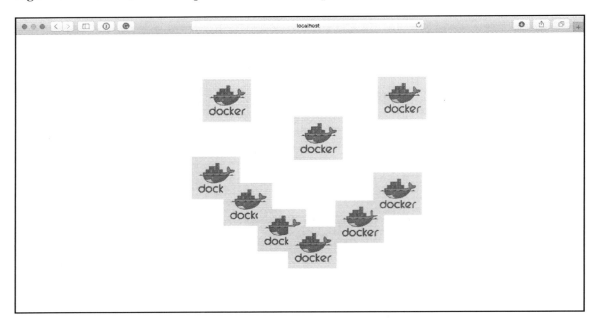

Once you have a pattern, let's remove the Redis container again by running:

```
$ docker container stop redis
$ docker container rm redis
```

As we discussed earlier in the chapter, losing the data in the container is to be expected. However, as we used the official Redis image from `https://store.docker.com/images/re dis/`, we haven't in fact lost any of our data.

The Dockerfile for the Redis offical image we used looks like the following:

```
FROM alpine:3.5

RUN addgroup -S redis && adduser -S -G redis redis
RUN apk add --no-cache 'su-exec>=0.2'

ENV REDIS_VERSION 3.0.7
ENV REDIS_DOWNLOAD_URL http://download.redis.io/releases/redis-3.0.7.tar.gz
ENV REDIS_DOWNLOAD_SHA e56b4b7e033ae8dbf311f9191cf6fdf3ae974d1c
```

```
RUN set -x \
  && apk add --no-cache --virtual .build-deps \
     gcc \
     linux-headers \
     make \
     musl-dev \
     tar \
  && wget -O redis.tar.gz "$REDIS_DOWNLOAD_URL" \
  && echo "$REDIS_DOWNLOAD_SHA *redis.tar.gz" | sha1sum -c - \
  && mkdir -p /usr/src/redis \
  && tar -xzf redis.tar.gz -C /usr/src/redis --strip-components=1 \
  && rm redis.tar.gz \
  && make -C /usr/src/redis \
  && make -C /usr/src/redis install \
  && rm -r /usr/src/redis \
  && apk del .build-deps

RUN mkdir /data && chown redis:redis /data
VOLUME /data
WORKDIR /data

COPY docker-entrypoint.sh /usr/local/bin/
RUN ln -s usr/local/bin/docker-entrypoint.sh /entrypoint.sh # backwards
compat
ENTRYPOINT ["docker-entrypoint.sh"]

EXPOSE 6379
CMD [ "redis-server" ]
```

If you notice, toward the end of the file, there are the VOLUME and WORKDIR directives declared; this means that when our container was launched, Docker actually created a volume and then ran redis-server from within the volume.

We can see this by running the following command:

```
$ docker volume ls
```

This should show at least two volumes:

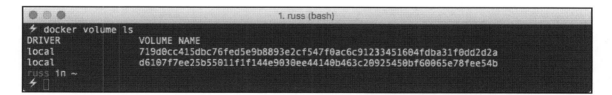

As you can see, the volume name is not very friendly at all, in fact, it is the unique ID of the volume. So how can we use the volume when we launch our Redis container? We know from the Dockerfile that the volume was mounted at /data within the container, so all we have to do is tell Docker which volume to use and where it should be mounted at runtime.

To do this, run the following command, making sure you replace the volume ID with that of your own:

```
$ docker container run -d --name redis -v
719d0cc415dbc76fed5e9b8893e2cf547f0ac6c91233451604fdba31f0dd2d2a:/data --
network moby-counter redis:alpine
```

If your application page looks like it is still trying to reconnect to the Redis container once you have launched your Redis container, then you may need to refresh your browser; failing that, restarting the application container by running `docker container restart moby-counter` and then refreshing your browser again should work.

You should be able to see the icons in their original positions. We can view the contents of the /data folder on the Redis container by running:

```
$ docker container exec redis ls -lhat /data
```

This will return something that looks like the following:

```
total 12
drwxr-xr-x 1 root root 4.0K Jun 25 14:55 ..
drwxr-xr-x 2 redis redis 4.0K Jun 25 14:00 .
-rw-r--r-- 1 redis redis 421 Jun 25 14:00 dump.rdb
```

You can also remove your running container and relaunch it, but this time using the ID of the second volume.

Finally, you can override the volume with your own. To create a volume, we need to use the `volume` command:

```
$ docker volume create redis_data
```

Once created, we will be able to use the `redis_data` volume to store our Redis on by running this command:

```
$ docker container run -d --name redis -v redis_data:/data --network moby-
counter redis:alpine
```

We can then use it as needed:

```
russ in ~
⚡ docker volume create redis_data
redis_data
russ in ~
⚡ docker container run -d --name redis -v redis_data:/data  --network moby-counter redis:alpine
fbe37a9162841a1ec04fe38ffc41461d63a73c0cf2aa7b4d38d07ffcdb98c35b
russ in ~
⚡ docker container restart moby-counter
moby-counter
russ in ~
⚡ docker container rm -f redis
redis
russ in ~
⚡ docker container run -d --name redis -v redis_data:/data  --network moby-counter redis:alpine
177937e2f058bb424d7b461b4257fd09e41f61f1465c4b0b0988192b005a0f65
russ in ~
⚡
```

Like the `network` command, we can view more information on the volume using the `inspect` command:

```
$ docker volume inspect redis_data
```

Look at the following output:

```
[
  {
    "Driver": "local",
    "Labels": {},
    "Mountpoint":
"/var/lib/docker/volumes/redis_data/_data",
    "Name": "redis_data",
    "Options": {},
    "Scope": "local"
  }
]
```

You can see that there is not much to a volume when using the local driver; one interesting thing to note is that the path to where the data is stored on the Docker host machine is `/var/lib/docker/volumes/redis_data/_data`. If you are using Docker for Mac or Docker for Windows, then this path will be your Docker host VM and not your local machine, meaning that you do not have direct access to the data inside the volume.

Don't worry though; we will be looking at Docker volumes and how you can interact with data in later chapters. For now, we should tidy up. First of all, remove the two containers and network:

```
$ docker container stop redis moby-counter
$ docker container prune
$ docker network prune
```

Then we can remove the volumes by running the following:

```
$ docker volume prune
```

You should see something similar to the following Terminal output:

```
● ● ●                           1. russ (bash)
⚡ docker container stop redis moby-counter
redis
moby-counter
russ in ~
⚡ docker container prune
WARNING! This will remove all stopped containers.
Are you sure you want to continue? [y/N] y
Deleted Containers:
177937e2f058bb424d7b461b4257fd09e41f61f1465c4b0b0988192b005a0f65
8ed5183eded1c904b86c279ab15ac44ffe15c2a57f1fb2287170f221dc320633

Total reclaimed space: 0 B
russ in ~
⚡ docker network prune
WARNING! This will remove all networks not used by at least one container.
Are you sure you want to continue? [y/N] y
Deleted Networks:
moby-counter

russ in ~
⚡ docker volume prune
WARNING! This will remove all volumes not used by at least one container.
Are you sure you want to continue? [y/N] y
Deleted Volumes:
719d0cc415dbc76fed5e9b8893e2cf547f0ac6c91233451604fdba31f0dd2d2a
d6107f7ee25b55011f1f144e9030ee44140b463c20925450bf60065e78fee54b
redis_data

Total reclaimed space: 743 B
russ in ~
⚡ ▯
```

As you can see, we are now back to having a clean slate.

Summary

In this chapter, we looked at how you can use the Docker command-line client to manage both individual containers as well as launch multi-container applications in their own isolated Docker networks. We also discussed how we can persist data on the filesystem using Docker volumes.

So far in this and the previous chapters, we have covered in detail the majority of the available commands used in the following sections:

```
$ docker container [command]
$ docker network [command]
$ docker volume [command]
$ docker image [command]
```

We have covered the four main areas of using Docker locally; we can now start to look at how we can interact with remote Docker hosts.

In the next chapter, we will use Docker Machine and revisit Docker networking.

5

Docker Machine

In this chapter, we will take a look at Docker Machine. It can be used to easily launch and bootstrap Docker hosts targeting various platforms, including locally or in a cloud environment. You can control your Docker hosts with it as well. Let's take a look at what we will be covering in this chapter:

- An introduction to Docker Machine
- Using Docker Machine to set up local Docker hosts
- Launching Docker hosts in the cloud
- More Docker networking
- Using other base operating systems

An introduction to Docker Machine

Before we roll our sleeves up and get stuck in with Docker Machine, we should take a moment to discuss what place it has in the overall Docker ecosystem.

Docker Machine's biggest strength is that it provides a consistent interface to several public cloud providers:

- **Amazon Web Services**: `https://aws.amazon.com/`
- **Microsoft Azure**: `https://azure.microsoft.com/`
- **DigitalOcean**: `https://www.digitalocean.com/`
- **Exoscale**: `https://www.exoscale.ch/`
- **Google Compute Engine**: `https://cloud.google.com/`
- **Rackspace**: `https://www.rackspace.com/`
- **IBM SoftLayer**: `https://www.softlayer.com/`

It also supports the following self-hosted VM/cloud platforms:

- **Microsoft Hyper-V**: `https://www.microsoft.com/en-gb/cloud-platform/server-virtualization/`
- **OpenStack**: `https://www.openstack.org/`
- **VMware vSphere**: `https://www.vmware.com/uk/products/vsphere.html`

And finally, the following locally hosted hypervisors are supported as well:

- **Oracle VirtualBox**: `https://www.virtualbox.org/`
- **VMware Fusion**: `https://www.vmware.com/uk/products/fusion.html`
- **VMware Workstation**: `https://www.vmware.com/uk/products/workstation.html`

Being able to target all of these technologies using a single command with minimal user interaction is a very big time saver if you need to quickly access a Docker host in Amazon Web Services one day and then DigitialOcean the next: you know you are going to get a consistent experience.

As it is a command-line tool, it is also very easy to pass instructions to colleagues or even script the launch and tear down on Docker hosts: imagine starting work with your environment built fresh for you each morning and then, to save costs, it is torn down each evening.

Deploying local Docker hosts with Docker Machine

Before we journey out into the cloud, we are going to look at the basics of Docker Machine locally by launching it, using Oracle VirtualBox to provide the VM.

To launch the machine, all you need to do is run the following command:

```
$ docker-machine create --driver virtualbox docker-local
```

This will start the deployment, during which you will get a list of tasks that Docker Machine is running. To launch your Docker host, each host launched with Docker Machine goes through the same steps.

First of all, Docker Machine runs a few basic checks, such as confirming that VirtualBox is installed:

```
Running pre-create checks...
```

Once the checks have passed, it creates the virtual machine using the selected driver:

```
Creating machine...
(docker-local) Copying /Users/russ/.docker/machine/cache/boot2docker.iso to
/Users/russ/.docker/machine/machines/docker-local/boot2docker.iso...
(docker-local) Creating VirtualBox VM...
(docker-local) Creating SSH key...
(docker-local) Starting the VM...
(docker-local) Check network to re-create if needed...
(docker-local) Waiting for an IP...
Waiting for machine to be running, this may take a few minutes...
```

As you can see, Docker Machine creates a unique SSH key for the virtual machine, this means that you will be able to access the virtual machine over SSH, more on that later. Once the virtual machine has booted, Docker Machine then makes a connection to the virtual machine:

```
Detecting operating system of created instance...
Waiting for SSH to be available...
Detecting the provisioner...
Provisioning with boot2docker...
Copying certs to the local machine directory...
Copying certs to the remote machine...
Setting Docker configuration on the remote daemon...
Checking connection to Docker...
```

As you can see, Docker Machine detects the operating system being used and chooses the appropriate bootstrap script to deploy Docker. Once Docker is installed, Docker Machine generates and shares certificates between your local host and the Docker host. It then configures the remote Docker installation for certificate authentication, meaning that your local client can connect to and interact with the remote Docker server:

Once Docker is installed, Docker Machine generates and shares certificates between your local host and the Docker host, it then configures the remote Docker installation for certificate authentication meaning that your local client can connect to and interact with the remote Docker server:

```
Docker is up and running!
To see how to connect your Docker Client to the Docker Engine running on
this virtual machine, run: docker-machine env docker-local
```

Finally, it checks whether your local Docker client can make the remote connection and completes the task by giving you instructions on how to configure your local client to the newly launched Docker host.

If you open VirtualBox, you should be able to see your new virtual machine:

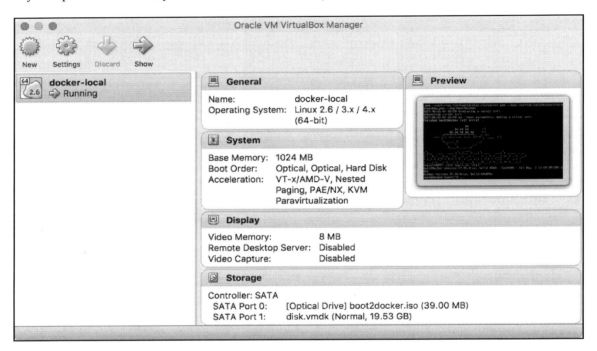

Next, we need to configure our local Docker client to connect to the newly launched Docker host; as already mentioned in the output of launching the host, running the following command will show you how to make the connection:

```
$ docker-machine env docker-local
```

This returns the following:

```
export DOCKER_TLS_VERIFY="1"
export DOCKER_HOST="tcp://192.168.99.100:2376"
export DOCKER_CERT_PATH="/Users/russ/.docker/machine/machines/docker-local"
export DOCKER_MACHINE_NAME="docker-local"
# Run this command to configure your shell:
# eval $(docker-machine env docker-local)
```

As you can see, this overrides the local Docker installation by giving the IP address and port number of the newly launched Docker host as well as the path to the certificates used for authentication. At the end of the output, it gives you a command to run and to configure your terminal session to make the connection.

Before we run the command, let's run `docker version` to get information on the current setup:

```
●  ●  ●                          1. russ (bash)
russ in ~
⚡ docker version
Client:
 Version:        17.03.1-ce
 API version:    1.27
 Go version:     go1.7.5
 Git commit:     c6d412e
 Built:          Tue Mar 28 00:40:02 2017
 OS/Arch:        darwin/amd64

Server:
 Version:        17.03.1-ce
 API version:    1.27 (minimum version 1.12)
 Go version:     go1.7.5
 Git commit:     c6d412e
 Built:          Fri Mar 24 00:00:50 2017
 OS/Arch:        linux/amd64
 Experimental:   true
russ in ~
⚡ 
```

As you can see, this is basically the Docker for Mac installation I am running. Running the following command and then `docker version` again should show some changes to the server:

```
$ eval $(docker-machine env docker-local)
```

The output of the command is given here:

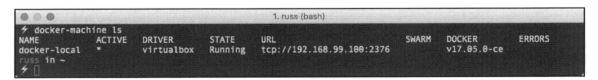

```
russ in ~
⚡ eval $(docker-machine env docker-local)
russ in ~
⚡ docker version
Client:
 Version:      17.03.1-ce
 API version:  1.27
 Go version:   go1.7.5
 Git commit:   c6d412e
 Built:        Tue Mar 28 00:40:02 2017
 OS/Arch:      darwin/amd64

Server:
 Version:      17.05.0-ce
 API version:  1.29 (minimum version 1.12)
 Go version:   go1.7.5
 Git commit:   89658be
 Built:        Thu May  4 21:43:09 2017
 OS/Arch:      linux/amd64
 Experimental: false
russ in ~
⚡ 
```

As you can see, the version of Docker has changed, along with the API version and build date. From here, we can interact with the Docker host in the same way as if it were a local Docker installation.

Before we move on to launching Docker hosts in the cloud, there are a few other basic Docker Machine commands to cover.

The first is listing the currently configured Docker hosts:

```
$ docker-machine ls
```

The output of the command is given here:

```
⚡ docker-machine ls
NAME           ACTIVE   DRIVER       STATE     URL                         SWARM   DOCKER        ERRORS
docker-local   *        virtualbox   Running   tcp://192.168.99.100:2376           v17.05.0-ce
russ in ~
⚡ 
```

As you can see, it lists the details on the machine name, the driver used and the Docker endpoint URL, and the version of Docker the hosts are running.

You will also notice that there is a * in the ACTIVE column; this indicates which Docker host your local client is currently configured to interact with. You can also find out the active machine by running docker-machine active.

The next command connects you to the Docker host using SSH:

```
$ docker-machine ssh docker-local
```

The output of the command is given here:

This is useful if you need to install additional software or configuration outside of Docker Machine. It is also useful if you need to look at logs and so on. You can find out the IP address of your Docker host by running the following:

```
$ docker-machine ip docker-local
```

We will be using this a lot later in the chapter. There are also commands to `stop`, `start`, `restart`, and `remove` your Docker host, though for now let's keep it running:

```
$ docker-machine stop docker-local
$ docker-machine start docker-local
$ docker-machine restart docker-local
$ docker-machine rm docker-local
```

There are also commands to find out more details about your Docker host:

```
$ docker-machine inspect docker-local
$ docker-machine config docker-local
$ docker-machine status docker-local
$ docker-machine url docker-local
```

Now that we have had a very quick rundown of the basics, let's try something more adventurous.

Launching Docker hosts in the cloud

In this section, we are going to take a look at two different public cloud drivers. As already mentioned, there are plenty available, but part of the appeal of Docker Machine is that it offers consistent experiences, so there are not too many differences between the drivers.

DigitalOcean

To launch a Docker host in DigitalOcean using Docker Machine, you only need an API access token. Rather than explaining how to generate one here, you can follow the instructions at https://www.digitalocean.com/help/api/.

Launching a Docker host using the API token will incur cost; ensure you keep track of the Docker hosts you launch. Details on DigitalOcean's pricing can be found at https://www.digitalocean.com/pricing/. Also, keep your API token secret as it could be used to gain unauthorized access to your account. All of the tokens used in this chapter have been revoked. Due to the additional flags that we need to pass to the Docker Machine command, I will be using \ to split the command across multiple lines to make it more readable.

To launch a Docker host called `docker-digtialocean`, we need to run the following command:

```
$ docker-machine create \
  --driver digitalocean \
  --digitalocean-access-token
ba46b9f97d16edb5a1f145093b50d97e50665492e9101d909295fa8ec35f20a1 \
  docker-digitalocean
```

As the Docker host is a remote machine, it will take a little while to launch, configure, and be accessible. As you can see from the following output, there are also a few changes to how Docker Machine bootstraps the Docker host:

```
Running pre-create checks...
Creating machine...
(docker-digitalocean) Creating SSH key...
(docker-digitalocean) Creating Digital Ocean droplet...
(docker-digitalocean) Waiting for IP address to be assigned to the
Droplet...
Waiting for machine to be running, this may take a few minutes...
Detecting operating system of created instance...
Waiting for SSH to be available...
```

```
Detecting the provisioner...
Provisioning with ubuntu(systemd)...
Installing Docker...
Copying certs to the local machine directory...
Copying certs to the remote machine...
Setting Docker configuration on the remote daemon...
Checking connection to Docker...
Docker is up and running!
To see how to connect your Docker Client to the Docker Engine running on
this virtual machine, run: docker-machine env docker-digitalocean
```

Once launched, you should be able to see the Docker host in your DigitalOcean control panel:

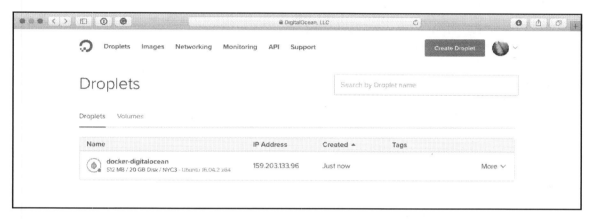

Reconfigure your local client to connect to the remote host by running:

```
$ eval $(docker-machine env docker-digitalocean)
```

Also, you can run `docker version` and `docker-machine inspect digitalocean` to find out more information about the Docker host.

Finally, running `docker-machine ssh docker-digitalocean` will SSH you into the host; as you can see from the following output and also from the output when you first launched the Docker host, there is a difference in the operating system used:

```
● ● ●                    1. root@docker-digitalocean: ~ (docker-machine)
⚡ docker-machine ssh docker-digitalocean
Welcome to Ubuntu 16.04.2 LTS (GNU/Linux 4.4.0-81-generic x86_64)

 * Documentation:  https://help.ubuntu.com
 * Management:     https://landscape.canonical.com
 * Support:        https://ubuntu.com/advantage

  Get cloud support with Ubuntu Advantage Cloud Guest:
    http://www.ubuntu.com/business/services/cloud

5 packages can be updated.
0 updates are security updates.


root@docker-digitalocean:~#
```

As you can see, we didn't have to tell Docker Machine which operating system to use, the size of the Docker host, or even where to launch it. That is because each driver has some pretty sound defaults. Adding these defaults to our command makes it look like the following:

```
$ docker-machine create \
    --driver digitalocean \
    --digitalocean-access-token
ba46b9f97d16edb5a1f145093b50d97e50665492e9101d909295fa8ec35f20a1 \
    --digitalocean-image ubuntu-16-04-x64 \
    --digitalocean-region nyc3 \
    --digitalocean-size 512mb \
    --digitalocean-ipv6 false \
    --digitalocean-private-networking false \
    --digitalocean-backups false \
    --digitalocean-ssh-user root \
    --digitalocean-ssh-port 22 \
    docker-digitalocean
```

As you can see, there is scope for you to customize the size, region, operating system, and even networking your Docker host is launched with.

Amazon Web Services

Amazon Web Services (AWS) is very big and extremely powerful. Explaining how to create a user, generate security credentials, and then install and the configure the AWS command-line tools will take several pages. Because of this, I will assume that you have this already configured. If you haven't and you would like to follow along, then refer to the following URLs first:

- **AWS security credentials**: http://docs.aws.amazon.com/general/latest/gr /aws-sec-cred-types.html
- **AWS command line interface docs**: http://docs.aws.amazon.com/cli/latest /userguide/cli-chap-welcome.html

Before we launch our Docker host in AWS, we need to know the ID of the **Virtual Private Cloud (VPC)** in the us-east-1 region, which is where Docker Machine will launch hosts by default. To do this, run the following command:

```
$ aws ec2 --region us-east-1 describe-vpcs
```

For me, running the command returned the following JSON array:

```
{
    "Vpcs": [
        {
            "VpcId": "vpc-35c91750",
            "InstanceTenancy": "default",
            "State": "available",
            "DhcpOptionsId": "dopt-b0bfafd2",
            "CidrBlock": "172.30.0.0/16",
            "IsDefault": false
        }
    ]
}
```

As you can see, the VPC ID is clearly visible. Once you have your VPC ID, run the following command:

```
docker-machine create \
    --driver amazonec2 \
    --amazonec2-vpc-id vpc-35c91750 \
    docker-aws
```

This will connect to the AWS API and launch your Docker host:

```
Running pre-create checks...
Creating machine...
(docker-aws) Launching instance...
Waiting for machine to be running, this may take a few minutes...
Detecting operating system of created instance...
Waiting for SSH to be available...
Detecting the provisioner...
Provisioning with ubuntu(systemd)...
Installing Docker...
Copying certs to the local machine directory...
Copying certs to the remote machine...
Setting Docker configuration on the remote daemon...
Checking connection to Docker...
Docker is up and running!
To see how to connect your Docker Client to the Docker Engine running on
this virtual machine, run: docker-machine env docker-aws
```

As you can see, there are no differences between the tasks executed by Docker machine in AWS and DigitalOcean; you can check the status of your Docker host by running the following command:

```
$ aws ec2 --region us-east-1 describe-instances
```

You can also check in the AWS Console for information on your Docker host:

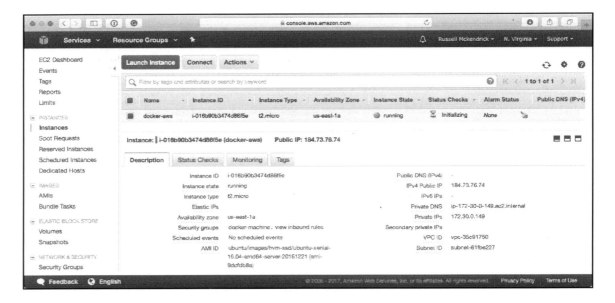

As with DigitalOcean, Docker Machine has a set of default settings; adding these to our `create` command extends it to the following:

```
docker-machine create \
  --driver amazonec2 \
  --amazonec2-ami AWS_AMI ami-5f709f34 \
  --amazonec2-region us-east-1 \
  --amazonec2-vpc-id vpc-35c91750 \
  --amazonec2-zone a \
  --amazonec2-instance-type t2.micro \
  --amazonec2-device-name /dev/sda1 \
  --amazonec2-root-size 16 \
  --amazonec2-volume-type gp2 \
  --amazonec2-ssh-user ubuntu \
  docker-aws
```

Again, there is plenty of scope for controlling where and at what size your Docker host launches. One thing you may have also noticed is that we never had to provide our AWS security credentials to Docker Machine; this is because it has taken them straight from your AWS CLI configuration, which can be found at `~/.aws/credentials`.

From here, we can run the same Docker Machine commands to interact with our AWS Docker host as we did for the DigitalOcean and local Docker hosts.

More Docker networking

While we have three Docker hosts running in different providers, we can look a little more at Docker networking. This time, rather than using the default networking driver, we are going to look at the **Weave Net** extension. This allows multihost networking and is a third-party extension written and provided by *Weave* (`https://weave.works/`).

So far, the networks we have been launching our containers into have all been confined to a single Docker host. Multi-host networking expands this so that our container networks span multiple Docker hosts, meaning that, for example, a container running a web server on one Docker host can talk to a container running a database on a completely different Docker host using the same DNS host, as well as having the isolation you would get when running on a single host.

First of all, check that our three Docker hosts are running by using the following command:

```
$ docker-machine ls
```

The output of the command is given here:

As you can see, in my current setup, the `docker-digitalocean` host is currently active; we do not need to worry about which machine is active as we will be using machine names in combination with our `docker-machine` and `docker container` commands.

Before we start to launch containers, we need to install and configure Weave on all three of our Docker hosts. For ease of use, as it is publicly accessible and does not have any external firewall like the AWS host, we will be using our DigitalOcean host as the master server.

To install and configure Weave on our `docker-digitalocean` host, run the following commands:

```
$ docker-machine ssh docker-digitalocean 'sudo curl -L git.io/weave -o
/usr/local/bin/weave; sudo chmod a+x /usr/local/bin/weave'
$ docker-machine ssh docker-digitalocean sudo weave launch --password
Wdmv3DzAvqR8NMGZEmZrJDdh
```

The password I supplied was randomly generated; feel free to use your own. Once our `docker-digitalocean` host is configured, we can add the two remaining hosts. There is a third step, which we will discuss once the configuration has been applied.

For the `docker-aws` host, run the following:

```
$ docker-machine ssh docker-aws 'sudo curl -L git.io/weave -o
/usr/local/bin/weave; sudo chmod a+x /usr/local/bin/weave'
$ docker-machine ssh docker-aws sudo weave launch --password
Wdmv3DzAvqR8NMGZEmZrJDdh
$ docker-machine ssh docker-aws sudo weave connect "$(docker-machine ip
docker-digitalocean)"
```

Finally, for our `docker-local` host, run this:

```
$ docker-machine ssh docker-local 'sudo curl -L git.io/weave -o
/usr/local/bin/weave; sudo chmod a+x /usr/local/bin/weave'
$ docker-machine ssh docker-local sudo weave launch --password
Wdmv3DzAvqR8NMGZEmZrJDdh
$ docker-machine ssh docker-local sudo weave connect "$(docker-machine ip
docker-digitalocean)"
```

As you can see from the preceding commands, other than providing the name of the Docker host, we haven't had to worry about finding out the IP address of the `docker-digitalocean` host; instead, we have used the `docker-machine ip` command to generate it dynamically for us.

Also, we have been passing the command we wish to execute on each of the three host machines after the `docker-machine ssh` command; this means that we never use SSH to connect to a host.

We can check the status of the Weave Net installation at any time by running the following:

```
$ docker-machine ssh docker-digitalocean sudo weave status
```

As you can see from the output returned, all of our hosts are connected to the network and communicating with each other:

```
Version: 2.0.0 (up to date; next check at 2017/06/26 16:02:13)

Service: router
       Protocol: weave 1..2
           Name: 7e:f1:8e:70:0c:87(docker-digitalocean)
     Encryption: enabled
  PeerDiscovery: enabled
        Targets: 0
    Connections: 2 (2 established)
          Peers: 3 (with 4 established connections)
  TrustedSubnets: none

Service: ipam
         Status: idle
          Range: 10.32.0.0/12
  DefaultSubnet: 10.32.0.0/12

Service: dns
         Domain: weave.local.
       Upstream: 8.8.4.4, 8.8.8.8
            TTL: 1
        Entries: 0
```

```
Service: proxy
        Address: unix:///var/run/weave/weave.sock

Service: plugin (legacy)
     DriverName: weave
```

You can also run the `status` command from the `docker-aws` and `docker-local` hosts:

```
$ docker-machine ssh docker-aws sudo weave status
$ docker-machine ssh docker-local sudo weave status
```

Now that we have our multihost networking installed and configured, we can start to launch containers. Let's look at launching the `moby-counter` application we used in the previous chapter. First of all, let's launch our Redis container:

```
docker $(docker-machine config docker-local) container run -d \
  --name redis \
  --hostname="redis.weave.local" \
  --network weave \
  --dns="172.17.0.1" \
  --dns-search="weave.local" \
  redis:alpine
```

Then we launch our `moby-counter` container:

```
docker $(docker-machine config docker-digitalocean) container run -d \
  --name moby-counter \
  --network weave \
  --dns="172.17.0.1" \
  --dns-search="weave.local" \
  -p 80:80 \
  russmckendrick/moby-counter
```

Also, let's launch a second copy:

```
docker $(docker-machine config docker-aws) container run -d \
  --name moby-counter \
  --network weave \
  --dns="172.17.0.1" \
  --dns-search="weave.local" \
  -p 80:80 \
  russmckendrick/moby-counter
```

As you can see, we have to add a few additional flags to configure our containers to use Weave Net's built-in DNS services as well as having to explicitly configure the hostname for our Redis container; this means that the DNS is correctly registered with Weave Net.

We have also used the `docker-machine config` command to reconfigure our Docker client to connect to our desired host on the fly, meaning that we do not open multiple terminals and reconfigure the host environment for each one.

Open your browser and go to the IP address of your DigitalOcean and AWS hosts; Mac and Linux users can do this by running the following commands:

```
$ open http://$(docker-machine ip docker-digitalocean)/
$ open http://$(docker-machine ip docker-aws)/
```

You should be able to place icons in one window and refresh the other to see the icons you added.

Also, you can ping the Redis container by running the following commands:

```
$ docker $(docker-machine config docker-digitalocean) container exec moby-
counter ping -c 3 redis
```

The output of the command is given here:

The following command will ping the Moby Counter from the Redis container:

```
$ docker $(docker-machine config docker-aws) container exec moby-counter
ping -c 3 redis
```

The output of the command is given here:

The same IP address is returned for the two pings; in my case, this was `10.32.0.1`.

There is one other thing: our two `moby-counter` application containers hosted in the public cloud have both been communicating with a container running on a VirtualBox VM on our local PC! Isn't that cool?

If you have ever tried to configure this kind of network in the past, I am sure you will agree that being able to launch a multi host network that communicates at a local VM level as well as a public cloud using just eight commands is quite impressive.

Before we finish this section of the chapter and move on to the next, we should remove our three hosts:

```
$ docker-machine rm docker-local docker-digitalocean docker-aws
```

You should see the following:

```
About to remove docker-local, docker-digitalocean, docker-aws
WARNING: This action will delete both local reference and remote instance.
Are you sure? (y/n): y
Successfully removed docker-local
Successfully removed docker-digitalocean
Successfully removed docker-aws
```

 Also double-check in the DigitalOcean control panel and the AWS Console that the Docker hosts have been properly terminated; if there were any problems during the removal process, you could incur an unexpected cost.

Using other base operating systems

You don't have to use the default operating systems with Docker Machine; it does come with provisioners for other base operating systems, including ones that are geared towards running containers. Before we finish the chapter, we are going to take a look at launching RancherOS and CoreOS on two different platforms.

Both of the distributions we are going to look at have just enough of an operating system to run a kernel, networking stack, and containers, just like Docker's own MobyOS, which is used as the base for Docker for Mac and Docker for Windows.

CoreOS on DigitalOcean

While CoreOS supports its own container runtime, called RKT (pronounced Rocket), it also ships with Docker; however, as we will see, the version of Docker currently shipping with the stable version of CoreOS is a little behind.

To launch the DigitalOcean-managed `coreos-stable` version, run the following command:

```
docker-machine create --driver=digitalocean \
  --digitalocean-access-
token=ba46b9f97d16edb5a1f145093b50d97e50665492e9101d909295fa8ec35f20a1 \
  --digitalocean-image=coreos-stable \
  --digitalocean-size=1GB \
  --digitalocean-ssh-user=core \
  docker-coreos
```

As with launching our other Docker hosts on public clouds, the output is pretty much the same. You will notice that Docker Machine uses the CoreOS provisoner. Once launched, you can run the following:

```
$ docker-machine ssh docker-coreos cat /etc/*release
```

This will let you check the contents of the release file:

```
DISTRIB_ID="Container Linux by CoreOS"
DISTRIB_RELEASE=1409.5.0
DISTRIB_CODENAME="Ladybug"
DISTRIB_DESCRIPTION="Container Linux by CoreOS 1409.5.0 (Ladybug)"
NAME="Container Linux by CoreOS"
ID=coreos
VERSION=1409.5.0
VERSION_ID=1409.5.0
BUILD_ID=2017-06-22-2222
PRETTY_NAME="Container Linux by CoreOS 1409.5.0 (Ladybug)"
ANSI_COLOR="38;5;75"
HOME_URL="https://coreos.com/"
BUG_REPORT_URL="https://issues.coreos.com"
COREOS_BOARD="amd64-usr"
```

Running the following will show you more information on the version of Docker that is running on the CoreOS host:

```
$ docker $(docker-machine config docker-coreos) version
```

You can see this from the following output; also, as already mentioned, it is behind the current release:

```
Client:
 Version: 17.03.1-ce
 API version: 1.24 (downgraded from 1.27)
 Go version: go1.7.5
 Git commit: c6d412e
 Built: Tue Mar 28 00:40:02 2017
 OS/Arch: darwin/amd64

Server:
 Version: 1.12.6
 API version: 1.24 (minimum version )
 Go version: go1.7.5
 Git commit: a82d35e
 Built: Mon Jun 19 23:04:34 2017
 OS/Arch: linux/amd64
 Experimental: false
```

This means not all of the commands we are using in this book will work. To remove the CoreOS host, run the following command:

```
$ docker-machine rm docker-coreos
```

For more information on CoreOS--the Linux distribution, not the company--visit the website at `https://coreos.com/os/docs/latest/`, and for more information on RKT, go to `https://coreos.com/rkt/`.

RancherOS on VirtualBox

While Chapter 9, *Rancher*, is dedicated entirely to Rancher, it does not cover the container-optimized operating system. Instead, it talks about Rancher the orchestration tool. The Rancher project (`https://rancher.com/`) distributes RancherOS to compliment its orchestration system.

To launch a RancherOS host locally using VirtualBox, run the following:

```
docker-machine create -d virtualbox \
    --virtualbox-boot2docker-url
https://releases.rancher.com/os/latest/rancheros.iso
    docker-rancher
```

You'll receive the following message:

```
(docker-rancher) Boot2Docker URL was explicitly set to
"https://releases.rancher.com/os/latest/rancheros.iso" at create time, so
Docker Machine cannot upgrade this machine to the latest version.
```

This means that you will not be able to use the `docker-machine upgrade` command. Docker Machine will use the RancherOS provisioner, and once it's complete, you will be able to check the release file by running the following:

```
$ docker-machine ssh docker-rancher cat /etc/*release
```

This will return something similar to the following:

```
DISTRIB_ID=RancherOS
DISTRIB_RELEASE=v1.0.2
DISTRIB_DESCRIPTION="RancherOS v1.0.2"
NAME="RancherOS"
VERSION=v1.0.2
ID=rancheros
ID_LIKE=
VERSION_ID=v1.0.2
PRETTY_NAME="RancherOS v1.0.2"
HOME_URL="http://rancher.com/rancher-os/"
SUPPORT_URL="https://forums.rancher.com/c/rancher-os"
BUG_REPORT_URL="https://github.com/rancher/os/issues"
BUILD_ID=
```

Let's check the version of Docker that is installed by running this command:

```
$ docker $(docker-machine config docker-rancher) version
```

It shows that the Docker version bundled with RanchOS is more recent than the version that is part of CoreOS:

```
Client:
 Version: 17.03.1-ce
 API version: 1.27
 Go version: go1.7.5
 Git commit: c6d412e
 Built: Tue Mar 28 00:40:02 2017
 OS/Arch: darwin/amd64

Server:
 Version: 17.03.1-ce
 API version: 1.27 (minimum version 1.12)
 Go version: go1.7.5
 Git commit: c6d412e
```

```
Built: Tue Mar 28 00:40:02 2017
OS/Arch: linux/amd64
Experimental: false
```

To remove the local RancherOS host, just run `docker-machine rm -f docker-rancher`.

For more information on RancherOS, you can view the project's website at `http://rancher.com/rancher-os/` or the code base on GitHub at `https://github.com/rancher/os/`.

Summary

In this chapter, we looked at Docker Machine. We first looked at how to use Docker Machine to create the Docker hosts locally on VirtualBox and reviewed the commands you can use to both interact with and manage your Docker Machine-launched Docker hosts. We then looked at how to use Docker Machine to deploy Docker hosts to your cloud environments, namely DigitalOcean and Amazon Web Services.

While we had three Docker Machine-managed hosts online, we took a look at multihost container networking by installing and configuring Weave Net by Weave. Once Weave Net was installed, we launched our multi-container application, but this time, we launched the containers on different Docker hosts.

Finally, we took a very quick look at how to launch two different container-optimized Linux operating systems, CoreOS and RancherOS, and the differences between them.

I am sure you will agree that using Docker Machine made running these tasks, which typically have very different approaches, a very consistent experience, which in the long run will save a lot of time as well as explaining.

In the next chapter, we will look at Docker Compose to launch multi-container applications. Docker Compose is a core component of the Docker ecosystem that you will find yourself using almost daily.

6

Docker Compose

In this chapter, we will be taking a look at another core Docker tool called Docker Compose. We will break the chapter down into the following sections:

- Docker Compose introduction
- Our Docker Compose application
- Docker Compose YAML file
- Docker Compose commands

Introducing Docker Compose

In Chapter 1, *Docker Overview*, we discussed a few of the problems that Docker has been designed to solve. We discussed how it solves problems such as running two applications side by side by isolating a single process in a single container, meaning that you can run two totally different versions of the same software stack, say PHP 5.6 and PHP 7, on the same host.

In the previous two chapters, we started to launch multi-container applications rather than running our entire stack.

The moby-counter application, which is written in Node.js, uses Redis as its database backend, so we have been launching two containers, one for the application and one of the database.

While it was quite simple to do this as the application itself was quite basic, there are some disadvantages to manually launching single containers.

For example, if I wanted a colleague to deploy the same application, I would have to pass them the following commands:

```
$ docker image pull redis:alpine
$ docker image pull russmckendrick/moby-counter
$ docker network create moby-counter
$ docker container run -d --name redis --network moby-counter redis:alpine
$ docker container run -d --name moby-counter --network moby-counter -p
8080:80 russmckendrick/moby-counter
```

Okay, I could get away with losing the first two commands as the image will be pulled during the run if they haven't already pulled it, but as the application starts to get more complex, I will have to start passing on an ever-growing set of commands and instructions.

I would also make it clear that they would have to take into account the order the commands need to be executed. Furthermore, my notes would have to include details of any potential issues to support them through any problems.

While Docker's responsibility should end at creating the images and launching containers using these images, they saw this as a scenario that the technology is meant to stop us from finding ourselves in. Thanks to Docker, people no longer have to worry about inconsistencies in the environment they are launching their applications in as they can now be shipped in images.

For this reason, back in July 2014, Docker purchased a small British start-up called **Orchard Laboratories**; their website is still accessible at `https://www.orchardup.com/`.

Orchard Laboratories offered two products. The first was a Docker-based hosting platform: think of it as a hybrid of Docker Machine and Docker itself. From a single command, `orchard`, you could launch a host machine and then proxy your Docker commands through to the newly launched host; for example, consider the following commands:

```
$ orchard hosts create
$ orchard docker run -p 6379:6379 -d orchardup/redis
```

These would have launched a Docker host on Orchard's platform and then a Redis container.

The second product was an open source project called **Fig**. Fig lets you use a YAML file to define how you would like your multi-container application to be structured. It would then take the YAML file and automate the launch of the containers as defined. The advantage of this was because it was a YAML file, it was really easy for developers to start shipping `fig.yml` files alongside their `Dockerfiles` within their code bases.

Of these two products, Docker purchased Orchard Laboratories for Fig. After a short while, the Orchard service was discontinued, and in February 2015, Fig became Docker Compose.

 You can read more about Orchard Laboratories joining Docker in the announcement blog post at `https://blog.docker.com/2014/07/welcomi ng-the-orchard-and-fig-team/`.

As part of our installation of Docker for Mac, Docker for Windows, and Docker on Linux in the first chapter, we installed Docker Compose, so rather than discussing what it does any further, let's try and bring up our two-container application using Docker Compose.

Our Docker Compose application

As already mentioned, Docker Compose uses a YAML file, typically named `docker-compose.yml`, to define what your multi-container application should look like. The Docker Compose representation of the two-container application we launched in `Chapter 4`, *Managing Containers*, and `Chapter 5`, *Docker Machine* is as follows:

```
version: "3"

services:
  redis:
    image: redis:alpine
    volumes:
      - redis_data:/data
    restart: always
  mobycounter:
    depends_on:
      - redis
    image: russmckendrick/moby-counter
    ports:
      - "8080:80"
    restart: always

volumes:
  redis_data:
```

Even without working through each of the lines in the file, it should be quite straightforward to follow along with what is going on. To launch our application, we simply change to the folder that contains your `docker-compose.yml` file and run the following:

```
$ docker-compose up
```

As you can see from the following Terminal output, a lot happened when it launched:

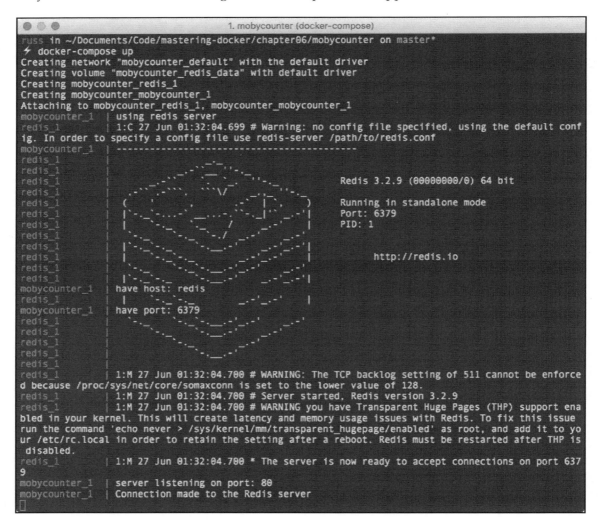

As you can see, from the first few lines, Docker Compose did the following:

1. Created a network called `mobycounter_default` using the default network driver--nowhere did we ask Docker Compose to do this. More on this in a minute.
2. Created a volume called `mobycounter_redis_data`, again using the default driver. This time we did actually instruct Docker Compose to create us this part of the multi-container application.
3. Launched two containers, one called `mobycounter_redis_1` and the second `mobycounter_mobycounter_1`.

You may have also spotted the Docker Compose namespace in our multi-container application and prefixed everything with `mobycounter`. It took this name from the folder our Docker Compose file was being stored in.

Once launched, Docker Compose attached to `mobycounter_redis_1` and `mobycounter_mobycounter_1` and streamed the output to our Terminal session. In the Terminal screen, you can see both `redis_1` and `mobycounter_1` starting and interacting with each other.

When running Docker Compose using `docker-compose up`, it will run in the foreground. Pressing *Ctrl* + *C* will stop the containers and return access to your Terminal session.

Docker Compose YAML file

Before we look at using Docker Compose more, we should have a deeper dive into `docker-compose.yml` files as these are the heart of Docker Compose.

 YAML is a recursive acronym which stands for **YAML Ain't Markup Language**. It is used by a lot of different applications for both configuration and also for defining data in a human-readable structured data format. The indentation you see in the examples is very important as it helps define the structure of the data. For more information, see the project's home page at `http://www.yaml.org/`.

Mobycounter YAML

The `docker-compose.yml` file we used to launch our multi-container application is split into three separate sections.

The first section simply specifies which version of the Docker Compose definition language we are using; in our case, as we are running a recent version of Docker and Docker Compose, we are using version 3:

```
version: "3"
```

The next section is where our containers are defined; this section is the services section. It takes the following format:

```
services:
--> container name:
----> container options
--> container name:
----> container options
```

In our example, we defined two containers. I have separated them out to make it easy to read:

```
services:

  redis:
    image: redis:alpine
    volumes:
      - redis_data:/data
    restart: always

  mobycounter:
    depends_on:
      - redis
    image: russmckendrick/moby-counter
    ports:
      - "8080:80"
    restart: always
```

The syntax for defining the service is close to how you would launch a container using the `docker container run` command. I say close because although it makes perfect sense when you read the definition, it is only on closer inspection that you realize there is actually a lot of difference between the Docker Compose syntax and the `docker container run` command.

For example, there are no flags for the following when running the `docker container run` command:

- `image`: This tells Docker Compose which image to download and use. This does not exist as an option when running `docker container run` on the command line as you can only run a single container; as we have seen in previous chapters, the image is always defined toward the end of the command without the need of a flag being passed.
- `volume`: This is the equivalent of the `-- volume` flag, but it can accept multiple volumes. It only uses the volumes that are declared in the Docker Compose YAML file; more on that in a moment.
- `depends_on`: This would never work as a `docker container run` invocation because the command is only targeting a single container. When it comes to Docker Compose, `depends_on` is used to help build some logic into the order your containers are launched in. For example, only launch container B when container A has successfully started.
- `ports`: This is basically the `--publish` flag, which accepts a list of ports.

The only part of the command we used that has an equivalent flag when running `docker container run` is this:

- `restart`: This is the same as using the `--restart` flag and accepts the same input.

The final section of our Docker Compose YAML file is where we declare our volumes:

```
volume:
  redis_data:
```

The voting application

As mentioned already, our Docker Compose file is quite a simple example. Let's take a look at a more complex Docker Compose file and see how we can introduce building containers and multiple networks.

In the repository for this book, which is available at `https://github.com/russmckendrick/mastering-docker/`, you will find a folder in the `chapter06` directory called `example-voting-app`. This is a fork of the voting application from the official Docker sample repository, which can be found at `https://github.com/dockersamples/`.

As you can see, the application is made up of five containers, two networks, and a single volume. Let's walk through the YAML file as there is a lot going on:

```
version: "3"

services:
```

Our first container is called `vote`; it is a Python application that allows users to submit their vote. As you can see from its following definition, rather than downloading an image, we are actually building an image from scratch by using `build` instead of `image`:

```
vote:
  build: ./vote
  command: python app.py
  volumes:
    - ./vote:/app
  ports:
    - "5000:80"
  networks:
    - front-tier
    - back-tier
```

The build instruction here tells Docker Compose to build a container using the Dockerfile, which can be found in the `./vote` folder. The Dockerfile itself is quite straightforward for a Python application.

Once the container launches, we are then mounting the `./vote` folder from our host machine into the container, which is achieved by passing the path of the folder we want to mount and where within the container we would like it mounted.

We are telling the container to run the `python app.py` when it launches. We are mapping port `5000` on our host machine to port `80` on the container, and finally, we are further attaching two networks to the container, one called `front-tier` and the second called `back-tier`.

The `front-tier` network will have the containers that have to have ports mapped to the host machine; the back-tier network is reserved for containers that do not need their ports to be exposed and acts as a private isolated network.

The `vote` application sends the votes to the `redis` container:

```
redis:
  image: redis:alpine
  container_name: redis
  ports: ["6379"]
  networks:
    - back-tier
```

This container uses the official Redis image and is not built from a Dockerfile; we are making sure that port `6379` is available, but only on the `back-tier` network.

We are also specifying the name of the container, setting it to `redis` by using `container_name`. This is to avoid us having to make any considerations on the default names generated by Docker Compose within our code.

Once our vote has been cast and it has found its way into the Redis database, a `worker` process is executed:

```
worker:
  build:
    context: ./worker
  networks:
    - back-tier
```

The worker container runs a .NET application whose only job is to connect to `redis` and register each vote by transferring it into a PostgreSQL database running on a container called `db`. The container is again built using a Dockerfile, but this time rather than passing the path to the folder where the Dockerfile and application are stored, we are using context. This sets the working directory for the `docker build` and also allows you to define additional options such as labels and changing the name of the Dockerfile.

As this container is doing nothing other than connecting to `redis` and the `db` container, it does not need any ports exposed; it also does not need to communicate with either of the containers running on the `front-tier` network, meaning we just have to add the `back-tier` network.

The next container is `db`, one we have already mentioned:

```
db:
  image: postgres:9.4
  container_name: db
  volumes:
    - "db-data:/var/lib/postgresql/data"
  networks:
    - back-tier
```

As you can see, it looks quite similar to the `redis` container in that we are using the official image; however, you may notice that we are not exposing a port as this is a default option in the official image. We are also specifying the name of the container.

As this is where our votes will be stored, we are creating and mounting a volume to act as persistent storage for our PostgreSQL database.

The final container launched is the result container; this is a Node.js application that connects to the PostgreSQL database running on `db` and displays the results in real time as votes are cast using the `vote` container:

```
result:
  build: ./result
  command: nodemon --debug server.js
  volumes:
    - ./result:/app
  ports:
    - "5001:80"
    - "5858:5858"
  networks:
    - front-tier
    - back-tier
```

The image is built using a Dockerfile in a similar fashion to the `vote` container. We are exposing port `5001`, which is where we can connect to see the results.

The final part of the `docker-compose.yml` file declares the volume for the PostgreSQL database and our two networks:

```
volumes:
  db-data:

networks:
  front-tier:
  back-tier:
```

Running `docker-compose up` gives a lot of feedback on what is happening during the launch; it takes about 5 minutes to launch the application for the first time. If you are not following along and launching the application yourself, what follows is an abridged version of the launch.

We start by creating the networks and getting the volume ready for our containers to use:

```
Creating network "examplevotingapp_front-tier" with the default driver
Creating network "examplevotingapp_back-tier" with the default driver
Creating volume "examplevotingapp_db-data" with default driver
```

We then build the vote container image:

```
Building vote
Step 1/7 : FROM python:2.7-alpine
2.7-alpine: Pulling from library/python
90f4dba627d6: Pull complete
19bc0bb0be9f: Pull complete
61bef6da706e: Pull complete
3e41fdc0d6e2: Pull complete
Digest:
sha256:10be70ff30d71a7bb3e8e7cb42f4e76ad8c28696ebce8c2faf89c33a2521a0f6
Status: Downloaded newer image for python:2.7-alpine
 ---> 8a72f6fe0cf4
Step 2/7 : WORKDIR /app
 ---> f555eeac2fe1
Removing intermediate container 0ac950f7ec78
Step 3/7 : ADD requirements.txt /app/requirements.txt
 ---> 2e86103004ae
Removing intermediate container 9c676447514c
Step 4/7 : RUN pip install -r requirements.txt
 ---> Running in 644ea3ffe44e
[lots of python build output here]
 ---> 46e89f5a6d00
Removing intermediate container 644ea3ffe44e
Step 5/7 : ADD . /app
 ---> 562c96f91d0d
Removing intermediate container ff8d462cd77c
Step 6/7 : EXPOSE 80
 ---> Running in f681463674c1
 ---> c601a2812a00
Removing intermediate container f681463674c1
Step 7/7 : CMD gunicorn app:app -b 0.0.0.0:80 --log-file - --access-logfile
- --workers 4 --keep-alive 0
 ---> Running in f0a6128dba6c
 ---> bbebc8f099cd
Removing intermediate container f0a6128dba6c
Successfully built bbebc8f099cd
Successfully tagged examplevotingapp_vote:latest
WARNING: Image for service vote was built because it did not already exist.
To rebuild this image you must use `docker-compose build` or `docker-
compose up --build`.
```

Once this vote image has been built, the worker image is built:

```
Building worker
Step 1/5 : FROM microsoft/dotnet:1.1.1-sdk
1.1.1-sdk: Pulling from microsoft/dotnet
10a267c67f42: Pull complete
```

```
fb5937da9414: Pull complete
9021b2326a1e: Pull complete
c63131473568: Pull complete
a4274048307f: Pull complete
61820b027a34: Pull complete
Digest:
sha256:7badca85a6b29361f7cf2a9b68cbaa111f215943bfe6d87910a1943db8a2a02f
Status: Downloaded newer image for microsoft/dotnet:1.1.1-sdk
 ---> a97efbca0c48
Step 2/5 : WORKDIR /code
 ---> 16894fefd6b9
Removing intermediate container 90ccc84a396b
Step 3/5 : ADD src/Worker /code/src/Worker
 ---> 826032994894
Removing intermediate container af0d371cc328
Step 4/5 : RUN dotnet restore -v minimal src/Worker && dotnet publish -c
Release -o "./" "src/Worker/"
 ---> Running in 21db89055f71
 Restoring packages for /code/src/Worker/Worker.csproj...
 [lots of .net build output here]
 Restore completed in 8.16 sec for /code/src/Worker/Worker.csproj.
NuGet Config files used:
 /root/.nuget/NuGet/NuGet.Config
Feeds used:
 https://api.nuget.org/v3/index.json
Installed:
 84 package(s) to /code/src/Worker/Worker.csproj
Microsoft (R) Build Engine version 15.1.548.43366
Copyright (C) Microsoft Corporation. All rights reserved.
Worker -> /code/src/Worker/bin/Release/netcoreapp1.0/Worker.dll
 ---> 0654c936945a
Removing intermediate container 21db89055f71
Step 5/5 : CMD dotnet src/Worker/Worker.dll
 ---> Running in 40068deb9dc3
 ---> 10fd31632c6c
Removing intermediate container 40068deb9dc3
Successfully built 10fd31632c6c
Successfully tagged examplevotingapp_worker:latest
WARNING: Image for service worker was built because it did not already
exist. To rebuild this image you must use `docker-compose build` or
`docker-compose up --build`.
```

Then the redis image is pulled:

```
Pulling redis (redis:alpine)...
alpine: Pulling from library/redis
88286f41530e: Pull complete
07b1ac6c7a50: Pull complete
```

```
91e2e140ea27: Pull complete
08957ceaa2b3: Pull complete
acd3d12a6a79: Pull complete
4ad88df09080: Pull complete
Digest:
sha256:2b1600c032e7653d079e9bd1eb80df5c99733795691f5ae9bca451bec325b7ea
Status: Downloaded newer image for redis:alpine
```

This is followed by the PostgreSQL image for the db container:

```
Pulling db (postgres:9.4)...
9.4: Pulling from library/postgres
9f0706ba7422: Pull complete
df3070b9fd62: Pull complete
945954562465: Pull complete
820e17b80256: Pull complete
4f9e8f8bc763: Pull complete
Digest:
sha256:4f831cae0dff7c1cbb8b35e3e31f7d0da622bee4af1735993c66bfefeec1e618
Status: Downloaded newer image for postgres:9.4
```

Now it is time for the big one; the build of the result image. Node.js is quite verbose, so you will get quite a bit of output being printed to the screen as the NPM sections of the Dockerfile are executed:

```
Building result
Step 1/11 : FROM node:5.11.0-slim
5.11.0-slim: Pulling from library/node
8b87079b7a06: Pull complete
a3ed95caeb02: Pull complete
1bb8eaf3d643: Pull complete
5674f5dccbc4: Pull complete
96a79bcf8a3b: Pull complete
Digest:
sha256:fb4e332730514c393a78a3f0be6b6e1a7f7f3a63c9e670d6ccb0d54d3b9c4985
[lots and lots of nodejs output]
npm WARN optional Skipping failed optional dependency
/nodemon/chokidar/fsevents:
npm WARN notsup Not compatible with your operating system or architecture:
fsevents@1.1.2
npm info ok
---> bad5c376013a
Removing intermediate container dc0060b5cc1d
Step 4/11 : ADD package.json /app/package.json
---> 8b1b09e5e073
Removing intermediate container 92a2233c2608
Step 5/11 : RUN npm config set registry http://registry.npmjs.org
---> Running in 5dffa4d8fa69
```

```
npm info it worked if it ends with ok
npm info using npm@3.8.6
npm info using node@v5.11.0
npm info config set "registry" "http://registry.npmjs.org"
npm info ok
---> 40860dc8d467
Removing intermediate container 5dffa4d8fa69
Step 6/11 : RUN npm install && npm ls
---> Running in 1f57b2914af3
[lots more nodejs output]
npm info ok
---> bdbe2d653e45
Removing intermediate container 1f57b2914af3
Step 7/11 : RUN mv /app/node_modules /node_modules
---> Running in 7957e5f08c8a
---> d309bf17c968
Removing intermediate container 7957e5f08c8a
Step 8/11 : ADD . /app
---> 507a74fd7ff6
Removing intermediate container e5c5227af370
Step 9/11 : ENV PORT 80
---> Running in 959913cc7838
---> f8eb2f5eec79
Removing intermediate container 959913cc7838
Step 10/11 : EXPOSE 80
---> Running in 2371b833bcdc
---> 3f7228a42540
Removing intermediate container 2371b833bcdc
Step 11/11 : CMD node server.js
---> Running in ce472d3bde87
---> 4117d314ff4a
Removing intermediate container ce472d3bde87
Successfully built 4117d314ff4a
Successfully tagged examplevotingapp_result:latest
WARNING: Image for service result was built because it did not already
exist. To rebuild this image you must use `docker-compose build` or
`docker-compose up --build`.
```

Now that our container images have been built and pulled, Docker Compose can launch our application:

```
Creating examplevotingapp_worker_1 ... done
Creating examplevotingapp_vote_1 ... done
Creating redis ... done
Creating db ... done
Creating examplevotingapp_result_1 ... done
Attaching to redis, db, examplevotingapp_worker_1,
examplevotingapp_result_1, examplevotingapp_vote_1
```

The `result` part of the application can be accessed at `http://localhost:5001`. By default, there are no votes and it is split 50/50:

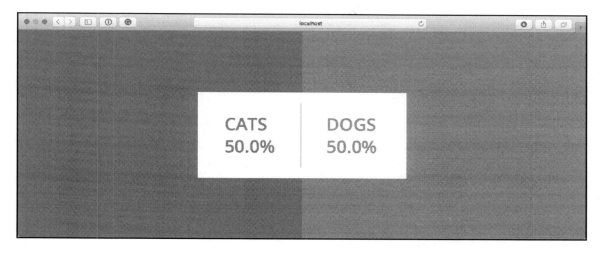

The vote part of the application can be found at `http://localhost:5000`:

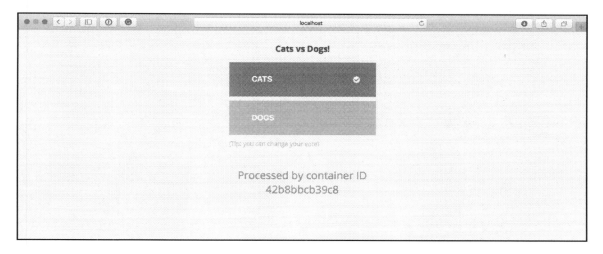

Clicking on either **CATS** or **DOGS** will register a vote; you should be able to see this logged in the Docker Compose output in your Terminal:

```
●  ●  ●                    1. example-voting-app (docker-compose)
db         |  LOG:   database system was shut down at 2017-07-01 15:36:25 UTC
db         |  FATAL:  the database system is starting up
result_1   |  Waiting for db
db         |  FATAL:  the database system is starting up
worker_1   |  Waiting for db
db         |  LOG:   MultiXact member wraparound protections are now enabled
db         |  LOG:   database system is ready to accept connections
db         |  LOG:   autovacuum launcher started
result_1   |  Connected to db
db         |  ERROR:  relation "votes" does not exist at character 38
db         |  STATEMENT:  SELECT vote, COUNT(id) AS count FROM votes GROUP BY vote
result_1   |  Error performing query: error: relation "votes" does not exist
worker_1   |  Connected to db
db         |  ERROR:  relation "votes" does not exist at character 38
db         |  STATEMENT:  SELECT vote, COUNT(id) AS count FROM votes GROUP BY vote
result_1   |  Error performing query: error: relation "votes" does not exist
worker_1   |  Found redis at 172.19.0.3
worker_1   |  Connecting to redis
vote_1     |  172.19.0.1 - - [01/Jul/2017 15:36:31] "POST / HTTP/1.1" 200 -
worker_1   |  Processing vote for 'a' by 'd52dbc1098f60334'
[]
```

There are a few errors as the Redis table structure is only created when the `vote` application registers the first vote; once a vote has been cast, the `redis` table structure will be created and the `worker` container will take that vote and process it by writing to the `db` container. Once the vote has been cast, the result container will update in real time:

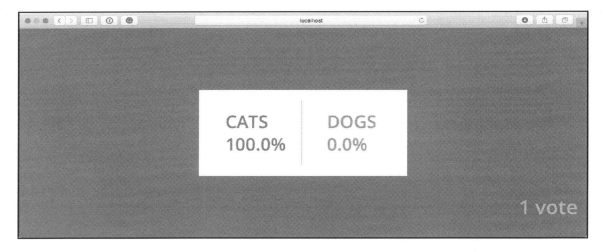

We will be looking at the Docker Compose YAML files again in the next chapter, when we will look at launching a Docker Swarm stack. For now, let's get back to Docker Compose and look at some of the commands we can run.

Docker Compose commands

We are over halfway through the chapter and the only Docker Compose command we have run is `docker-compose up`. If you have been following along and you run `docker container ls -a`, you will see something similar to the following Terminal screen:

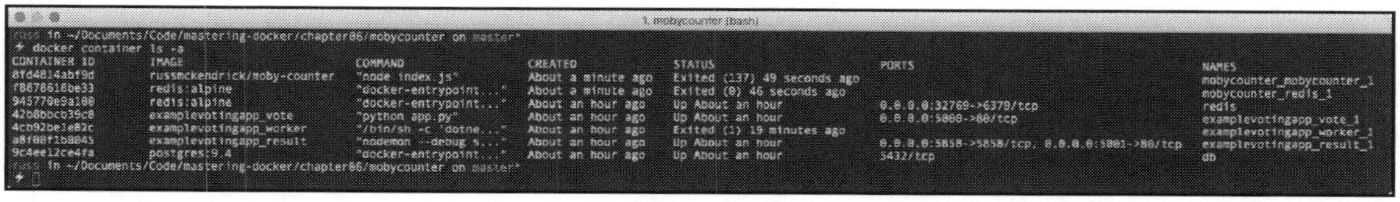

Choose one of the Docker Compose applications and change to the folder that contains the `docker-compose.yml` file, and we will work through some more Docker Compose commands.

Up and PS

The first one is `docker-compose up`, but this time, we will be adding a flag. In your chosen application folder, run the following:

```
$ docker-compose up -d
```

This will start your application back up, this time in detached mode:

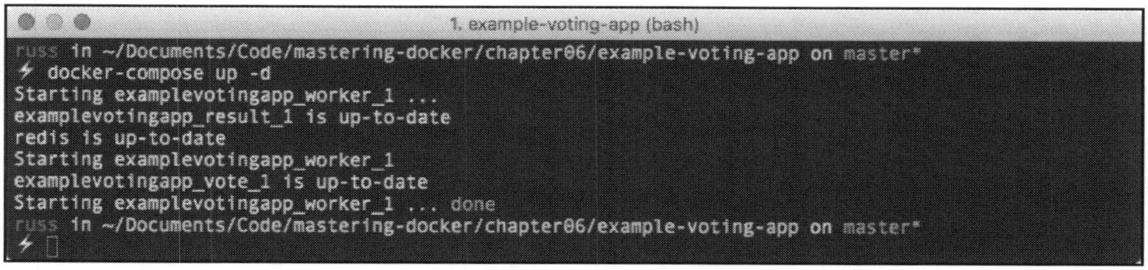

Once control of your Terminal is returned, you should be able to check that the containers are running using the following command:

```
$ docker-compose ps
```

As you can see from the following Terminal output, all of the containers have the State of Up:

```
● ● ●                          1. example-voting-app (bash)
russ in ~/Documents/Code/mastering-docker/chapter06/example-voting-app on master*
⚡ docker-compose ps
           Name                    Command            State              Ports
----------------------------------------------------------------------------------------
db                        docker-entrypoint.sh       Up       5432/tcp
                          postgres
examplevotingapp_resu     nodemon --debug            Up       0.0.0.0:5858->5858/tc
lt_1                      server.js                           p,
                                                              0.0.0.0:5001->80/tcp
examplevotingapp_vote     python app.py              Up       0.0.0.0:5000->80/tcp
_1
examplevotingapp_work     /bin/sh -c dotnet          Up
er_1                      src/Work ...
redis                     docker-entrypoint.sh       Up       0.0.0.0:32769->6379/t
                          redis ...                           cp
russ in ~/Documents/Code/mastering-docker/chapter06/example-voting-app on master*
⚡ []
```

When running these commands, Docker Compose will only be aware of the containers defined in the service section of your docker-compose.yml file; all other containers will be ignored as they don't belong to our service stack.

Config

Running the following command will validate our docker-compose.yml file:

```
$ docker-compose config
```

If there are no issues, it will print a rendered copy of your Docker Compose YAML file to screen; this is how Docker Compose will interpret your file. If you don't want to see this output and just want to check for errors, then you can run:

```
$ docker-compose config -q
```

This is shorthand for `--quiet`. If there are any errors, which the examples we have worked through so far shouldn't have, they will be displayed as follows:

```
ERROR: yaml.parser.ParserError: while parsing a block mapping
in "./docker-compose.yml", line 1, column 1
expected <block end>, but found '<block mapping start>'
in "./docker-compose.yml", line 27, column 3
```

Pull, build, and create

The next two commands will help you prepare to launch your Docker Compose application. The following command will read your Docker Compose YAML file and `pull` any of the images it finds:

```
$ docker-compose pull
```

The following command will execute any `build` instructions it finds in your file:

```
$ docker-compose build
```

These commands are useful when you are first defining your Docker Compose-powered application and want to test without launching your application. The `docker-compose build` command can also be used to trigger a build if there are updates to any of the Dockerfiles used to originally build your images.

The `pull` and `build` commands only generate/pull the images needed for our application; they do not configure the containers themselves. For this, we need to use the following command:

```
$ docker-compose create
```

This will `create` but not launch the containers. In the same way that the `docker container create` command does, they will have an `Exited` state until you start them. The `create` command has a few useful flags you can pass:

- `--force-recreate`: This recreates the container even if there is no need to as nothing within the configuration has changed
- `--no-recreate`: This doesn't recreate a container if it already exists; this flag cannot be used with the preceding flag
- `--no-build`: This doesn't build the images, even if an image that needs to be built is missing
- `--build`: This builds the images before creating the containers

Start, stop, restart, pause, and unpause

The following commands work exactly in the same way as their `docker container` counterparts, the only difference being they effect change on all of the containers:

```
$ docker-compose start
$ docker-compose stop
$ docker-compose restart
$ docker-compose pause
$ docker-compose unpause
```

It is possible to target a single service by passing its name; for example, to pause and unpause the db service we would run:

```
$ docker-compose pause db
$ docker-compose unpause db
```

Top, logs, and events

The next three commands all give us feedback on what is happening within our running containers and Docker Compose.

The following command, like its `docker container` counterpart, displays information on the processes running within each of our Docker Compose-launched containers:

```
$ docker-compose top
```

As you can see from the following Terminal output, each container is split into its own section:

```
●  ●  ●                          1. example-voting-app (bash)
russ in ~/Documents/Code/mastering-docker/chapter06/example-voting-app on master*
⚡ docker-compose top
db
PID     USER    TIME                        COMMAND
-----------------------------------------------------------------------------
3135    999     0:00    postgres
3472    999     0:00    postgres: checkpointer process
3473    999     0:00    postgres: writer process
3474    999     0:00    postgres: wal writer process
3475    999     0:00    postgres: autovacuum launcher process
3476    999     0:00    postgres: stats collector process
3480    999     3:50    postgres: postgres postgres 172.19.0.2(60348) idle
3517    999     0:00    postgres: postgres postgres 172.19.0.3(50578) idle

examplevotingapp_result_1
PID     USER    TIME                        COMMAND
-----------------------------------------------------------------------------
3212    root    0:00    node /usr/local/bin/nodemon --debug server.js
3506    root    0:00    sh -c node --debug server.js
3507    root    0:01    node --debug server.js

examplevotingapp_vote_1
PID     USER    TIME            COMMAND
-----------------------------------------------------------------------------
3400    root    0:00    python app.py
3496    root    0:02    /usr/local/bin/python app.py

examplevotingapp_worker_1
PID     USER    TIME                COMMAND
-----------------------------------------------------------------------------
2994    root    0:00    /bin/sh -c dotnet src/Worker/Worker.dll
3099    root    16:14   dotnet src/Worker/Worker.dll

redis
PID     USER     TIME     COMMAND
-----------------------------------------------------------------------------
3311    chrony   1:46     redis-server
russ in ~/Documents/Code/mastering-docker/chapter06/example-voting-app on master*
⚡ 
```

If you would like to see just one of the services, you simply have to pass its name when running the command:

```
$ docker-compose top db
```

The next command streams the logs from each of the running containers to screen:

```
$ docker-compose logs
```

Like the `docker container` command, you can pass flags such as `-f` or `--follow` to keep the stream flowing until you press *Ctrl + C*. Also, you can stream the logs for a single service by appending its name to the end of your command.

```
● ● ●                    1. example-voting-app (docker-compose)
russ in ~/Documents/Code/mastering-docker/chapter06/example-voting-app on master*
⚡ docker-compose logs -f db
Attaching to db
db     | LOG:  database system was shut down at 2017-07-01 18:42:04 UTC
db     | LOG:  MultiXact member wraparound protections are now enabled
db     | LOG:  database system is ready to accept connections
db     | LOG:  autovacuum launcher started
```

The `events` command again works like the `docker container` version; it streams events, such as the ones triggered by the other commands we have been discussing, in real time. For example, run this command:

```
$ docker-compose events
```

Then, running `docker-compose pause` gives the following output:

```
● ● ●                    1. example-voting-app (docker-compose)
russ in ~/Documents/Code/mastering-docker/chapter06/example-voting-app on master*
⚡ docker-compose events
2017-07-02 11:13:14.089008 container pause 826ff65e71a9f92c6de32898f794073d3d993d05d94ffd0e06a558225
b40ed63 (image=postgres:9.4, name=db)
2017-07-02 11:13:14.248001 container pause 8647670adddf6068a61e807deca6cf4bf23198ffd2f25b2f69ec037cf
1899537 (image=redis:alpine, name=redis)
2017-07-02 11:13:14.248001 container pause c36650d033026dee86359436933f426decb999838f636fc9155f40f4f
1e50de1 (image=examplevotingapp_vote, name=examplevotingapp_vote_1)
2017-07-02 11:13:14.248186 container pause d4caa1b2c9af9334b228cf6fa3615d66680870f60d4fcb0209068e8b9
484bc18 (image=examplevotingapp_result, name=examplevotingapp_result_1)
2017-07-02 11:13:14.248370 container pause 2d82adcad614aa11d297b4c891ebc5094e3917dd2225dd4e2c0f8ba97
c188c45 (image=examplevotingapp_worker, name=examplevotingapp_worker_1)
```

Exec and run

These two commands run similar to their `docker container` equivalents. Run the following:

```
$ docker-compose exec worker ping -c 3 db
```

This will launch a new process in the already running worker container and `ping` the db container 3 times, as seen here:

```
● ● ●                          1. example-voting-app (bash)
russ in ~/Documents/Code/mastering-docker/chapter06/example-voting-app on master*
⚡ docker-compose exec worker ping -c 3 db
PING db (172.19.0.4): 56 data bytes
64 bytes from 172.19.0.4: icmp_seq=0 ttl=64 time=0.082 ms
64 bytes from 172.19.0.4: icmp_seq=1 ttl=64 time=0.037 ms
64 bytes from 172.19.0.4: icmp_seq=2 ttl=64 time=0.035 ms
--- db ping statistics ---
3 packets transmitted, 3 packets received, 0% packet loss
round-trip min/avg/max/stddev = 0.035/0.051/0.082/0.000 ms
russ in ~/Documents/Code/mastering-docker/chapter06/example-voting-app on master*
⚡
```

The run command is useful if you need to run a containerized command as a one-off within your application. For example, if you use a package manager such as `composer` to update the dependencies of your project that is stored on a volume, you could run something like this:

```
$ docker-compose run --volume data_volume:/app composer install
```

This would run the `composer` container with the `install` command and mount the `data_volume` to `/app` within the container.

Scale

The `scale` command will take the service you pass the command and scale it to the number you define; for example, to add more `worker` containers I just need to run:

```
$ docker-compose scale worker=3
```

However, this actually gives the following warning:

```
WARNING: The scale command is deprecated. Use the up command with the --
scale flag instead.
```

What we should now be using is the following command:

```
$ docker-compose up -d --scale worker=3
```

While the scale command is in the current version of Docker Compose, it will be removed from future versions.

You will notice that I chose to scale the number of `worker` containers. There is a good reason for this as you will see for yourself if you try running the following command:

```
$ docker-compose up -d --scale vote=3
```

You will notice that while Docker Compose creates the additional two containers, they fail to start with the following error:

```
russ in ~/Documents/Code/mastering-docker/chapter06/example-voting-app on master*
⚡ docker-compose up -d --scale vote=3
examplevotingapp_worker_1 is up-to-date
Starting examplevotingapp_vote_1 ...
Starting examplevotingapp_vote_1 ... done
redis is up-to-date
examplevotingapp_result_1 is up-to-date
Creating examplevotingapp_vote_2 ...
Creating examplevotingapp_vote_3 ...
Creating examplevotingapp_vote_2 ... error
Creating examplevotingapp_vote_3 ... error

ERROR: for examplevotingapp_vote_3  Cannot start service vote: driver failed programming external co
nnectivity on endpoint examplevotingapp_vote_3 (51d49c1b3061a48298bc62802971dd7f84e5ecf86d7db860437c
e0cddde5045c): Bind for 0.0.0.0:5000 failed: port is already allocated

ERROR: for examplevotingapp_vote_2  Cannot start service vote: driver failed programming external co
nnectivity on endpoint examplevotingapp_vote_2 (875d59f687d6c11508c80a8a47547f2e7509a64ec05429711860
ef6bd26d9d6c): Bind for 0.0.0.0:5000 failed: port is already allocated

ERROR: for vote  Cannot start service vote: driver failed programming external connectivity on endpo
int examplevotingapp_vote_3 (51d49c1b3061a48298bc62802971dd7f84e5ecf86d7db860437ce0cddde5045c): Bind
 for 0.0.0.0:5000 failed: port is already allocated
ERROR: Encountered errors while bringing up the project.
russ in ~/Documents/Code/mastering-docker/chapter06/example-voting-app on master*
⚡ 
```

That is because we cannot have three individual containers all trying to map to the same port. There is a workaround for this and we will look at that in more detail in our next chapter.

Kill, rm, and down

The three Docker Compose commands we are finally going to look at are the ones that remove/terminate our Docker Compose application. The first command stops our running containers by immediately stopping running container processes. This is the `kill` command:

```
$ docker-compose kill
```

Be careful when running this as it does not wait for containers to gracefully stop like when running `docker-compose stop`, meaning that using the `docker-compose kill` command may result in data loss.

Next up is the `rm` command; this removes any containers with the state of exited:

```
$ docker-compose rm
```

Finally, we have the `down` command. This, as you might have already guessed, has the opposite effect of running `docker-compose up`:

```
$ docker-compose down
```

That will remove the containers and the networks created when running `docker-compose up`. If you want to remove everything, you can do so by running the following:

```
$ docker-compose down --rmi all --volumes
```

This will remove all of the containers, networks, volumes and images (both pulled and built) when you ran the `docker-compose up` command; this includes images that may be in use outside of your Docker Compose application--there will, however, be an error if the images are in use, and they will not be removed.

Summary

I hope you have enjoyed this chapter on Docker Compose, and I hope that like I did, you can see that it has evolved from being an incredibly useful third-party tool to an extremely important part of the core Docker experience.

Docker Compose introduces some key concepts in how you should approach running and managing your containers. We will be taking these concepts one step further as well as revisiting Docker Compose in `Chapter 7`, *Docker Swarm*.

7
Docker Swarm

In this chapter, we will be taking a look at Docker Swarm. With Docker Swarm, you can create and manage Docker clusters. Swarm can be used to distribute containers across multiple hosts. Swarm also has the ability to scale containers.

We will look at:

- Installing Docker Swarm
- Docker Swarm roles
- Docker Swarm usage
- Docker Swarm services and stacks
- Docker Swarm load balancing and scheduling

Before we look at launching a Docker Swarm cluster, I should mention that there are currently two different versions of Docker Swarm available.

In the first edition of this book, this chapter covered what is now the standalone legacy version of Docker Swarm; this was supported up until Docker 1.12 and is no longer being actively developed. Should you want to find out more about the standalone version of Docker Swarm, you can find the project documentation at `https://docs.docker.com/swarm/`.

 It isn't recommended that you use the standalone Docker Swarm as Docker ended support for version 1.11.x in the first quarter of 2017.

Docker 1.12 introduced Docker Swarm mode. This introduced all of the functionality that was available in standalone Docker Swarm into the core Docker engine along with additional features. As we are covering Docker version 1.13 and preceding in this book, we will be using Docker Swarm mode, which for the remainder of the chapter we will refer to as Docker Swarm.

Installing Docker Swarm

As you are already running a version of Docker with inbuilt support for Docker Swarm, there isn't anything you need to do to install Docker Swarm; you can verify that Docker Swarm is available on your installation by running the following command:

```
$ docker swarm --help
```

You should see something that looks like the following Terminal output when running the command:

```
1. russ (bash)
russ in ~
⚡ docker swarm --help

Usage:  docker swarm COMMAND

Manage Swarm

Options:
      --help    Print usage

Commands:
  init        Initialize a swarm
  join        Join a swarm as a node and/or manager
  join-token  Manage join tokens
  leave       Leave the swarm
  unlock      Unlock swarm
  unlock-key  Manage the unlock key
  update      Update the swarm

Run 'docker swarm COMMAND --help' for more information on a command.
russ in ~
⚡ 
```

If you get an error, ensure that you are running Docker version 1.13 or above; at the time of writing, the current version of Docker is 17.03.

Docker Swarm roles

Which roles are involved with Docker Swarm? Let's take a look at the two roles a host can assume when running within a Docker Swarm cluster:

- Swarm manager
- Swarm worker

Swarm manager

The Swarm manager is the host that is the central management point for all Swarm hosts. The Swarm manager is where you issue all your commands to control those nodes. You can switch between the nodes, join nodes, remove nodes, and manipulate those hosts.

Each cluster can run several Swarm managers. For production, it is recommended that you run a minimum of five Swarm managers: this would mean that our cluster can take a maximum of two Swarm manager nodes failures before you start to have any errors. Swarm managers use the **Raft Consensus Algorithm** to maintain a consistent state across all of the manager nodes.

For a detailed explanation of the Raft consensus algorithms, I recommend working through the excellent presentation by The Secret Lives of Data, which can be found at http://thesecretlivesofdata.com/raft. It explains the processes taking place in the background on the manager nodes.

Swarm worker

The Swarm workers; which we have seen earlier referred to as Docker hosts, are those that run the Docker containers. Swarm workers are managed from the **Swarm manager**.

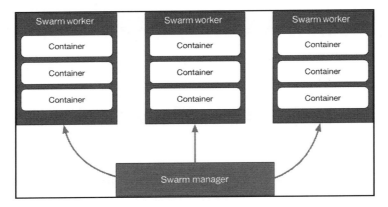

This is an illustration of all the Docker Swarm components. We see that the Docker **Swarm manager** talks to each Swarm host that is running the Swarm container.

Using Docker Swarm

Let's now take a look at using Swarm and how we can perform the following tasks:

- Creating a cluster
- Joining workers
- Listing nodes
- Managing a cluster

Creating a cluster

Let's start by creating a cluster, which starts with a Swarm manager. Since we are going to be creating a multi-node cluster on our local machine, we should use Docker Machine to launch a host by running this command:

```
$ docker-machine create \
    -d virtualbox \
    swarm-manager
```

An abridged version of the output you get is shown here:

```
(swarm-manager) Creating VirtualBox VM...
(swarm-manager) Creating SSH key...
(swarm-manager) Starting the VM...
Docker is up and running!
To see how to connect your Docker Client to the Docker Engine running on
this virtual machine, run: docker-machine env swarm-manager
```

The `swarm-manager` node is now up running using VirtualBox. we can confirm this by running:

```
$ docker-machine ls
```

You should see something similar to the following output:

```
russ in ~
 docker-machine ls
NAME          ACTIVE  DRIVER      STATE    URL                           SWARM  DOCKER      ERRORS
swarm-manager -       virtualbox  Running  tcp://192.168.99.100:2376            v17.04.0-ce
russ in ~
```

Now let's point Docker Machine at the new Swarm manager. From the preceding output when we created the Swarm manager, we can see it tells us how to point to the node:

```
$ docker-machine env swarm-manager
```

This will show you the commands needed to configure your local Docker client to talk to our newly launched Docker host: following you can see the configuration I had returned when I ran the command:

```
export DOCKER_TLS_VERIFY="1"
export DOCKER_HOST="tcp://192.168.99.100:2376"
export DOCKER_CERT_PATH="/Users/russ/.docker/machine/machines/swarm-
manager"
export DOCKER_MACHINE_NAME="swarm-manager"
# Run this command to configure your shell:
# eval $(docker-machine env swarm-manager)
```

Upon running the previous command, we are told to run the following command to point to the Swarm manager:

```
$ eval $(docker-machine env swarm-manager)
```

Now if we look at which machines are on our host, we can see that we have the `swarm-master` host as well as it now set to `ACTIVE`, which means we can now run commands on it:

```
$ docker-machine ls
```

It should show you something like the following:

Now that we have the first host up-and-running, we should add the two worker nodes. To do this, simply run the following command to launch two more Docker hosts:

```
$ docker-machine create \
    -d virtualbox \
    swarm-worker01
$ docker-machine create \
    -d virtualbox \
    swarm-worker02
```

Once you have launched the two additional hosts, you can get the list of hosts using this command:

```
$ docker-machine ls
```

It should show you something like the following:

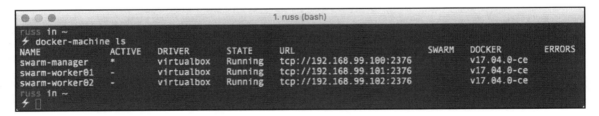

It is worth pointing out that, so far, we have not done anything to create our Swarm cluster; we have only launched the hosts it will be running on.

You may have noticed that one of the columns when running the `docker-machine ls` command is SWARM. This only contains information if you have launched your Docker hosts using the standalone Docker Swarm command, which is built into Docker Machine.

Let's bootstrap our Swarm manager. To do this, we will pass the results of a few Docker Machine commands to our host. The command to run to create our manager is:

```
$ docker $(docker-machine config swarm-manager) swarm init \
    --advertise-addr $(docker-machine ip swarm-manager):2377 \
    --listen-addr $(docker-machine ip swarm-manager):2377
```

You should receive a message similar to this one:

```
Swarm initialized: current node (qha7m9bf55wwd8p3e0jiyk7yf) is now a
manager.
To add a worker to this swarm, run the following command:

docker swarm join \
--token
SWMTKN-1-3fxwovyzh24120myqbzolpen303uzk562y26q4z1wgxto5avm3-4aiagep3e2a1nwy
af4yjp7ic5 \
192.168.99.100:2377

To add a manager to this swarm, run 'docker swarm join-token manager' and
follow the instructions.
```

As you can see from the output, once your manager is initialized, you are given a unique token. This token will be needed for the worker nodes to authenticate themselves and join our cluster.

Joining workers

To add our two workers to the cluster, run the following commands, making sure you replace the token with the one you received when initializing your own manager:

```
$ docker $(docker-machine config swarm-worker01) swarm join \
    $(docker-machine ip swarm-manager):2377 \
    --token
SWMTKN-1-3fxwovyzh24120myqbzolpen303uzk562y26q4z1wgxto5avm3-4aiagep3e2a1nwy
af4yjp7ic5
```

For the second worker, you need to run this:

```
docker $(docker-machine config swarm-worker02) swarm join \
    $(docker-machine ip swarm-manager):2377 \
    --token
SWMTKN-1-3fxwovyzh24120myqbzolpen303uzk562y26q4z1wgxto5avm3-4aiagep3e2a1nwy
af4yjp7ic5
```

Both times, you should get confirmation that your node has joined the cluster:

```
This node joined a swarm as a worker.
```

Listing nodes

You can check the Swarm by running the following command:

```
$ docker-machine ls
```

Check that your local Docker client is still configured to connect to the `swarm-manager` node, and if it isn't, rerun the following command:

```
$ eval $(docker-machine env swarm-manager)
```

Now that we are connecting to the `swarm-manager` node, you can run the following:

```
$ docker node ls
```

This will connect to the `swarm-master` and query all of the nodes that form our cluster. You should see that all three of our nodes are listed:

```
● ● ●                            1. russ (bash)
russ in ~
⚡ docker-machine ls
NAME            ACTIVE    DRIVER       STATE     URL                            SWARM    DOCKER        ERRORS
swarm-manager   *         virtualbox   Running   tcp://192.168.99.100:2376               v17.04.0-ce
swarm-worker01  -         virtualbox   Running   tcp://192.168.99.101:2376               v17.04.0-ce
swarm-worker02  -         virtualbox   Running   tcp://192.168.99.102:2376               v17.04.0-ce
russ in ~
⚡ docker node ls
ID                          HOSTNAME        STATUS   AVAILABILITY   MANAGER STATUS
qg3ycvryuccvsslo2cc4aa8r4   swarm-worker02  Ready    Active
qha7m9bf55wwd8p3e0jiyk7yf * swarm-manager   Ready    Active         Leader
wgtfdnhcau7fcr7xsj08uo7do   swarm-worker01  Ready    Active
russ in ~
⚡ 
```

Managing a cluster

Let's see how we can perform some management of all of these cluster nodes that we are creating.

So there are two ways you can go about managing these Swarm hosts and the containers on each host that you are creating, but first, you need to know some information about them.

As we have already seen, we can list the nodes within the cluster using our local Docker client, as it is already configured to connect to the Swarm manager host. We can simply type this:

```
$ docker info
```

It will give us lots of information about the host, as you can see from the following output:

```
Containers: 0
  Running: 0
  Paused: 0
  Stopped: 0
Images: 0
Server Version: 17.04.0-ce
Storage Driver: aufs
Root Dir: /mnt/sda1/var/lib/docker/aufs
Backing Filesystem: extfs
Dirs: 0
Dirperm1 Supported: true
Logging Driver: json-file
Cgroup Driver: cgroupfs
Plugins:
  Volume: local
  Network: bridge host macvlan null overlay
Swarm: active
  NodeID: qha7m9bf55wwd8p3e0jiyk7yf
  Is Manager: true
  ClusterID: n5akyh6xsnc15qnx5ccp54vrr
  Managers: 1
  Nodes: 3
  Orchestration:
    Task History Retention Limit: 5
  Raft:
    Snapshot Interval: 10000
    Number of Old Snapshots to Retain: 0
    Heartbeat Tick: 1
    Election Tick: 3
  Dispatcher:
    Heartbeat Period: 5 seconds
```

```
    CA Configuration:
      Expiry Duration: 3 months
    Node Address: 192.168.99.100
    Manager Addresses:
      192.168.99.100:2377
Runtimes: runc
Default Runtime: runc
Init Binary:
containerd version: 422e31ce907fd9c3833a38d7b8fdd023e5a76e73
runc version: 9c2d8d184e5da67c95d601382adf14862e4f2228
init version: 949e6fa
Security Options:
  seccomp
    Profile: default
Kernel Version: 4.4.59-boot2docker
Operating System: Boot2Docker 17.04.0-ce (TCL 7.2); HEAD : c69677f - Thu
Apr 6 16:26:16 UTC 2017
OSType: linux
Architecture: x86_64
CPUs: 1
Total Memory: 995.8 MiB
Name: swarm-manager
ID: VKLO:MKJK:Y4UD:2IXV:WBA3:LTZE:J4MU:MGAD:VF7Z:QVVI:XNQG:SMAB
Docker Root Dir: /mnt/sda1/var/lib/docker
Debug Mode (client): false
Debug Mode (server): true
  File Descriptors: 32
  Goroutines: 149
  System Time: 2017-04-26T09:51:29.683890515Z
  EventsListeners: 0
Username: russmckendrick
Registry: https://index.docker.io/v1/
Labels:
  provider=virtualbox
Experimental: false
Insecure Registries:
  127.0.0.0/8
Live Restore Enabled: false
```

As you can see, there is information about the cluster in the Swarm section; however, we are only able to run the docker info command against the host our client is currently configured to communicate with; luckily, the docker node command is cluster aware, so we can use that to get information on each node within our cluster, like this, for example:

```
$ docker node inspect swarm-manager --pretty
```

Passing the `--pretty` flag with the `docker node inspect` command will render the output in the easy-to-read format you see as follows. If `--pretty` is left out, Docker will return the raw JSON object containing the results of the query the inspect command runs against the cluster.

This should provide the following information on our Swarm manager:

```
ID: qha7m9bf55wwd8p3e0jiyk7yf
Labels:
Hostname: swarm-manager
Joined at: 2017-04-25 16:56:47.092119605 +0000 utc
Status:
  State: Ready
  Availability: Active
  Address: 192.168.99.100
Manager Status:
  Address: 192.168.99.100:2377
  Raft Status: Reachable
  Leader: Yes
Platform:
  Operating System: linux
  Architecture: x86_64
Resources:
  CPUs: 1
  Memory: 995.8 MiB
Plugins:
  Network: bridge, host, macvlan, null, overlay
  Volume: local
Engine Version: 17.04.0-ce
Engine Labels:
  - provider = virtualbox
```

Run the same command, but this time targeting one of the worker nodes:

```
$ docker node inspect swarm-worker01 --pretty
```

It gives us similar information:

```
ID: wgtfdnhcau7fcr7xsj08uo7do
Labels:
Hostname: swarm-worker01
Joined at: 2017-04-25 17:11:03.532507218 +0000 utc
Status:
  State: Ready
  Availability: Active
  Address: 192.168.99.101
Platform:
  Operating System: linux
```

```
    Architecture: x86_64
Resources:
  CPUs: 1
  Memory: 995.8 MiB
Plugins:
  Network: bridge, host, macvlan, null, overlay
  Volume: local
Engine Version: 17.04.0-ce
Engine Labels:
  - provider = virtualbox
```

But as you can see, it is missing the information about the state of the manager functionality. This is because the worker nodes do not need to know about the status of the manager nodes; they just need to know they are allowed to receive instructions from the managers.

So we can see the information about this host, such as the number of containers, the numbers of images on the host, and information about the CPU and memory as well as other interesting information about the host.

Promoting a worker node

Say you wanted to perform some maintenance on your single manager node, but you wanted to maintain the availability of your cluster. No problem; you can promote a worker node to a manager node.

While we have our local three-node cluster up and running, let's promote `swarm-worker01` to be a new manager. To do this, run the following:

```
$ docker node promote swarm-worker01
```

You should receive a message confirming that your node has been promoted immediately after executing the command:

```
Node swarm-worker01 promoted to a manager in the swarm.
```

List the nodes by running this:

```
$ docker node ls
```

This should show you that you now have two nodes that now display something in the MANAGER STATUS column:

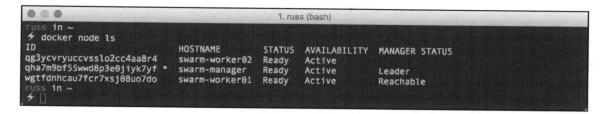

Our `swarm-manager` node is still the primary manager node though. Let's look at doing something about that.

Demoting a manager node

You may have already put two and two together, but to demote a manager node to a worker, you simply need to run this:

```
$ docker node demote swarm-manager
```

Again, you will receive immediate feedback saying the following:

Manager swarm-manager demoted in the swarm.

Now we have demoted our node, and you can check the status of the nodes within the cluster by running this command:

```
$ docker node ls
```

As your local Docker client is still pointing toward, the newly demoted node, you will receive a message saying the following:

Error response from daemon: This node is not a swarm manager. Worker nodes can't be used to view or modify cluster state. Please run this command on a manager node or promote the current node to a manager.

As we have already learned, it is easy to update our local client configuration to communicate with other nodes using Docker Machine. To point your local client to the new manager node, run the following:

```
$ eval $(docker-machine env swarm-worker01)
```

Now that out client is talking to a manager node again, rerun this:

```
$ docker node ls
```

It should list the nodes, as expected:

```
russ in ~
⚡ docker node ls
ID                            HOSTNAME        STATUS  AVAILABILITY  MANAGER STATUS
qg3ycvryuccvsslo2cc4aa8r4     swarm-worker02  Ready   Active
qha7m9bf55wwd8p3e0j1yk7yf     swarm-manager   Ready   Active
wgtfdnhcau7fcr7xsj08uo7do *   swarm-worker01  Ready   Active        Leader
russ in ~
⚡
```

Draining a node

To temporarily remove a node from our cluster so that we can perform maintenance, we need to set the status of the node to `Drain`. Let's look at draining our former manager node. To do this, we need to run the following command:

```
$ docker node update --availability drain swarm-manager
```

This will stop any new tasks, such as new containers launching or being executed against the node we are draining. Once new tasks have been blocked, all running tasks will be migrated from the node we are draining to nodes with an `ACTIVE` status.

As you can see from the following Terminal output, listing the nodes now shows that `swarm-manager` is listed as `Drain` in the `AVAILABILITY` column:

```
russ in ~
⚡ docker node ls
ID                            HOSTNAME        STATUS  AVAILABILITY  MANAGER STATUS
qg3ycvryuccvsslo2cc4aa8r4     swarm-worker02  Ready   Active
qha7m9bf55wwd8p3e0j1yk7yf     swarm-manager   Ready   Drain
wgtfdnhcau7fcr7xsj08uo7do *   swarm-worker01  Ready   Active        Leader
russ in ~
⚡
```

Now that our node is no longer accepting new tasks and all running tasks have been migrated to our two remaining nodes, we can safely perform our maintenance, such as rebooting the host. To reboot `swarm-manager`, run the following two commands, ensuring that you are connected to the Docker host (you should see the `boot2docker` banner, like the screenshot after the commands):

```
$ docker-machine ssh swarm-manager
$ sudo reboot
```

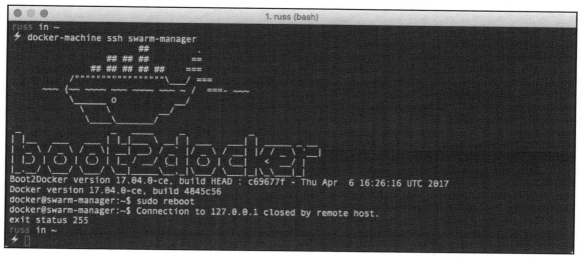

Once the host has been rebooted, run this:

```
$ docker node ls
```

It should show that the node has an AVAILABILITY of pause. To add the node back into the cluster, simply change the AVAILABILITY to active by running this:

```
$ docker node update --availability active swarm-manager
```

As you can see from the following Terminal output, our node is now active, meaning new tasks can be executed against it:

```
russ in ~
⚡ docker node ls
ID                          HOSTNAME         STATUS  AVAILABILITY  MANAGER STATUS
qg3ycvryuccvsslo2cc4aa8r4   swarm-worker02   Ready   Active
qha7m9bf55wwd8p3e0jiyk7yf   swarm-manager    Ready   Pause
wgtfdnhcau7fcr7xsj08uo7do * swarm-worker01   Ready   Active        Leader
russ in ~
⚡ docker node update --availability active swarm-manager
swarm-manager
russ in ~
⚡ docker node ls
ID                          HOSTNAME         STATUS  AVAILABILITY  MANAGER STATUS
qg3ycvryuccvsslo2cc4aa8r4   swarm-worker02   Ready   Active
qha7m9bf55wwd8p3e0jiyk7yf   swarm-manager    Ready   Active
wgtfdnhcau7fcr7xsj08uo7do * swarm-worker01   Ready   Active        Leader
russ in ~
⚡ 
```

Now that we have looked at how to create and manage a Docker Swarm cluster, we should look at how to run a task such as creating and scaling a service.

Docker Swarm services and stacks

So far, we have looked at the following commands:

```
$ docker swarm <command>
$ docker node <command>
```

These two commands allow us to bootstrap and manage our Docker Swarm cluster from a collection of existing Docker hosts. The next two commands we are going to look at are as follows:

```
$ docker service <command>
$ docker stack <command>
```

The Service and Stack commands allow us to execute tasks that in turn launch, scale, and manage containers within our Swarm cluster.

Services

The service command is a way of launching containers that take advantage of the Swarm cluster. Let's look at launching a really basic single-container service on our Swarm cluster. To do this, run the following command:

```
$ docker service create --name cluster --constraint "node.role == worker" -
p:80:80/tcp russmckendrick/cluster
```

This will create a service called `cluster` that consists of a single container with port `80` mapped from the container to the host machine, and it will only be running on nodes that have the role of worker.

Before we look at doing more with the service, we can check whether it worked on our browser. To do this, we will need the IP address of our two worker nodes. First of all, we need to double-check which are the worker nodes by running this command:

```
$ docker node ls
```

Once we know which node has which role, you can find the IP addresses of your nodes by running this:

```
$ docker-machine ls
```

Look at the following Terminal output:

My worker nodes are `swarm-manager` and `swarm-worker02`, whose IP addresses are `192.168.99.100` and `192.168.99.102` respectively.

Going to either of the IP addresses of your worker nodes, such as
`http://192.168.99.100/` or `http://192.168.99.102/`, in a browser will show the
output of the `russmckendrick/cluster` application, which is the Docker Swarm graphic
and the hostname of the container the page is being served from:

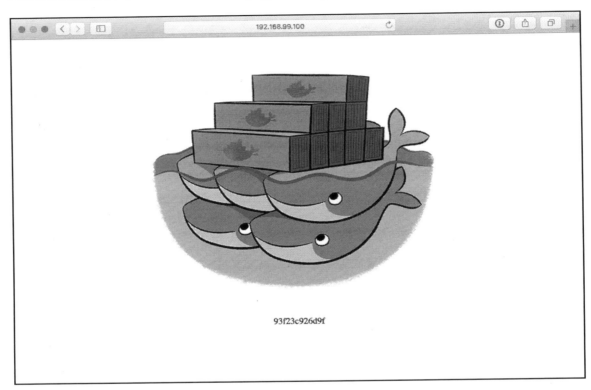

Now that we have our service running on our cluster, we can start to find out more
information about it. First of all, we can list the services again by running this command:

```
$ docker service ls
```

In our case, this should return the single service we launched, called cluster:

```
russ in ~
⚡ docker service ls
ID              NAME       MODE         REPLICAS   IMAGE
39t4voc7gp5y    cluster    replicated   1/1        russmckendrick/cluster:latest
russ in ~
⚡ 
```

As you can see, it is a replicated service and 1/1 containers active. Next, you can drill-down to find out more information about the service by running the inspect command:

```
$ docker service inspect cluster --pretty
```

This will return detailed information about the service:

```
1. russ (bash)
russ in ~
⚡ docker service inspect cluster --pretty

ID:                   39t4voc7gp5yiqcvbkff9tkr3
Name:                 cluster
Service Mode:         Replicated
 Replicas:            1
Placement:Contraints: [node.role == worker]
UpdateConfig:
 Parallelism:         1
 On failure:          pause
 Max failure ratio:   0
ContainerSpec:
 Image:               russmckendrick/cluster:latest@sha256:e7d6182aa203671889d940a12918278b1b193fd684e7de0a02c8b
1ca9492eb7b
 Resources:
Endpoint Mode:        vip
Ports:
 PublishedPort 80
  Protocol = tcp
  TargetPort = 80
russ in ~
⚡ 
```

You may have noticed that so far, we haven't had to care about which of our two Worker nodes the service is currently running on. This is quite an important feature of Docker Swarm, as it completely removes the need for you to worry about the placement of individual containers.

Before we look at scaling our service, we can take a quick look at which host our single container is running on by running these commands:

```
$ docker node ps
$ docker node ps swarm-manager
$ docker node ps swarm-worker02
```

This will list the containers running on each of our hosts. By default, it will list the host the command is being targeted against, which in my case is `swarm-worker01`:

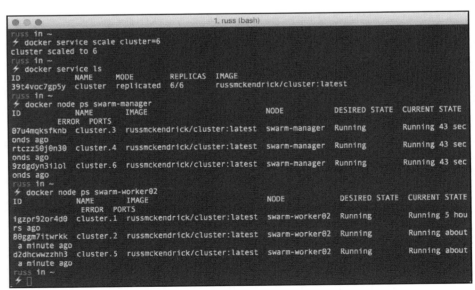

Let's look at scaling our service to six instances of our application container. Run the following commands to scale and check our service:

```
$ docker service scale cluster=6
$ docker service ls
$ docker node ps swarm-manager
$ docker node ps swarm-worker02
```

We are only checking two of the nodes since we originally told our service to launch on worker nodes. As you can see from the following Terminal output, we now have three containers running on each of our worker nodes:

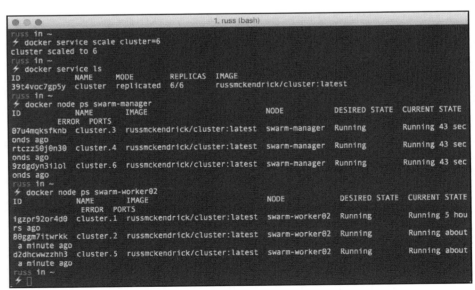

Before we move on to look at stacks, let's remove our service. To do this, run the following:

```
$ docker service rm cluster
```

This will remove all of the containers, while leaving the downloaded image on the hosts.

Stacks

It is more than possible to create quite complex, highly available multi-container applications using Swarm and services. In a non-Swarm cluster, manually launching each set of containers for a part of the application can get to be a little laborious and also difficult to share. To this end, Docker has created functionality that allows you to define your services in Docker Compose files.

The following Docker Compose file will create the same service we launched in the previous section:

```
version: "3"
services:
  cluster:
    image: russmckendrick/cluster
    ports:
      - "80:80"
    deploy:
      replicas: 6
      restart_policy:
        condition: on-failure
      placement:
        constraints:
          - node.role == worker
```

As you can see, the stack can be made up of multiple services, each defined under services section of the Docker Compose file.

In addition to the normal Docker Compose commands, you can add a deploy section; this is where you define everything relating to the Swarm element of your stack. In the previous example, we said we would like six replicas, which should be distributed across our two worker nodes. Also, we updated the default restart policy, which you saw when we inspected the service from the previous section and it showed up as paused, so that, if a container becomes unresponsive, it is always restarted.

To launch our stack, copy the previous contents into a file called `docker-compose.yml`, and then run the following command:

```
$ docker stack deploy --compose-file=docker-compose.yml cluster
```

Docker will, like when launching containers with Docker Compose, create a new network and then launch your services on it.

You can check the status of your stack by running this:

```
$ docker stack ls
```

This will show that a single service has been created. You can get details of the service created by the stack by running this command:

```
$ docker stack services cluster
```

Finally, running the following command will show where the containers within the stack are running:

```
$ docker stack ps cluster
```

Take a look at the Terminal output:

```
● ● ●                              1. cluster (bash)
russ in ~/Desktop/cluster
⚡ docker stack ls
NAME      SERVICES
cluster   1
russ in ~/Desktop/cluster
⚡ docker stack services cluster
ID              NAME             MODE        REPLICAS  IMAGE
ty0czqwd471c    cluster_cluster  replicated  6/6       russmckendrick/cluster:latest
russ in ~/Desktop/cluster
⚡ docker stack ps cluster
ID              NAME             IMAGE                          NODE           DESIRED STATE  CURRE
NT STATE        ERROR   PORTS
07wrabg5dso2    cluster_cluster.1  russmckendrick/cluster:latest  swarm-manager  Running        Runni
ng 8 minutes ago
onsslc92pos1    cluster_cluster.2  russmckendrick/cluster:latest  swarm-worker02  Running        Runni
ng 8 minutes ago
fbb2sk6but5y    cluster_cluster.3  russmckendrick/cluster:latest  swarm-manager  Running        Runni
ng 8 minutes ago
v2l2ngznjfo1    cluster_cluster.4  russmckendrick/cluster:latest  swarm-worker02  Running        Runni
ng 8 minutes ago
m0qvc5mth666    cluster_cluster.5  russmckendrick/cluster:latest  swarm-manager  Running        Runni
ng 8 minutes ago
ujkex1f8uv2d    cluster_cluster.6  russmckendrick/cluster:latest  swarm-worker02  Running        Runni
ng 8 minutes ago
russ in ~/Desktop/cluster
⚡ 
```

Chapter 7

Again, you will be able to access the stack using the IP addresses of your nodes, and you will be routed to one of the running containers.

To remove a stack, simply run this command:

```
$ docker stack rm cluster
```

This will remove all services and networks created by the stack when it is launched.

Deleting a Swarm cluster

Before moving on, as we no longer require it for the next section, you can delete your Swarm cluster by running the following command:

```
$ docker-machine rm swarm-manager swarm-worker01 swarm-worker02
```

Should you need to relaunch the Swarm cluster for any reason, simply follow the instructions from the start of the chapter to recreate a cluster.

Load balancing, overlays, and scheduling

In the last few sections, we looked at launching services and stacks. To access the applications we launched, we were able to use any of the host IP addresses in our cluster; how was this possible?

Ingress load balancing

Docker Swarm has an ingress load balancer built in, making it easy to distribute traffic to our public facing containers. This means that you can expose applications within your Swarm cluster to services, for example an external load balancer such as Amazon Elastic Load Balancer, knowing that your request will be routed to the correct container(s) no matter which host happens to be currently hosting it, as demonstrated by the following diagram:

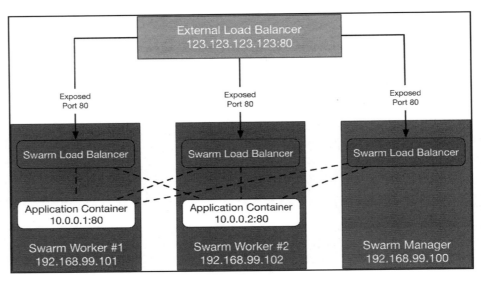

This means that our application can be scaled up or down, fail, or be updated, all without the need to have the external load balancer reconfigured.

Network overlays

In our example, we launched a simple service running a single application. Say we wanted to add a database layer in our application, which is typically a fixed point within the network; how could we do this?

Docker Swarm's network overlay layer extends the network you launch your containers in across multiple hosts, meaning that each service or stack can be launched into its own isolated network. This means that our database container, running MongoDB, will be accessible to all other containers running on the same overlay network on port 27017, no matter which of the hosts the containers are running on.

You may be thinking to yourself H*ang on a minute; does this mean I have to hard-code an IP address into my application's configuration?* Well that wouldn't fit well with the problems Docker Swarm is trying to resolve, so no, you don't.

Each overlay network has its own inbuilt DNS service, which means that every container launched within the network is able to resolve the hostname of another container within the same network to its currently assigned IP address. This means that when we configure our application to connect to our database instance, we simply need to tell it to connect to, say, `mongodb:27017`, and it will connect to our MongoDB container.

This will make our diagram look like the following:

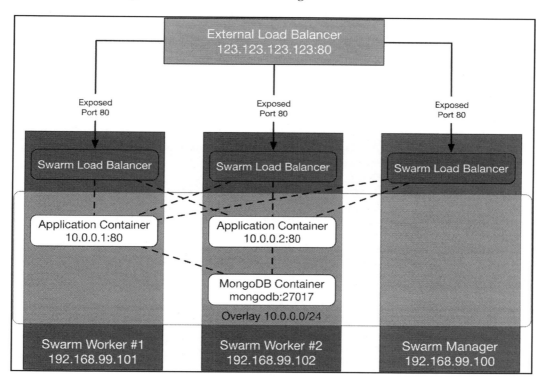

There are some other considerations you will need to take into account when adopting this pattern, but we will cover those in `Chapter 12`, *Docker Workflows*.

Scheduling

At the time of writing, there is only a single scheduling strategy available within Docker Swarm, called **Spread**. What this strategy does is to schedule tasks to be run against the least loaded node that meets any of the constraints you defined when launching the service or stack. For the most part, you should not need to add too many constraints to your services

One feature that is not currently supported by Docker Swarm is affinity and anti-affinity; while it is easy to get around this using constraints, I urge you not to overcomplicate things as it is very easy to end up overloading hosts or creating single points of failure if you put too many constraints in place when defining your services.

Summary

In this chapter, we explored Docker Swarm. We took a look at how to install Docker Swarm and the Docker Swarm components, which make up Docker Swarm. We took a look at how to use Docker Swarm: joining, listing, and managing Swarm manager and worker nodes. We reviewed the service and stack commands and how to use them and spoke about the Swarm inbuilt ingress load balancer, overlay networks, and scheduler.

In the next three chapters, we are going to be taking a look at some GUI applications that you can utilize to manage your Docker hosts, containers, and images. They are some very powerful tools and choosing one can be difficult so let's cover all three starting with Portainer.

8
Portainer

In this chapter, we will take a look at Portainer. Portainer is a tool that allows you to manage Docker resources from a web interface. The topics that will be covered are as follows:

- The road to Portainer
- Getting Portainer up and running
- Using Portainer
- Portainer and Docker Swarm

The road to Portainer

Before we roll up our sleeves and dive into installing and using Portainer, we should discuss the background of the project. The first edition of this book covered Docker UI. Docker UI was written by *Michael Crosby*, who handed the project over to *Kevan Ahlquist* after about a year of development. It was at this stage, due to trademark concerns, that the project was renamed UI for Docker.

Development of UI for Docker continued up until the point Docker started to accelerate the introduction of features such as Swarm mode into the core Docker Engine. It was around this time that the UI for Docker project was forked into the project that would become Portainer, which had its first major release in June 2016.

Since their first public release, the team behind Portainer estimate around 70 percent of the code has already been rewritten, and by mid-2017, new features were added, such as role-based controls and Docker Compose support. They believe that the remaining UI for Docker code will have been rewritten by the end of 2017.

In December 2016, a notice was committed to the UI for Docker GitHub repository stating that the project is now deprecated and that Portainer should be used.

The following is what you will see when navigating your browser to the Portainer website, `http://www.portainer.io`:

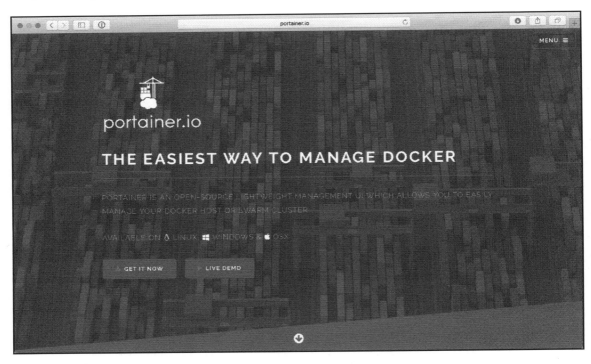

We won't be following the instructions in the **GET IT NOW** link. Instead, we will make a few tweaks.

Getting Portainer up and running

We are first going be looking at using Portainer to manage a single Docker instance running locally. I am running Docker for Mac so I will be using that, but these instructions should also work with other Docker installations.

First of all, let's grab the container image from the Docker Hub by running the following commands:

```
$ docker image pull portainer/portainer
```

```
$ docker image ls
```

As you can see when we ran the `docker image ls` command, the Portainer image is only 9.96 MB. To launch Portainer, we simply have to run the following command:

```
$ docker container run -d -p 9000:9000 -v
/var/run/docker.sock:/var/run/docker.sock portainer/portainer
```

 As you can see from the command we have just run, we are mounting the socket file for the Docker Engine on our Docker Host machine. Doing this will allow Portainer full unrestricted access to the Docker Engine on our host machine. It needs this so it can manage Docker on the host; however, it does mean that your Portainer container has full access to your host machine, so be careful in how you give access to it and also when publicly exposing Portainer on remote hosts.

For the most basic type of installation, that is all we need to run. There are a few more steps to complete the installation; they are all performed in the browser. To complete them, go to `http://localhost:9000/`.

The first screen you will be greeted by asks you to set a password for the admin user:

Once you have set the password, you will be taken to a login page: enter the username `admin` and the password you just configured. Once logged in, you will be asked about the Docker instance you wish to manage. There are two options:

- Manage the Docker instance where Portainer is running
- Manage a remote Docker instance

For the moment, we want to manage the instance where Portainer is running:

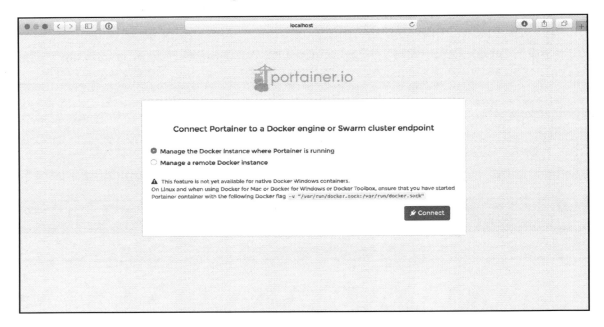

As you can see, there is a message that says the following:

This feature is not yet available for native Docker Windows containers. On Linux and when using Docker for Mac or Docker for Windows or Docker Toolbox, ensure that you have started Portainer container with the following Docker `flag -v` `"/var/run/docker.sock:/var/run/docker.sock"`

As we have already taken mounting the Docker socket file into account when launching our Portainer container, we can click on **Connect** to complete our installation. This will take us straight into Portainer itself, showing us the dashboard.

Using Portainer

Now that we have Portainer running and configured to communicate with our Docker installation, we can start to work through the features listed in the left-hand side menu, starting at the top with the **Dashboard**, which is also the default landing page of your Portainer installation.

The Dashboard

As you can see from the following screenshot, the **Dashboard** gives us an overview of the current state of the Docker instance that Portainer is configured to communicate with:

In my case, this shows how many containers I have running, which at the moment is just the already running Portainer container, as well as the number of images I have downloaded. We can also see the number of **Volumes** and **Networks** available on the Docker instance.

It also shows basic information on the Docker instance itself; as you can see, the Docker instance is running Moby Linux, has two CPUs and 2 GB of RAM: this is the default configuration for Docker for Mac.

The **Dashboard** will adapt to the environment you have Portainer running in, so we will revisit it when we look at attaching Portainer to a Docker Swarm cluster.

Application templates

Next up, we have **App Templates**. This section is probably the only feature not to be a direct feature available in the core Docker Engine; it is instead a way of launching common applications using containers downloaded from the Docker Hub:

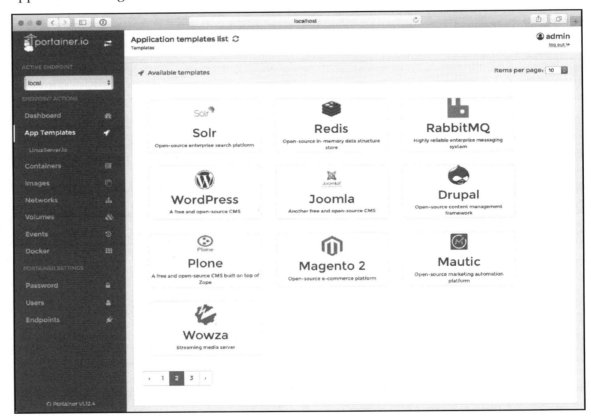

There are about 25 templates that ship with Portainer by default as well as templates from h ttps://www.linuxserver.io/.

The templates are defined in JSON format. For example, the MariaDB template looks like the following:

```
{
  "title": "MariaDB",
  "description": "Performance beyond MySQL",
  "logo":
"https://cloudinovasi.id/assets/img/logos/mariadb.png",
  "image": "mariadb:latest",
  "env": [
  {
   "name": "MYSQL_ROOT_PASSWORD",
   "label": "Root password"
  }
  ],
  "ports": [
  "3306/tcp"
  ],
  "volumes": ["/var/lib/mysql"]
}
```

As you can see, it looks similar to a Docker Compose file; however, this format is only used by Portainer. For the most part, the options are pretty self-explanatory, but we should touch upon the **Name** and **Label** options.

For containers that typically require options defined by passing custom values via environment variables, the **Name** and **Label** options allow you present the user with custom form fields that need to be completed before the container is launched, as demonstrated by the following screenshot:

As you can see, we have a field where we can enter the root password we would like to use for our MariaDB container. Filling this in will take that value and pass it as an environment variable, building the following command to launch the container:

```
$ docker container run --name [Name of Container] -p 3306 -e
MYSQL_ROOT_PASSWORD=[Root password] -d mariadb:latest
```

For more information on app templates, I recommend reviewing the documentation, which can be found at `http://portainer.readthedocs.io/en/latest/templates.html`.

Containers

Next up in the left-hand menu is **Containers**. This is where you launch and interact with the containers running on your Docker instance. Clicking on the **Containers** menu entry will bring up a list of all of the containers, both running and stopped, on your Docker instance.

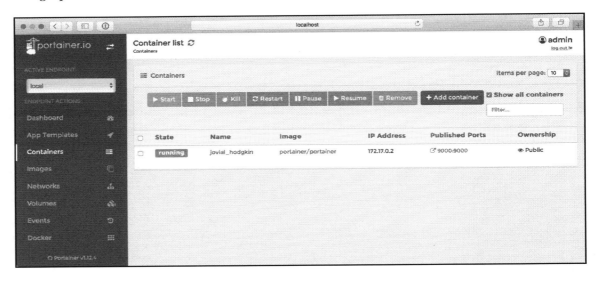

As you can see, I currently have only a single container running, and that just happens to be the Portainer one. Rather than interacting with that, let's press the **+ Add Container** button to launch a container running the cluster application we used in previous chapters.

There are several options on the **Create Container** page; these should be filled in as follows:

- **Name:** cluster
- **Image:** russmckendrick/cluster

- **Always pull the image**: On
- **Publish all exposed ports**: On

Finally, add a port mapping from port 80 on the host to port 80 on the container by clicking on **+ map additional port**. Your completed form should look something like the following screenshot:

Once that's done, click on **Start container**, and after a few seconds, you will be returned the list of running containers, where you should see your newly launched container:

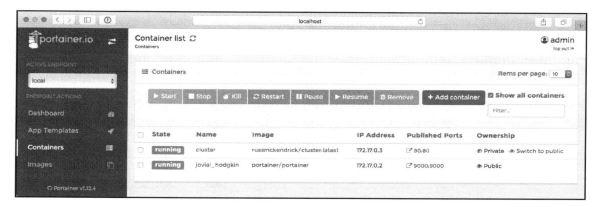

Using the tick box on the left of each container in the list will enable the buttons at the top, where you can control the status of your containers--make sure not to **Kill** or **Remove** the Portainer container. Clicking on the name of the container, in our case **cluster**, will bring up more information on the container itself:

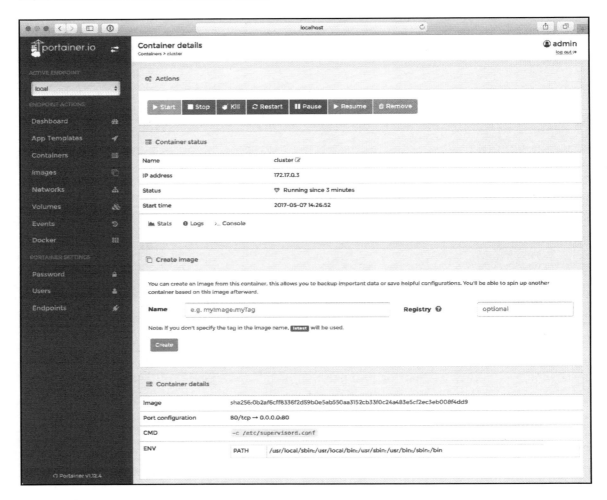

As you can see, the information about the container is the same information you would get if you were to run this command:

```
$ docker container inspect cluster
```

You will also notice that there are buttons for **Stats**, **Logs**, and **Console**.

Stats

Stats shows the CPU, memory, and network utilization, as well as a list of the processes for the container you are inspecting:

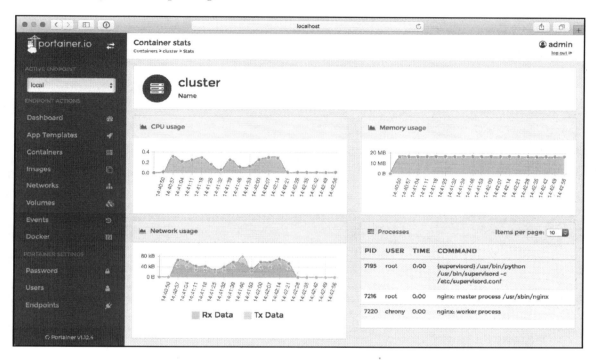

The graphs will automatically refresh if you leave the page open, and refreshing the page will zero the graphs and start afresh. This is because Portainer is receiving this information from the Docker API using the following command:

```
$ docker container stats cluster
```

Each time the page is refreshed, the command is started from scratch as Portainer currently does not poll Docker in the background to keep a record of statistics for each of the running containers.

Logs

Next up, we have `logs`. This shows you the results of running the following command:

```
$ docker container logs cluster
```

It displays both the STDOUT and STDERR logs:

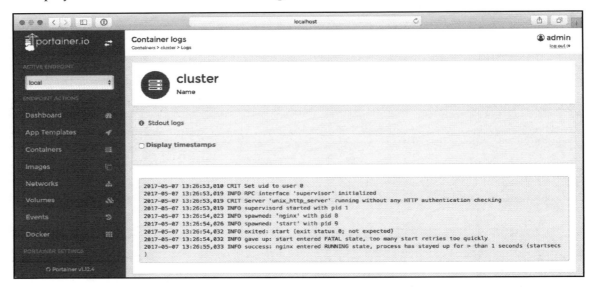

You also have the option of adding timestamps to the output; this is the equivalent of running the following:

```
$ docker container logs --timestamps cluster
```

Console

Finally, we have **Console**. This will open an HTML5 terminal and allow you to log in to your running container. Before you connect to your container, you need to choose a shell. You have the option of two shells to use: `/bin/bash` or `/bin/sh`. While the cluster image has both shells installed, I choose to use `sh`:

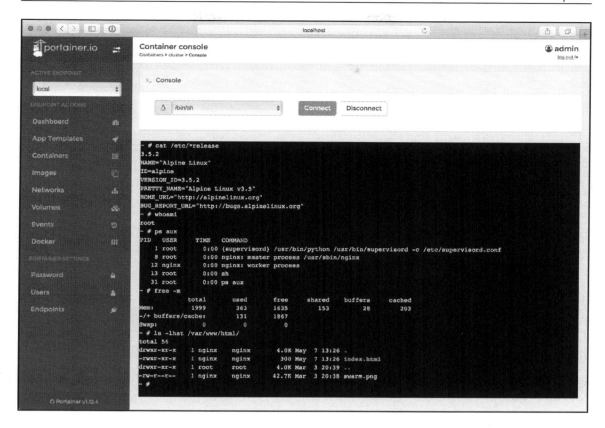

This is the equivalent of running the following command to gain access to your container:

```
docker container exec -it cluster /bin/sh
```

As you can see from the screenshot, the `sh` process has a PID of 13. This process was created by the `docker container exec` command, and that single process will be terminated once you disconnect from your shell session.

Images

Next up in the left-hand menu is **Images**. From here, you can manage, download, and upload images:

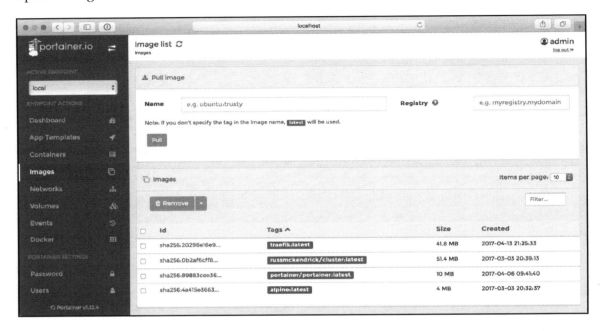

At the top of the page, you have the option of pulling an image. For example, simply entering `amazonlinux` into the box and then clicking on **Pull** will download a copy of the Amazon Linux container image from Docker Hub. The command executed by Portainer would be this:

```
$ docker image pull amazonlinux
```

You can find more information about each image by clicking on the image ID; this will take you to a page that nicely renders the output of running this command:

```
$ docker image inspect russmckendrick/cluster
```

Look at the following screenshot:

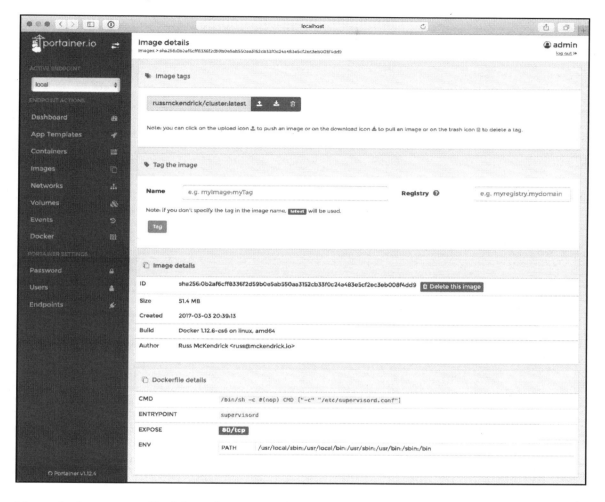

Not only do you get all of the information about the image, but you also get options to push a copy of the image to your chosen registry or, by default, the Docker Hub.

Networks and volumes

The next two items in the menu allow you to manage networks and volumes; I am not going to go into too much detail here as there is not much to them.

Networks

Here, you can quickly add a network using the default bridge driver. Clicking on **Advanced settings** will take you to a page with more options. These include using other drivers, defining the subnets, adding labels, and restricting external access to the network. As with other sections, you can also remove networks and inspect existing networks.

Volumes

There are not many options here other than adding or removing a volume. When adding a volume, you get a choice of drivers as well as being able to fill in options to pass to the driver, which allows the use of third-party driver plugins. Other than that, there is not much to see here, not even an inspect option.

Events

The events page shows you all of the events from the last 24 hours; you also have an option of filtering the results, meaning you can quickly find the information you are after:

This is the equivalent of running the following command:

```
$ docker events --since '2017-05-06T16:30:00' --until '2017-05-07T16:30:00'
```

Docker

The final entry simply shows you the output of the following:

```
$ docker info
```

The following shows the output of the command:

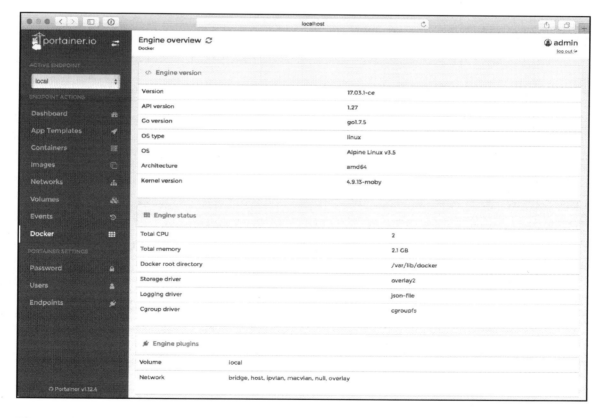

This can be useful if you are targeting multiple Docker instance endpoints and need information on the environment the endpoint is running on.

Portainer and Docker Swarm

In the previous section, we looked at how to use Portainer on a standalone Docker instance. Portainer also supports Docker Swarm clusters, and the options in the interface adapt to the clustered environment. We should look at spinning up a Swarm and then launching Portainer as a service and see what changes.

Creating the Swarm

As per the Docker Swarm chapter, we are going to be creating the Swarm locally using Docker Machine; to do this, run the following commands:

```
$ docker-machine create \
  -d virtualbox \
  swarm-manager

$ docker-machine create \
  -d virtualbox \
  swarm-worker01

$ docker-machine create \
  -d virtualbox \
  swarm-worker02
```

Once the three instances have launched, run the following command to initialize the Swarm:

```
$ docker $(docker-machine config swarm-manager) swarm init \
  --advertise-addr $(docker-machine ip swarm-manager):2377 \
  --listen-addr $(docker-machine ip swarm-manager):2377
```

Then run the following commands, inserting your own token, to add the worker nodes:

```
$ docker $(docker-machine config swarm-worker01) swarm join \
  $(docker-machine ip swarm-manager):2377 \
  --token
SWMTKN-1-5wz1e5n1c2oqlaojbbr1mlwvc3wjrh8iefvs889d1uzc5r8ag1-9rwp0n4q37jsw5f
wh30xn4h1d

$ docker $(docker-machine config swarm-worker02) swarm join \
  $(docker-machine ip swarm-manager):2377 \
  --token
SWMTKN-1-5wz1e5n1c2oqlaojbbr1mlwvc3wjrh8iefvs889d1uzc5r8ag1-9rwp0n4q37jsw5f
wh30xn4h1d
```

Now that we have our cluster formed, run the following to point your local Docker client to the manager node:

```
$ eval $(docker-machine env swarm-manager)
```

Finally, check the status of the Swarm using the following command:

```
$ docker node ls
```

The Portainer service

Now what we have a Docker Swarm cluster and our local client is configured to communicate with the manager node, we can launch the Portainer service by simply running:

```
docker service create \
  --name portainer \
  --publish 9000:9000 \
  --constraint 'node.role == manager' \
  --mount type=bind,src=/var/run/docker.sock,dst=/var/run/docker.sock \
  portainer/portainer \
  -H unix:///var/run/docker.sock
```

As you can see, this will launch Portainer as a service on the manager node and make the service mount the manager nodes socket file so that it has visibility of the rest of the Swarm. You can check that the service has launched without any errors using the following commands:

```
$ docker service ls
$ docker service inspect portainer --pretty
```

The following shows the output:

```
● ● ●                    2. russ (bash) 🐿
russ in ~
⚡ docker service inspect portainer --pretty

ID:                    1kcayhodyz6onbdj8l1103b7v
Name:                  portainer
Service Mode:          Replicated
 Replicas:             1
Placement:Constraints:   [node.role == manager]
UpdateConfig:
 Parallelism:          1
 On failure:           pause
 Max failure ratio:    0
ContainerSpec:
 Image:                portainer/portainer:latest@sha256:40bf7e42c9cd4b95ab70b9eca8c9b772e7ef65e78fa094ccb6
f745e117b5237c
 Args:                 -H unix:///var/run/docker.sock
Mounts:
  Target = /var/run/docker.sock
   Source = /var/run/docker.sock
   ReadOnly = false
   Type = bind
Resources:
Endpoint Mode:  vip
Ports:
 PublishedPort 9000
  Protocol = tcp
  TargetPort = 9000
russ in ~
⚡ 
```

Now that the service has launched, you can access Portainer on port 9000 on any of the IP addresses of the nodes in your cluster, or run the following command:

```
$ open http://$(docker-machine ip swarm-manager):9000
```

When the page opens, you will be once again be asked to set a password for the `admin` user; once set, you will be greeted with a login prompt. Once you have been logged in, you will be taken straight to the **Dashboard**. The reason for this is that when we launched Portainer this time, we passed it the argument `-H unix:///var/run/docker.sock`, which told Portainer to select the option we manually chose when we launched Portainer on our single host.

Swarm differences

As already mentioned, there are a few changes to the Portainer interface when it is connected to a Docker Swarm cluster. In this section, we will cover them. If a part of the interface is not mentioned, then there is no difference between running Portainer in single host mode.

Dashboard

One of the first changes you will notice is that the **Dashboard** now displays information on the Swarm cluster:

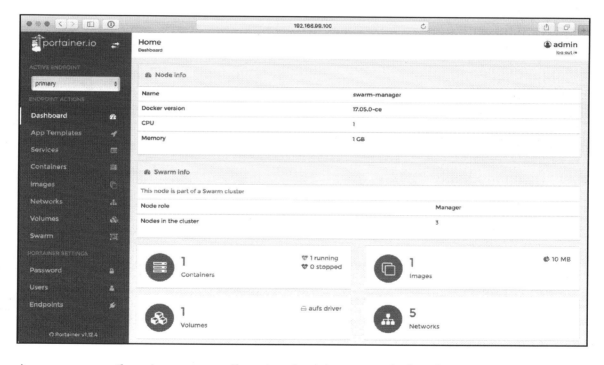

As you can see, there is now a small section that gives you a little information about the size of the cluster as well as the role of the node Swarm is currently configured to communicate with.

Swarm

For more information on the cluster, click on **Swarm** in the left-hand menu. This will give you more information on the cluster as well as letting you know the status of each of the nodes:

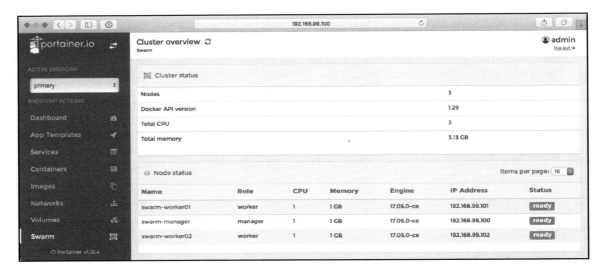

Clicking on the node name will take you to a page that gives you more options about the configuration of the selected node. You also have options around the availability of the node within the cluster as you can pause and drain the node, as shown in this screenshot:

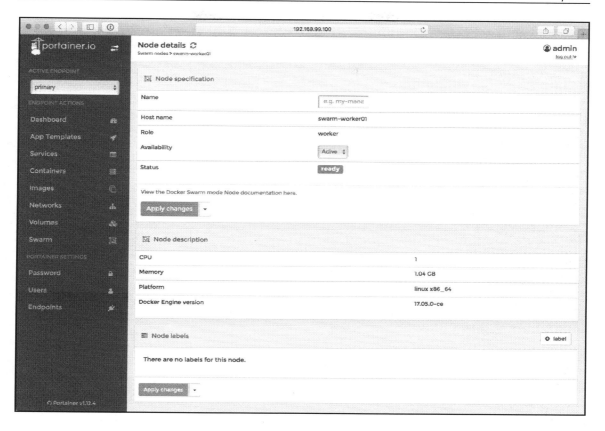

Services

This page is where you can create and manage services; it should show only one running service right now, which is Portainer. So that we don't cause any problems with the running Portainer container, we are going to create a new service. To do this, click on the **+ Add Service** button. On the page that loads, enter the following:

- **Name**: cluster
- **Image**: russmckendrick/cluster
- **Scheduling mode**: **Replicated**
- **Replicas**: 1

As before, add a port mapping for port 80 on the host to map to port 80 to the container:

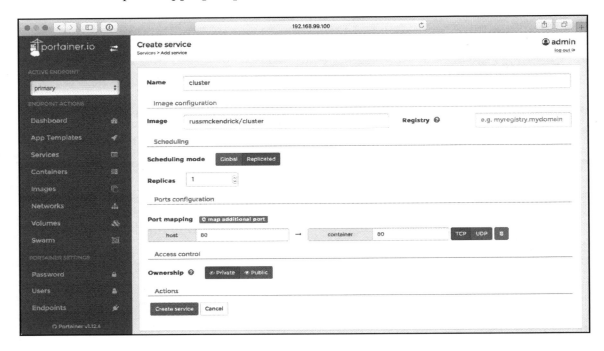

Once you have entered the information, click on **Create service**. You will be taken back to the list of services, which should now contain the cluster service we just added:

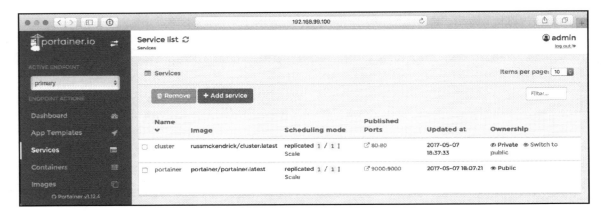

You may have noticed that in the scheduling mode column, there is an option to scale. Click on it and increase the number of replicas to 6 for our `cluster` service.

Clicking on `cluster` in the **Name** column takes us to an overview of the service. As you can see, there is a lot of information on the service:

You can make a lot of changes to the **Service** on the fly, including placement constraints, the restart policy, adding service labels, and more. Right at the bottom of the page is a list of the tasks associated with the service:

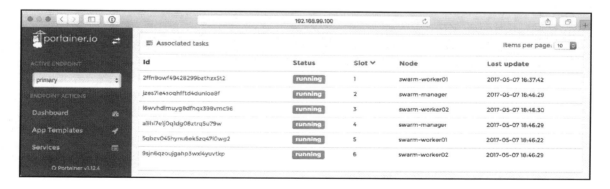

As you can see, we have six running tasks, two on each of our three nodes. Clicking on **Containers** in the left-hand menu may show something different than you expect:

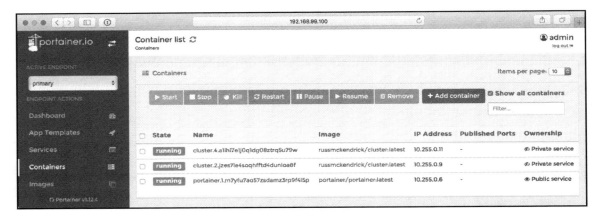

There are only three containers listed, and one of them is for the Portainer service. Why is that?

Well, if you remember in the Docker Swarm chapter, we learned that `docker container` commands only really apply to the node you are running them against, and as Portainer is only talking to our manager node, that is the only node which the Docker container commands are executed against. Remember that Portainer is only a web interface for the Docker API, so it mirrors the same results as you get running `docker container ls` on the command line.

Endpoints

However, we can add our two remaining cluster nodes to Portainer. To do this, click on the Endpoint entry in the left-hand menu.

To add the endpoint, we will need to know the endpoint URL and have access to the certificates so that Portainer can authenticate itself against the Docker daemon running on the node. Luckily, as we launched the hosts using Docker Machine, this is a simple task. To get the endpoint URLs, run the following command:

```
$ docker-machine ls
```

For me, the two endpoint URLs were `192.168.99.101:2376` and `192.168.99.102:2376`; yours may be different. The certificates we need to upload can be found in the `~/.docker/machine/certs/` folder on your machine. I recommend running the following commands to open the folder in your finder:

```
$ cd ~/.docker/machine/certs/
$ open .
```

Once you have added the node, you will be able to change to it using the **Active Endpoint** drop-down menu in the top left of the Portainer page. As you can see from the following screenshot, we can see that `swarm-worker-01` is running two containers and that it is in a swarm cluster as a worker node:

You will also notice that other than the small **Swarm info** section on the Dashboard, there's no mention of Swarm services. Again, this is because Portainer only knows as much as your Docker nodes, and Swarm mode only allows nodes with the role of manager to launch services and tasks and interact with the other nodes in your cluster.

Summary

That concludes our deep dive with Portainer. As we can see, Portainer is very powerful, yet simple to use, and will only continue to grow and integrate more of the Docker ecosystem as features are released. With Portainer, you can do a lot of manipulation with not only your hosts but also the containers and services running on single or cluster hosts.

In the next chapter, we will take a look at another GUI tool for managing your Docker hosts, containers, and images, and that is called Rancher.

9
Rancher

Rancher is another open source project that helps with the deployment of Docker environments by using a GUI to allow you to control just about everything that you can with the CLI, as well as many other additional features.

In this chapter, we will cover the following topics:

- Installing and configuring authentication
- Creating a herd
- Launching stacks
- Removing the herd
- Other cluster types

Installing and configuring authentication

As you can see from the homepage at `http://rancher.com/`, on the face of it, Rancher looks a lot like Portainer:

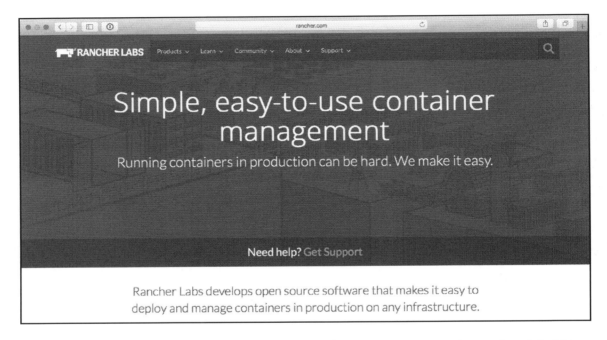

While it is true that both can be used to deploy and manage your containers, they inhabit two different spaces. The differences start with the installation process. Rancher does not currently support Docker for Mac or Docker for Windows. If you are using these platforms, you must use a local virtual machine running Ubuntu 16.04 or higher with a minimum of 1 GB of RAM. However, to take proper advantage of Rancher, I recommend that you use a server instance that is publicly accessible.

Installation

For our installation, I am going to be launching a single DigitalOcean droplet using Docker Machine and use that as the base for our Rancher services.

To launch the droplet in DigitalOcean, I simply have to run the following command:

```
$ docker-machine create \
  --driver digitalocean \
  --digitalocean-access-token
7b6216feba5d02669525bf8e7a86c773c9d17a438987c08040ce32f14b66d4cf \
  --digitalocean-size 1gb \
  rancher
```

 Ensure you use your own access token; you can generate one at `https://c loud.digitalocean.com/settings/api`.

Once the droplet has launched, we can point our local Docker client toward it by running this command:

```
$ eval $(docker-machine env rancher)
```

Once we have our client communicating with our droplet, we can launch Rancher by running the following command:

```
$ docker container run -d \
  --name=rancher \
  --restart=unless-stopped \
  -p 8080:8080 \
  rancher/server:stable
```

Rancher takes a few minutes to bootstrap itself; you can track its progress by running this command:

```
docker container logs rancher -f
```

If at any point during this process you see a message like the following and the container stops, then your instance does not have enough RAM:

```
# There is insufficient memory for the Java Runtime Environment to
continue.
# Native memory allocation (mmap) failed to map 31092736 bytes for
committing reserved memory.
```

Check that your droplet was launched with the `--digitalocean-size 1gb` flag. You will know that your installation has completed when the logs stop scrolling; the last messages in there should include several creation events, similar to the following Terminal output:

```
● ● ●                              1. russ (docker)
time="2017-05-13T13:04:11Z" level=info msg="Creating service metadata"
time="2017-05-13T13:04:11Z" level=info msg="[network-services:network-manager]: Created " eventId=df
bb4005-7940-4dc8-87d3-fd56c687c994 resourceId=1st4
time="2017-05-13T13:04:11Z" level=info msg="[network-services:metadata]: Created " eventId=dfbb4005-
7940-4dc8-87d3-fd56c687c994 resourceId=1st4
time="2017-05-13T13:04:11Z" level=info msg="[network-services:dns]: Creating " eventId=dfbb4005-7940
-4dc8-87d3-fd56c687c994 resourceId=1st4
time="2017-05-13T13:04:11Z" level=info msg="[network-services:dns]: Created " eventId=dfbb4005-7940-
4dc8-87d3-fd56c687c994 resourceId=1st4
time="2017-05-13T13:04:11Z" level=info msg="[network-services:]: Project created " eventId=dfbb4005-
7940-4dc8-87d3-fd56c687c994 resourceId=1st4
time="2017-05-13T13:04:11Z" level=info msg="[network-services:]: Creating project " eventId=dfbb4005
-7940-4dc8-87d3-fd56c687c994 resourceId=1st4
time="2017-05-13T13:04:11Z" level=info msg="[network-services:network-manager]: Creating " eventId=d
fbb4005-7940-4dc8-87d3-fd56c687c994 resourceId=1st4
time="2017-05-13T13:04:11Z" level=info msg="[network-services:metadata]: Creating " eventId=dfbb4005
-7940-4dc8-87d3-fd56c687c994 resourceId=1st4
time="2017-05-13T13:04:11Z" level=info msg="[network-services:metadata]: Created " eventId=dfbb4005-
7940-4dc8-87d3-fd56c687c994 resourceId=1st4
time="2017-05-13T13:04:11Z" level=info msg="[network-services:dns]: Creating " eventId=dfbb4005-7940
-4dc8-87d3-fd56c687c994 resourceId=1st4
time="2017-05-13T13:04:11Z" level=info msg="[network-services:dns]: Created " eventId=dfbb4005-7940-
4dc8-87d3-fd56c687c994 resourceId=1st4
time="2017-05-13T13:04:11Z" level=info msg="[network-services:network-manager]: Created " eventId=df
bb4005-7940-4dc8-87d3-fd56c687c994 resourceId=1st4
time="2017-05-13T13:04:11Z" level=info msg="[network-services:]: Project created " eventId=dfbb4005-
7940-4dc8-87d3-fd56c687c994 resourceId=1st4
time="2017-05-13T13:04:11Z" level=info msg="Stack Create Event Done" eventId=dfbb4005-7940-4dc8-87d3
-fd56c687c994 resourceId=1st4
```

At this point, press *Ctrl + C* to stop the logs from streaming to your Terminal. If you are running macOS you can open Rancher by running the following command:

```
$ open http://$(docker-machine ip rancher):8080
```

Or you can run the following command to get the IP address of your Rancher host:

```
$ docker-machine ip rancher
```

Once you have the IP address enter the IP with `:8080` in your browser, for example, `http://123.123.123.123:8080`. You should be greeted by a screen that looks like this:

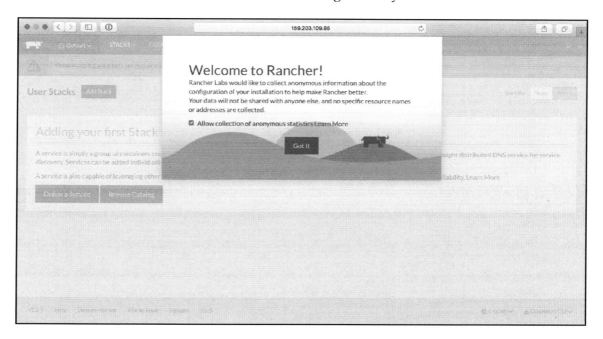

Click on **Got It** to move on to the next step.

Configuring authentication

The very first task we need to do is secure our installation as it is publicly accessible. To do this, go to the **Admin** menu and select **Access** from the drop-down menu. By default, Rancher will ask if you want to use GitHub as an authentication service:

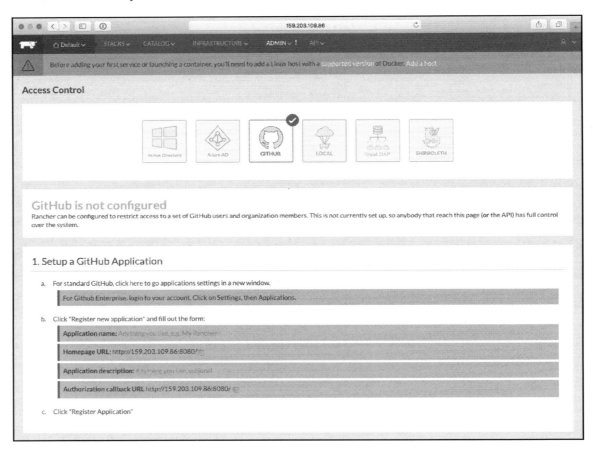

As you can see, there are instructions on how to configure this. Following the standard GitHub link will take you to `https://github.com/settings/developers/`. Once there, follow the onscreen instructions from Rancher until you have something that looks like the following:

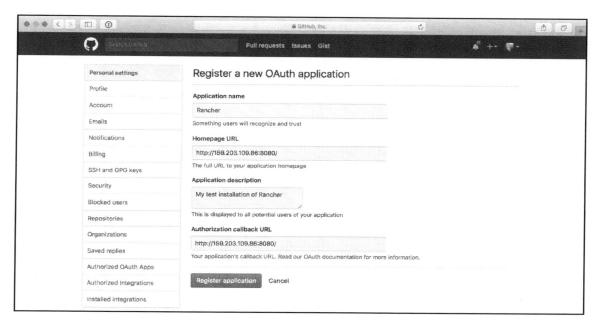

 The homepage URL and authorization callback URL should be the should be completed as per the instructions which were given to you by Rancher, these allow GitHub to return you to Rancher once you have logged in through GitHub. For more information on GitHub Applications and OAuth please see `https://developer.github.com/v3/guides/getting-started/`.

Once you have registered your application, enter the credentials in the boxes provided by Rancher and click on **Save**. After saving, you can the test the login; this will open the following window:

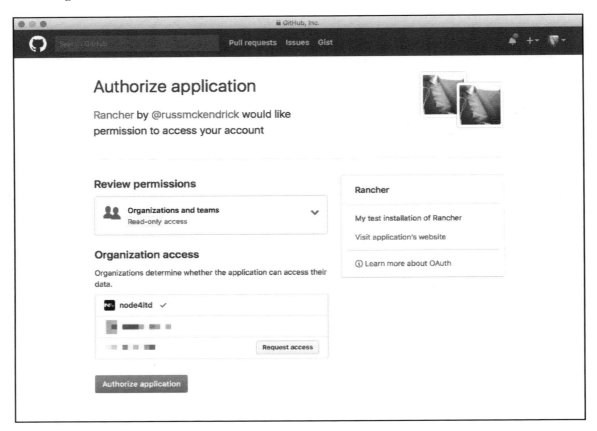

Once you click on **Authorize application**, your Rancher page will refresh and you will receive confirmation that **GitHub is enabled**:

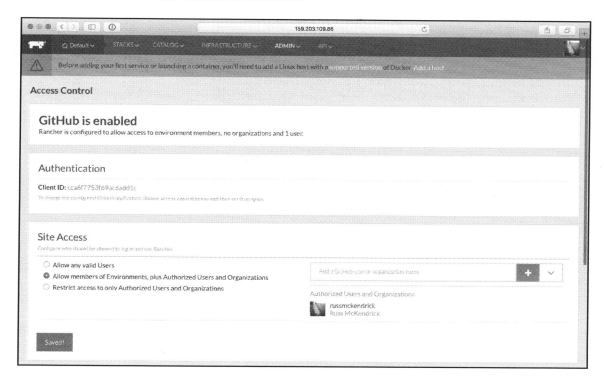

Now that we have our basic installation complete and secure, let's have a look at creating an environment and then adding some hosts. As you can see from the notice on each page of our Rancher installation, we need to do this before we can start launching services.

Creating a herd

The default environment created by Rancher uses it own orchestration technology called **Cattle**. Cattle is described by Rancher as follows:

> "Cattle is the orchestration engine that powers Rancher. Its primary role is meta data management and orchestration of external systems. Cattle, in fact, does no real work, but instead delegates to other components (agents) to do the actual work. You can look at cattle as the middle management layer in Rancher. Do middle managers really do anything?"

Before we can start to launch services using Cattle, we need to add hosts for them to be created on. To add a host to our herd, go to the **Infrastructure** menu and then select **Hosts** from the drop-down menu. This will take you to a mostly blank page that confirms you have no running hosts or containers.

Clicking on the **Add Host** button will bring up several options. As we are using **DigitalOcean**, click on that option and enter your API key where prompted:

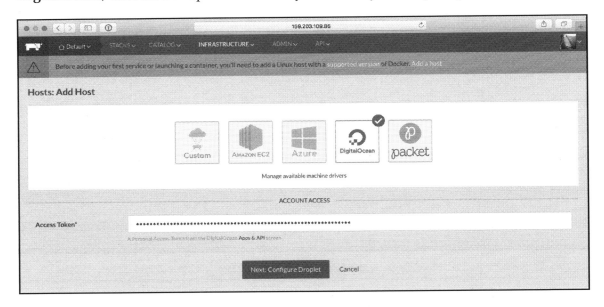

Clicking on **Next: Configure Droplet** will take you to a page where you choose a few options about the droplets that will go on to form our herd:

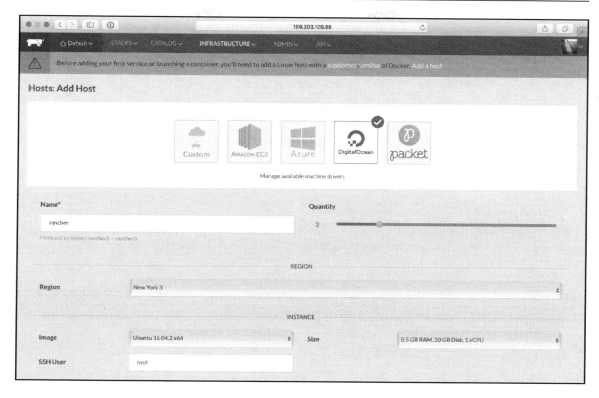

As you can see from the previous screen, I am launching three 512 MB Ubuntu 16.04 droplets in the `New York 3` region. Clicking on the **Create** button at the bottom of the page will create the droplets and register them with our Rancher installation.

After a few minutes, our three hosts should be visible, and the **Hosts** screen should have quite a bit of detail about each of the hosts:

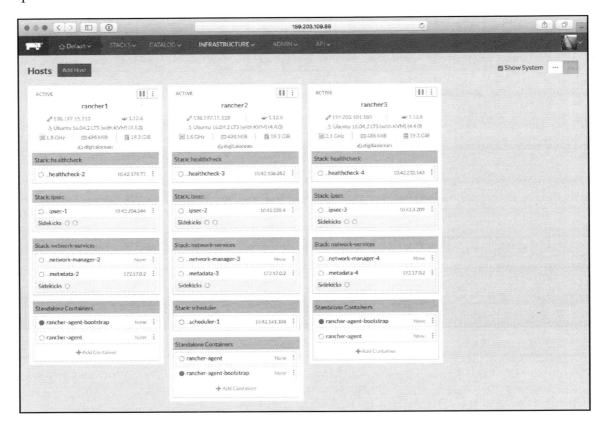

Now that we have hosts within our herd, we can look at launching a stack.

Launching stacks

There are two different types of stack you can launch within Rancher: user defined and infrastructure. Stacks are collections of services which are in turn made up containers typically these services are configured to interact with each other in much the same way that services are defined in Docker Compose files.

Infrastructure stacks extend the capabilities of Rancher by adding external features such as load balancers, persistent storage, and DNS services to name a few.

User Defined Stacks

We are going to look at launching a user-defined stack, this is a stack which you configure from the ground up. As in previous chapters, this will be the cluster application, which can be found at `https://hub.docker.com/r/russmckendrick/cluster/`.

Going to the **STACKS** menu item and then selecting **All** will show you that there are already some stacks running; these make up the Rancher and Cattle services we are using:

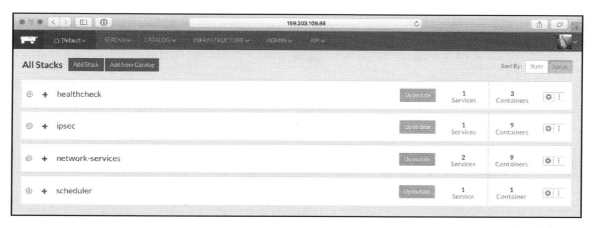

Clicking on the **Add Stack** button will take you to a simple form that defines your stack; here we simply need to name our stack and give it a description. There are also options for importing both Docker and Rancher compose files; we are going to ignore these options for now and just enter the name and description:

- **Name:** `MyClusterApplication` (note that names cannot contain spaces or other special characters)
- **Description:** `Testing Rancher with the cluster application`

As shown in the following screenshot:

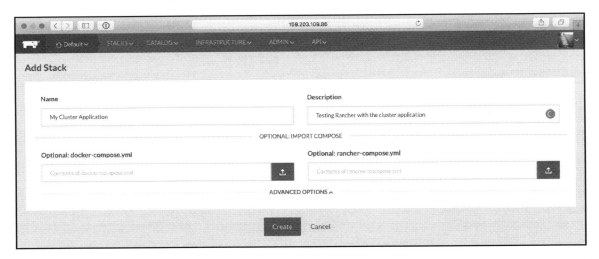

Once they've been entered, click on the **Create** button and you will be taken to our very sparse-looking new stack:

The next step in launching our stack is to add the cluster container. To do this, click on the **Add Service** button, and on the page that loads, enter the following information:

- **Scale: Run 1 container**
- **Name: cluster-service**

- **Description**: The containers running russmckendrick/cluster
- **Select Image**: russmckendrick/cluster
- **Always pull images before creating**: Leave ticked

As shown in the following screenshot:

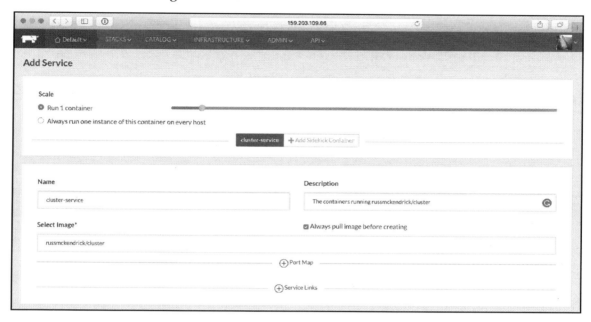

Leave the remaining options as they are and then click on the **Create** button at the bottom of the page; this will launch our lone container:

While we have a service up and running, we still won't be able to access it externally; to do this, we will need to add a load balancer. Click on the downward arrow on the **Add Service** button and select **Add Load Balancer** from the drop-down list:

- **Name:** `cluster-loadbalancer`
- **Description:** `The Load Balancer to expose the cluster service`
- **Port Rules:** Add port `80` and then select the `cluster-service`

Leave all of the other options at their defaults and click on **Create**:

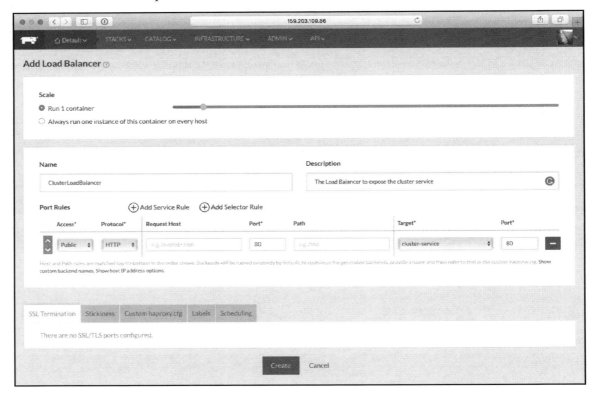

Our stack should now show two active services, `cluster-loadbalanacer` and `cluster-service`, running a total of two containers:

Clicking on `80/tcp` on the `cluster-loadbalancer` service will open up a new tab in your browser and take you to our cluster application:

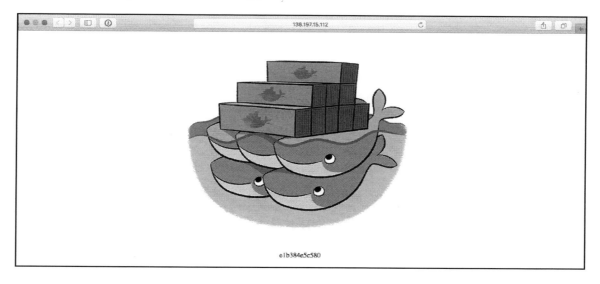

Back in Rancher, click on the **Info** (information) icon; next, the `cluster-service` name will slide in an information or edit box from the bottom of your browser. Here we can scale the service; for example, I have scaled my service so that there are six containers:

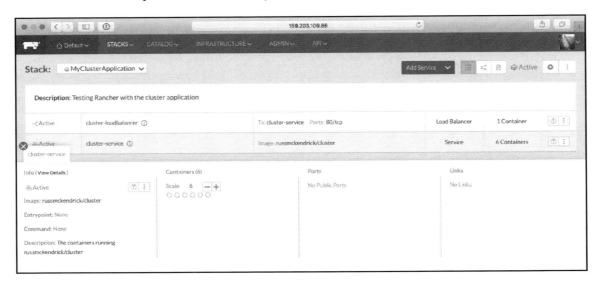

Refreshing the application page will show that the container UUID changes with each refresh, cycling through each of our six containers. Back in Rancher, you will notice that there are three buttons between the **Add Service** button and the status of the stack (it should currently say **Active**). These change the view of the current page, and the first one is the list view we are currently seeing.

The second changes the view to a graph one; this shows you the topology of your stack and how the services are connected to each other; as we are only running two services in our cluster stack, this is simply two boxes with a line between them. The final view is the compose YAML view; clicking this will change the view of our stack, showing the Docker and Rancher compose files, which we can use to recreate the stack with its current configuration:

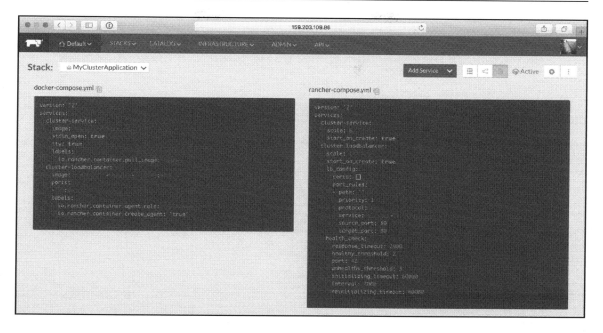

The `docker-compose.yml` file is a standard V2 compose file that defines our two services:

```
version: '2'
services:
  cluster-service:
    image: russmckendrick/cluster
    stdin_open: true
    tty: true
    labels:
      io.rancher.container.pull_image: always
  cluster-loadbalancer:
    image: rancher/lb-service-haproxy:v0.6.4
    ports:
      - 80:80/tcp
    labels:
      io.rancher.container.agent.role: environmentAdmin
      io.rancher.container.create_agent: 'true'
```

As you can see, it uses labels to define any Rancher-specific options. The `rancher-compose.yml` file contains all of the metadata to define the current state of the stack:

```yaml
version: '2'
services:
  cluster-service:
    scale: 6
    start_on_create: true
  cluster-loadbalancer:
    scale: 1
    start_on_create: true
    lb_config:
      certs: []
      port_rules:
        - path: ''
          priority: 1
          protocol: http
          service: cluster-service
          source_port: 80
          target_port: 80
    health_check:
      response_timeout: 2000
      healthy_threshold: 2
      port: 42
      unhealthy_threshold: 3
      initializing_timeout: 60000
      interval: 2000
      reinitializing_timeout: 60000
```

You can download the files for your stack by clicking on the button with the three dots right at the end and selecting the **Export Config** option from the drop-down menu.

Container view

Clicking on **INFRASTRUCTURE** in the top menu and selecting **Containers** from the drop-down menu will list all of the containers running within our herd, and entering **cluster** in the search box will filter the list down to just the ones running within our stack:

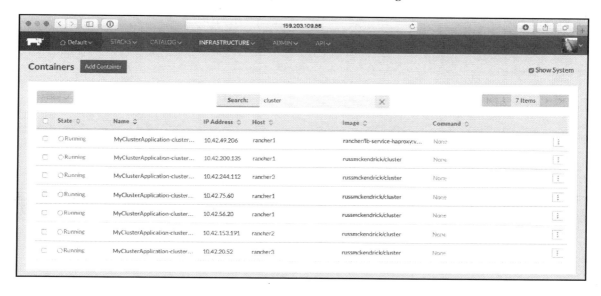

Clicking on the container name, for example, the load balancer `MyClusterApplication-cluster-loadbalancer-1`, will show you detailed information on the container, including all of the **CPU**, **Memory**, **Network**, and **Storage** graphs you would expect to see:

There are additional options, such as **Restarting**, **Stopping**, **Deleting** and even the **Execute Shell** option in the button with the three dots.

Catalog

You can also boot predefined stacks, and Rancher ships with a few dozen covering all types of application. These can all be accessed through the **Catalog** menu. The following screen shows a handful of the stacks available:

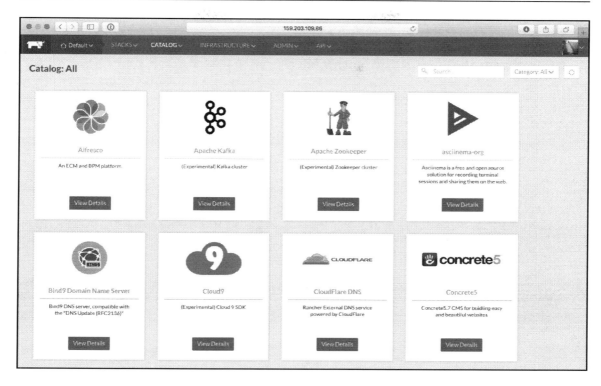

These enable us to quickly launch and configure stacks running your selected application. One thing I would mention is if you were to have a go at launching some of the items from the catalog, you may run into problems due to the low specification of the hosts within our herd. Remember that it is just a test environment, so Java-based applications such as Jenkins will not run.

Removing the herd

Before we progress any further, we should remove the hosts from within our herd. I would recommend launching the DigitalOcean control panel and terminating the droplets from there directly rather than using Rancher. In the past, I have had problems with timeouts and droplets that have not been fully terminated, which resulted in unexpected costs.

Terminate the three hosts, Rancher1, Rancher2, and Rancher3, and make sure they are no longer listed within your DigitalOcean control panel before moving on.

Other cluster options

As you may have already spotted, Rancher allows you to launch other cluster types, which are as follows:

- Kubernetes
- Mesos
- Docker Swarm (currently experimental)

Not only are you able to launch these clusters from within Rancher, but you are also able to use a single Rancher installation and switch between the different environments. Creating a new environment could not be easier. Click on **Default** in the top left and then go to **Environment.** From there, you will find the option to **Add Environment**. Clicking on this will take you to a simple page where you can name and select the template you wish to use:

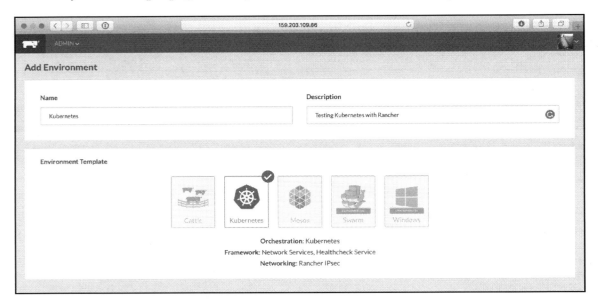

Once you have added your new environment, you simply have to add hosts as before:

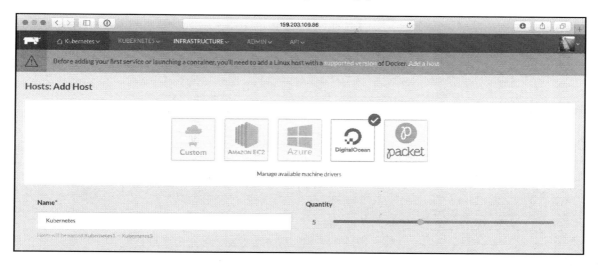

Depending on the environment template you selected, adding the hosts can take up to 10 minutes as not only does the Rancher client and networking need to be installed and configured, but the cluster environment also needs to be to bootstrapped.

Once this is complete, you may notice that the majority of the options in the top menu are missing. This is because Rancher is not trying to be a replacement for the GUI to manage your environment. For example, when launching a Kubernetes cluster, the **Kubernetes Dashboard** is installed:

Clicking the **Kubernetes UI** button will open up the dashboard, and as you are already authenticated and logged in to Rancher, you will be logged straight in:

There are other ways you can manage your Kubernetes cluster, such as the command-line `kubectl`. Don't worry, Rancher has you covered there as well by providing terminal access to a container running `kubectl` and an option to download the configuration so that you can use your local installation of `kubectl`:

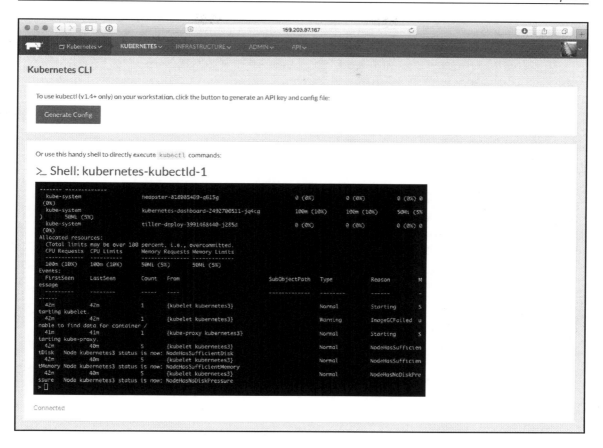

The other environment templates work in much the same way. Also, the Swarm template deploys Portainer for you to manage your Swarm cluster.

Summary

At the start of the chapter, I mentioned that on the face of it, Rancher looks to be the same as Portainer. I hope as you worked through the chapter that it has become apparent they are two very different tools.

While it can be said that Rancher does offer the same functionality when using its own orchestration technology, Cattle, its strengths are in that it makes launching quite complex clusters across multiple cloud providers quite a simple task without diluting the experience or functionality of your chosen environment. Having manually launched all of the supported environments, I can say that this is no easy task.

On top of that, there are features such as Rancher's API we haven't touched upon. Every command we have executed through the Rancher GUI in the chapter also has an equivalent in the API, meaning that Rancher can be used and integrated into your own projects and workflows. For more details on the API, refer to the documentation at `https://docs.ranch er.com/rancher/v1.6/en/api/v2-beta/`.

Next up, we are going to be looking at Docker's own cloud offering.

10
Docker Cloud

Docker Cloud is Docker's own hosted service that allows you to launch and manage Docker hosts in various public cloud providers. Docker Cloud started off life as a service called **Tutum**, which was purchased by Docker in October 2015.

 For more information on Docker's acquisition of Tutum, see the following blog post:
`https://blog.docker.com/2015/10/docker-acquires-tutum/`

Tutum's original goal was to help you run your containers in the cloud, providing you with a unified interface no matter which provider you are using. Docker has been supporting this vision with continued development and rebranding the service as Docker Cloud. In this chapter, we are going to look at both the Docker Cloud service and also Docker for Amazon Web Services. We will cover the following topics:

- Creating an account
- Linking providers
- Launching nodes
- Swarm mode
- Docker for Amazon Web Services

The first thing that should be mentioned is that Docker Cloud is a paid service, and it currently costs $15 per node per month. As we work through the chapter, I will point out which actions will incur costs.

Creating an account

When visiting the Docker Cloud website at `https://cloud.docker.com/`, you will notice that it has a signup on its front page:

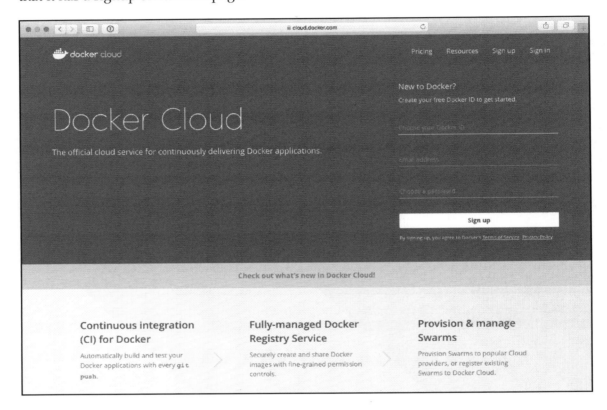

You may also notice that the form is creating a Docker ID. Odds are that if you have been following along with some of the previous chapters of this book, then you probably already have a Docker ID as Docker maintains a single identity service across all their products. This means if you have been using the Docker Hub, then you will be able to log straight into Docker Cloud.

Click on **Sign in** to be taken a familiar sign page:

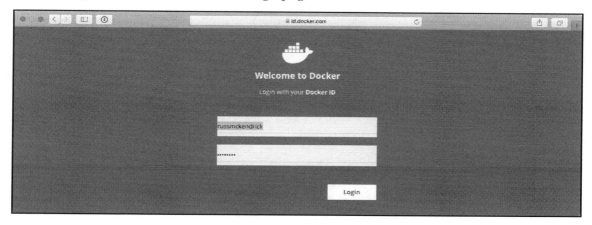

If you do not have a Docker ID, then you will be able to create one using the form on the Docker Cloud home page.

Once logged in with your Docker ID, you should be greeted by a blank screen with lots of menu options down on the left-hand side. In the following screenshot, I have extended the menu so you can see which item means what:

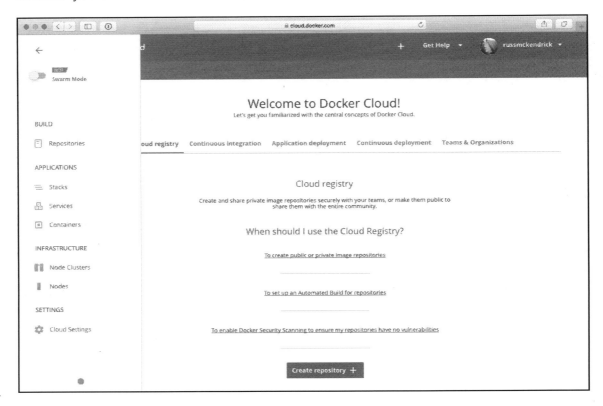

Before we look at **BUILD**, **APPLICATIONS**, or **INFRASTRUCTURE**, we are going to go to the **Cloud Settings**. Click here so that we can link Docker Cloud to our public cloud accounts.

Linking your accounts

When you first open the **Cloud Settings** page, you should see something that looks similar to the following screen:

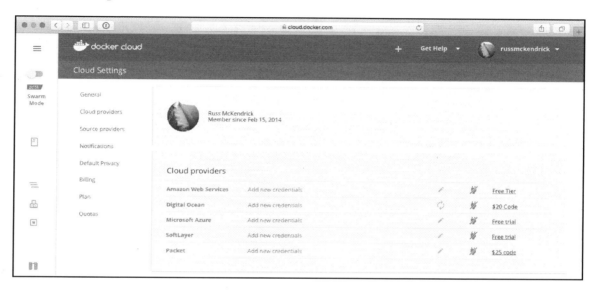

As you can see, there are several cloud providers listed. We are going to look at how to link **Digital Ocean** and **Amazon Web Services**. Let's start with the simpler of the two, DigitalOcean.

DigitalOcean

To link to a Cloud provider, click on the icon that looks like a power cord plug with a line going across it. When you do this with the DigitalOcean provider, you will be taken to DigitalOcean's application authorization page.

If you are not logged in to the DigitalOcean control panel (which can be found at `https://c loud.digitalocean.com/`), you will be asked to log in. Once logged in, you should be presented with a screen that asks you grant read or write privileges to Docker Cloud:

Tick the box next to your user and then click on the **Authorize application** button. Once you do so, you will be returned to Docker Cloud.

Amazon Web Services

Linking your Amazon Web Services account to Docker Cloud has a few more steps. To link the account, we need to provide Docker Cloud with the role **Amazon Resource Names (ARNs)**, which has the necessary privileges to access the resources required within our Amazon Web Services account to be able to launch instances.

To do this, we must first create a policy. To do so, log in to your Amazon Web Services account at `https://console.aws.amazon.com/` or your organization's custom sign-in page if you use one. Once logged in, go to the **Services** menu, which can be found in the top-left of the page, and find the IAM service.

The AWS **Identity and Access Management (IAM)** service allows you to manage both users and access to the AWS API at an extremely granular level. This service could potentially allow you to create credentials allowing a high level of access to your account--do not publish any credentials created here publicly. For more information, see `https://aws.amazon.com/iam/`.

Once you are on the **Welcome to Identity and Access Management** page, click on **Polices**, which can be found in the left-hand menu. This page lists all of the default policies supplied by Amazon, along with any custom ones you have created.

We are going to be creating our own policy. To do this, click on the **Create Policy** button; you will be taken to a page where you have three options: **Copy an AWS Managed Policy**, **Policy Generator**, and **Create Your Own Policy**. Click on **Select** next to **Create Your Own Policy**.

Enter the **Policy Name** as `dockercloud-policy`, leave the **Description** blank, and for the **Policy Document**, enter the following:

```
{
    "Version": "2012-10-17",
    "Statement": [
        {
          "Action": [
            "ec2:*",
            "iam:ListInstanceProfiles"
          ],
          "Effect": "Allow",
          "Resource": "*"
        }
    ]
}
```

You can see this in the following screenshot:

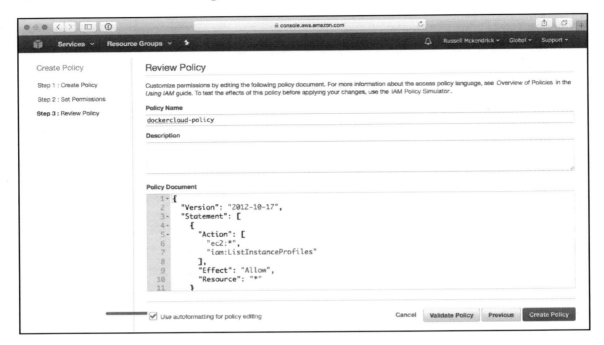

Once you have entered the details, click on **Create Policy.** Now that we have our policy, we need to attach it to a role. To do this, click on **Roles** in the left-hand side menu and then click the **Create new role** button.

There are four steps to create a role, the first of which is to select the type of role we want to create; in our case, we want to select **Role for cross-account access** as we will be allowing Docker Cloud access to our Amazon Web Services account:

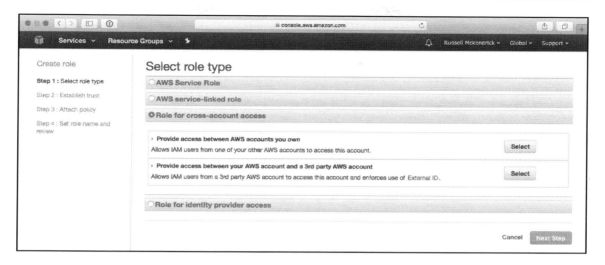

Now that in **Role for cross-account access** we have two options; as we going to be allowing third-party access, click on the **Select** button next to the **Provide access between your AWS account and a 3rd party AWS account** option.

This will take you to step two, where you will need to tell Amazon the **Account ID** of the third party you want to be able to use your role with, and also you will need to provide your Docker ID username. The account number you need for this is 689684103426; enter it in the **Account ID** field, and in the **External ID** field, enter your Docker ID. Leave **Require MFA** unticked:

Once you have entered the details, click on **Next Step** to attach the policy we created earlier. To do this, enter `docker cloud` in the **Filter** and check the box next to the `dockercloud-policy` result:

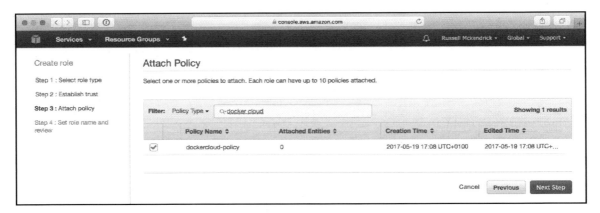

Click on **Next Step** to move onto the final step. Here we need to give our role a name, so enter `dockercloud-role` in the **Role** name field. Review the rest of the information, such as the account number, which should read `689684103426`, and then click on **Create role**.

This will create our Docker Cloud role and take you back to the list of roles. The final piece of information we need before we return to Docker Cloud is the ARN name for the role we just created. To get this, click on the role name in the list of roles and make a note of the **Role ARN:**

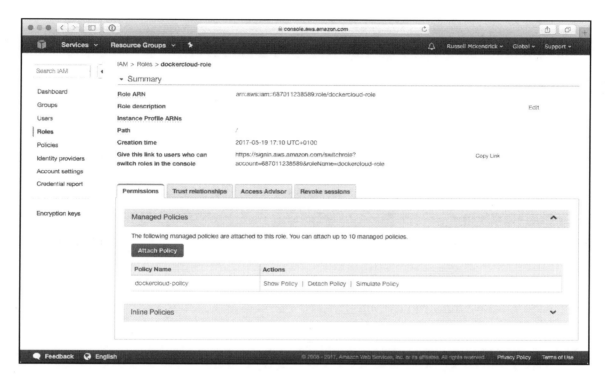

Now that we have the role ARN, return to Docker Cloud and click on the power cord plug next to Amazon Web Services; this will open a prompt that asks you for the role ARN. Enter it and click on **Save**:

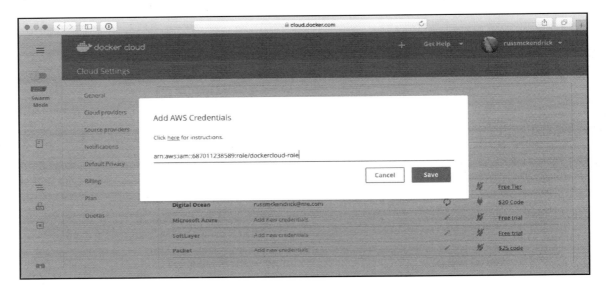

You should now have two different cloud providers linked to your Docker Cloud account, and your **Cloud Settings** page should look something like the following:

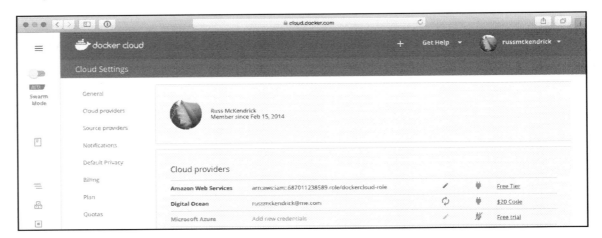

Launching nodes

Now that we have our two cloud providers connected, we can start to launch nodes. To start with, we are going to create a two-node cluster in DigitalOcean. To do this, click on the **Node Clusters** icon in the in the left-hand menu in Docker Cloud and then click on the **Create** button. The form will adapt as you fill parts in, so do not worry if you do not see all of the options listed. To create our creatively titled `Testing` cluster, enter the following:

- **NAME**: `Testing`
- **LABELS**: Leave blank
- **PROVIDER**: `Digital Ocean`
- **REGION**: [Select which ever is closest to you]
- **TYPE/SIZE**: `1GB [1 CPUs, 1 GB RAM]`
- **DISK SIZE**: This will be automatically populated when you choose the **TYPE/SIZE**
- **Number of nodes**: `2`

Once the form is complete, it should look like the following:

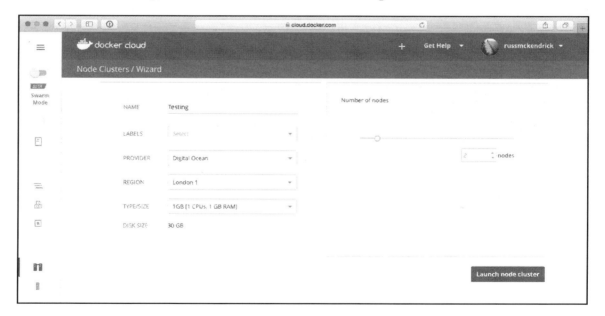

Be aware that moving pass this stage will incur cost both with DigitalOcean and Docker Cloud. I will be providing screenshots to the next stages in case you do not want to follow along with your accounts.

Clicking on **Launch node cluster** will do just that. Checking your DigitalOcean account, you should see two freshly launched droplets:

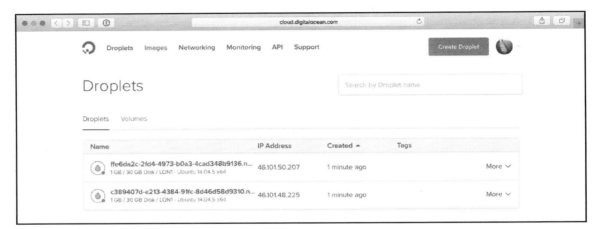

After a few minutes, you will see your cluster listed as **DEPLOYED**:

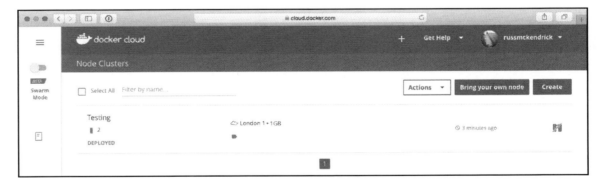

Clicking on the cluster name will give you more details on the cluster itself:

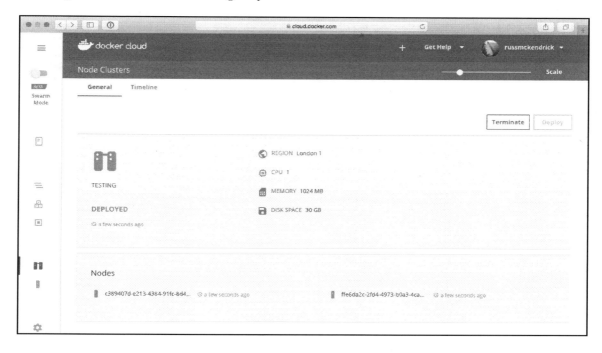

Clicking on one of the two nodes will give you a breakdown of the node itself:

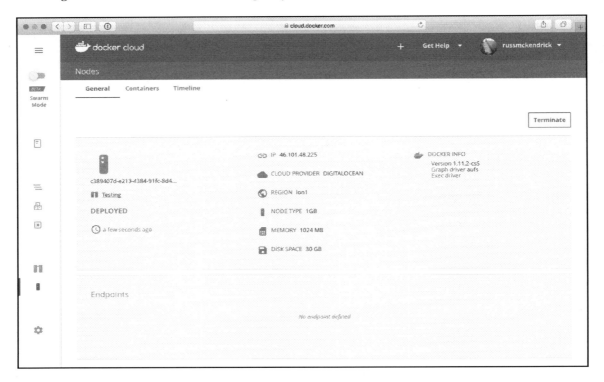

You may notice that the Docker version on the nodes is actually different than what we have been using so far; it is actually the **Commercially Supported** (**CS**) version of the Docker Engine. Feature-wise, it matches the functionality of the open source version (Docker 1.11.2), but it includes back-ported fixes for both security-related and priority defects from other versions.

Launching a stack

Now that we have a cluster with a few nodes up and running, we can launch some containers. Like previous chapters, we are going to be launching our cluster application. To do this, we are going to be using a stackfile, which is very similar to the stackfile we looked at in Chapter 8, *Portainer*. However, the syntax is slightly different as this was the forerunner to the stackfile now being used by Docker Swarm.

The following shows the stackfile for our application:

```
lb:
  image: dockercloud/haproxy
  autorestart: always
  links:
    - web
  ports:
    - "80:80"
  roles:
    - global
web:
  image: russmckendrick/cluster
  autorestart: always
  deployment_strategy: high_availability
  target_num_containers: 4
```

As you can see, we are creating two services: a load balancer and a web app (web). The load balancer is using the Docker Cloud HAProxy image and the web app is using our own image from the Docker Hub. To launch the stack, click on the **Stacks** icon in the left-hand side menu and enter the preceding stackfile in the space provided. Ensure that the spacing is correct or Docker Cloud will not be able to interpret the file correctly; I have called my stack **ClusterApp**:

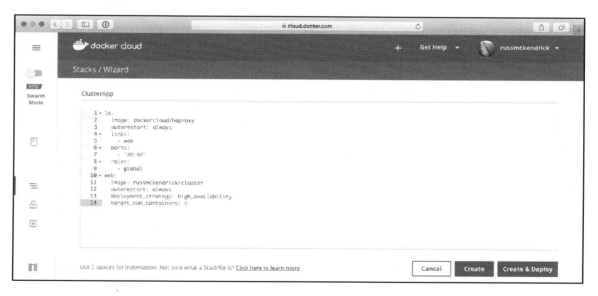

Once you have entered the stackfile, click on **Create & Deploy**. This will take you straight to your stack; as you can see, you get an overview of the services and also you get an endpoint:

The endpoint is a full URL to your application using the `dockerapp.io` domain. Mine was `http://lb.clusterapp.94d6a6e7.svc.dockerapp.io/` (the URL is no longer live). Entering your own endpoint into your browser should take you to your running application:

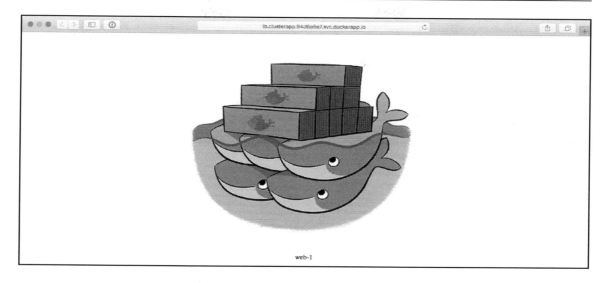

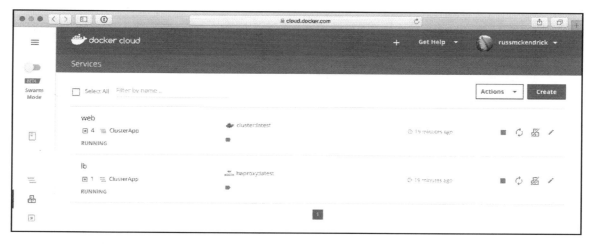

Clicking on the **Services** icon will list our two services:

From here, you can **Stop**, **Start**, **Redeploy**, and **Terminate** your services. Clicking on a service will give you a little more information about how the service is deployed as well as giving you a list of the currently running containers that form the service:

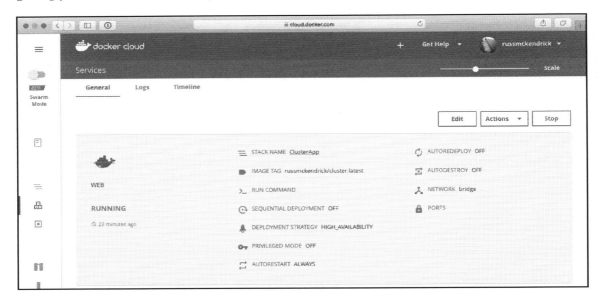

Clicking on **Containers** in the left-hand side menu will give you the list of the containers active in your Docker Cloud account:

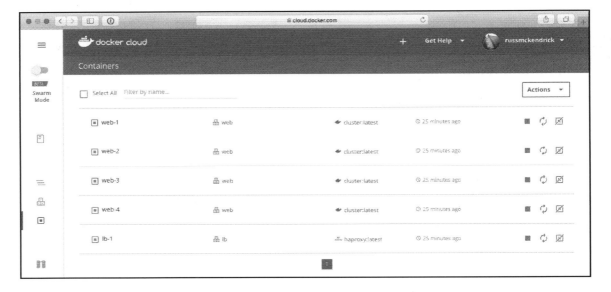

As you can see from the preceding list, we have five containers running: the four that make up our web app service and a single container for the load balancer service. Clicking on the container name will give you more detail on the container:

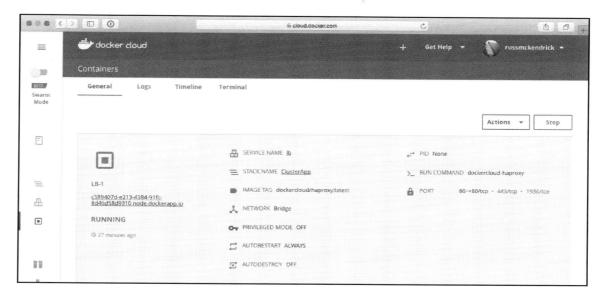

As you can see, you also get the option to view the container logs. Click on **Logs** gives you a streaming view of the log output you would expect to see from the command line when running `docker container logs` command. Clicking **Terminal** will open a web-based interactive Terminal giving you command line access to the container itself.

As I have already mentioned, you should be able to run the preceding steps and launch a **Node Cluster** in Amazon Web Services.

At this point, if you have been following along, it is probably a good time to terminate your **Stacks** and **Node Clusters** to save yourself any unexpected charges.

Swarm mode

I am sure you have noticed the **Swarm mode** (beta) switch at the top of the left-hand side menu. Clipping this switch will take you to the beta of the new Docker Cloud. It does not just add more functionality--it completely replaces the current Docker Cloud with a new application altogether.

If you go to the **Cloud Settings**, which can now be found in the drop-down menu near your username, you will notice that not only are there only two **Service providers** listed, but also your role ARN is not there:

At this point, you may think you would be able to use the role ARN we set up earlier in the chapter, but unfortunately, **Swarm mode** needs a lot more permissions than we originally granted. Rather than working through how to add a new role for **Swarm mode**, we are going to look at launching the configuration that **Swarm mode** launches using Docker for Amazon Web Services.

We are not going to cover Docker Clouds Swarm mode. If you would like more information on how you would create the role ARN and use the service, I would recommend reading through the excellent documentation at https://docs.docker.com/docker-cloud/cloud-swarm/.

Before moving on to the next section of the chapter, please ensure that all stacks and cluster nodes launched by Docker Cloud have been removed if you no-longer require them.

Docker for AWS

Docker for AWS is an Amazon CloudFormation template created by Docker that is designed to easily launch a Docker Swarm mode cluster in AWS with Docker best practices and recommendations applied.

 Amazon CloudFormation is a service offered by Amazon that allows you to define how you would like your infrastructure to look in a template file that can then be shared or brought under version control. For more information on the service, see http://aws.amazon.com/cloudformation /.

The first thing we need to do, and it's also the only thing we need to configure ahead of launching Docker for AWS, is to ensure that we have an SSH assigned to our account in the region we will be launching our cluster. To do this, log in to the AWS console at https://co nsole.aws.amazon.com/ or your organisation's custom sign-in page if you use one. Once logged in, go to the **Service** menu, which can be found in the top-left of the page, and find the EC2 service.

To make sure that you are in your desired region, you can use the region switcher in the top right between your username and the support menu. Once you are in the right region, click on **Key Pairs**, which can be found under **Network & Security** in the left-hand menu. Once on the **Key Pairs** page, you should see a list of your current key pairs. If you have none listed or don't have access to them, you can either click on **Create Key Pair** or **Import Key Pair** and follow the onscreen prompts.

Docker for AWS can be found in the Docker Store at https://store.docker.com/edition s/community/docker-ce-aws. You have two choices of Docker for AWS: stable and Edge version. The Edge version contains experimental features from upcoming versions of Docker; because of that, we are going to look at launching Docker for AWS (stable). To do that, just click on the button and you will be taken straight to CloudFormation with the Docker template already loaded.

You can view the raw template by going to `https://editions-us-east-1.s3.amazonaws.com/aws/stable/Docker.tmpl`, or you can visualize the template in the CloudFormation designer. As you can see from the following visualization, there is a lot going on to launch the cluster:

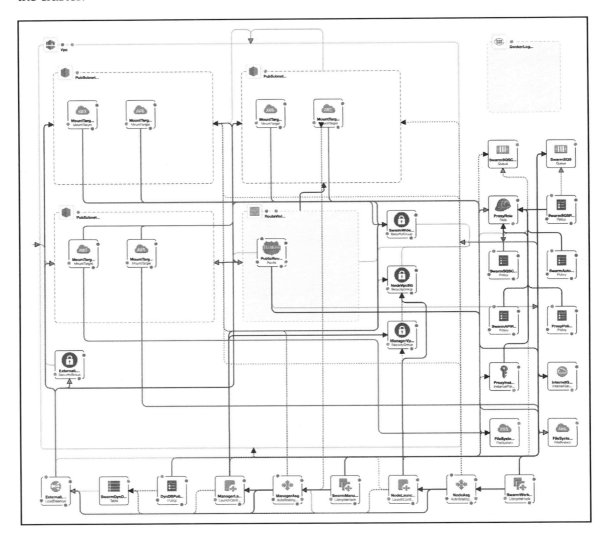

The beauty of this approach is that you don't have to worry about any of these complications; Docker has you covered and has taken on all of the heavy lifting.

The first step in launching the cluster has already been sorted for you; all you have to do is click on **Next** on the **Select Template** page:

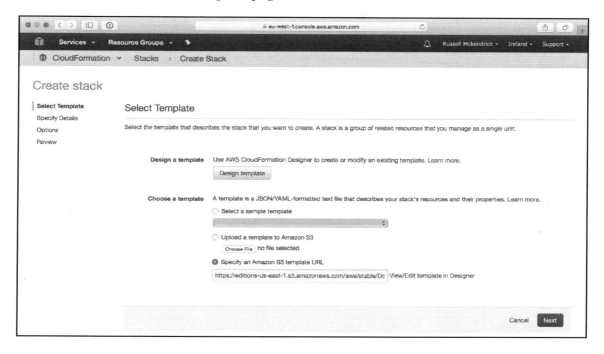

Next up, we have to **Specify Details** about our cluster. Other than the **SSH Key**, we are going to be leaving everything at their default values:

- **Stack name:** `Docker`
- **Number of Swarm managers?:** 3
- **Number of Swarm worker nodes?:** 5
- **Which SSH key to use?:** (select your key from the list)
- **Enable daily resource cleanup?:** `No`
- **Use Cloudwatch for container logging?:** `yes`
- **Swarm manager instance type?:** `t2.micro`
- **Manager ephemeral storage volume size?:** `20`
- **Manager ephemeral storage volume type:** `standard`
- **Agent worker instance type?:** `t2.micro`
- **Worker ephemeral storage volume size?:** `20`
- **Worker ephemeral storage volume type:** `standard`

Once you have checked that everything is OK, click on the **Next** button. In the next step, we can leave everything as it is and click on the **Next** button to be taken to a review page. On the review page, you will find a link that gives you the estimated cost:

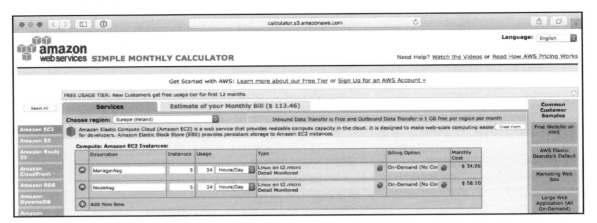

As you can see, the monthly estimate for my cluster is $113.46. The final thing you need to do before launching the cluster is to tick the box that says **I acknowledge that AWS CloudFormation might create IAM resources** and click on the **Create** button. As you can imagine, it takes a while to launch the cluster; you can check on the status of the launch by selecting your CloudFormation stack in the AWS console and selecting the **Events** tab:

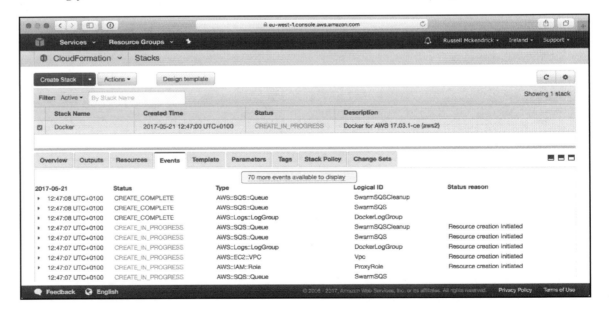

After about 10 minutes, you should see the status change from **CREATE_IN_PROGRESS** to **CREATE_COMPLETE**. When you see this, click on the **Outputs** tab and you should see a list of URLs and links:

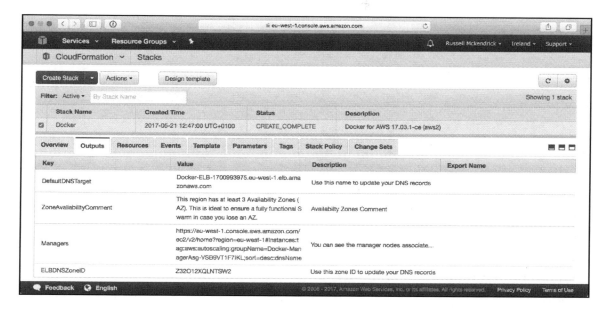

To log in to our Swarm cluster, click on the link next to managers to be taken to a list of EC2 instances, which are our manager nodes. Select one of the instances and then make a note of its public IP address. In a terminal, SSH to the node using `docker` as the username. For example, I ran the following commands to log in and get a list of all nodes:

```
$ ssh docker@54.246.218.236
$ docker node ls
```

If you downloaded a SSH key from the AWS Console when you added a key you should update the command above to include the path to your download key e.g. `ssh -i /path/to/private.key docker@54.246.218.236`

The preceding commands to log in and get a list of all nodes are shown in the following screenshot:

```
● ● ●                                     1. russ (ssh)
russ in ~
⚡ ssh docker@54.246.218.236
The authenticity of host '54.246.218.236 (54.246.218.236)' can't be established.
ECDSA key fingerprint is SHA256:QSpg4Uc/AJT2yVe5Sdh5QEMGjs3Y1HzinFxTUtnMrWk.
Are you sure you want to continue connecting (yes/no)? yes
Warning: Permanently added '54.246.218.236' (ECDSA) to the list of known hosts.
Welcome to Docker!
~ $ docker node ls
ID                            HOSTNAME                                 STATUS  AVAILABILITY  MANAGER STATUS
d8smypycnt0o5osl80ncvvr1p     ip-172-31-1-133.eu-west-1.compute.internal    Ready   Active
itei3odzhudtw2p1knr0zkztm     ip-172-31-22-67.eu-west-1.compute.internal    Ready   Active        Reachable
jw11qvp6f6lku823qqoiefkqy *   ip-172-31-44-79.eu-west-1.compute.internal    Ready   Active        Leader
nd2g2pk1cxp0i0w9va1onyc7o     ip-172-31-26-81.eu-west-1.compute.internal    Ready   Active
s1dru2ewgtad5pe1h8k7dk4ds     ip-172-31-35-46.eu-west-1.compute.internal    Ready   Active
vgch3a75rmmh9wfytu59xaigk     ip-172-31-6-0.eu-west-1.compute.internal      Ready   Active        Reachable
w5zqd0z771xjz40pn8fkw30u5     ip-172-31-36-40.eu-west-1.compute.internal    Ready   Active
zj85d1b78lpppzqzgwzg7bt84     ip-172-31-1-229.eu-west-1.compute.internal    Ready   Active
~ $ 
```

From here, you can treat it like any other Docker Swarm cluster. For example, we can launch and scale the cluster service by running this:

```
$ docker service create --name cluster --constraint "node.role == worker" -
p:80:80/tcp russmckendrick/cluster
$ docker service scale cluster=6
$ docker service ls
$ docker service inspect --pretty cluster
```

Now thaty your service has been launched, you can view your application at the URL given as the `DefaultDNSTarget`. This is an Amazon Elastic load balancer that has all of our nodes sat behind it.

Once you have finished with your cluster, return to the CloudFormation page within the AWS console, select your stack, and then select **Delete Stack** from the `Actions` drop-down menu. This will remove all traces of your Docker for Amazon Web Services cluster and stop you from getting any unexpected charges.

 Docker for Azure is also available; it works in a similar way to Docker for Amazon Web Services. However, it does require a little more upfront configuration. For more information on Docker for Azure, see its Docker Store page at `https://store.docker.com/editions/community/docker-ce-azure`.

Summary

We have now looked at three very powerful GUI tools that you can add to your Docker arsenal. With these tools, you can manipulate everything from your host environments to the images that live on those hosts as well as the containers running on those hosts. You can scale them, manipulate them, and even remove them as needed.

In the next chapter we are going to take a look at how to secure your Docker host as well as how to run scans against your container images.

11
Docker Security

In this chapter, we will be taking a look at Docker security, the topic on the forefront of everyone's minds these days. We will be splitting up the chapter into five sections:

- Container considerations
- Docker commands
- Best practices
- The Docker Bench Security application
- Third-party security services

Container considerations

When Docker was first released, there was a lot of talk about Docker versus virtual machines. I remember reading articles in magazines, commenting on threads on Reddit, and reading endless blog posts. In the early days of the Docker alpha and beta versions, people used to approach Docker containers like virtual machines because there really weren't any other points of references and we viewed them as tiny VMs.

I would enable SSH, run multiple processes in containers, and even create my container images by launching a container and running the commands to install my software stack, which is something we discussed you should never do in `Chapter 2`, *Building Container Images* as it is considered to be bad practice.

So rather than discussing containers versus virtual machines here, let's look at some of the considerations you need to make when running containers rather than virtual machines.

The advantages

When you start a Docker container, the Docker Engine is doing a lot of work behind the scenes. Two of the tasks that the Docker Engine performs when launching your containers is to set up namespaces and control groups. What does that mean? By setting up namespaces, Docker keeps the processes isolated in each container, not only from other containers but also from the host system. The control groups ensure that each container gets its own share of items such as CPU, memory, and disk I/O. More importantly, they ensure that one container doesn't exhaust all the resources on a given Docker host.

By setting up namespaces, Docker keeps the processes isolated in each container; not only from other containers but also from the host system. The control groups ensure that each container gets its own share of items such as CPU, memory, and disk I/O. More importantly, they ensure that one container doesn't exhaust all the resources on a given Docker host.

As we have seen in previous chapters, being able to launch our containers into a Docker-controlled network means that we can isolate our containers at the application level, meaning that all of the containers for Application A will not have any access at the network layer to the containers for Application B.

Add to this that this network isolation can run on a single Docker host using the default network driver or span multiple Docker hosts using Docker Swarm's built-in multi-host networking driver or the Weave Net driver from Weave.

Lastly, what I consider one of the biggest advantages of Docker over a typical virtual machine is that you shouldn't have to log in into the container. Docker is trying its hardest to keep you from needing to log in to a container to manage the process it is running. With commands such as `docker container exec`, `docker container top`, `docker container logs`, and `docker container stats`, you can do everything you need to do without exposing any more services than you need to.

Your Docker host

When you are dealing with virtual machines, you can control who has access to which virtual machine. Let's say you only want **User1**, who is a developer, to have access to the development VMs. However, **User2** is an operator who is responsible for both the development and production environments so he needs access to all the VMs. Most virtual machine management tools allow you to grant role-based access to your VMs.

With Docker, you have a little disadvantage because whoever has access to the Docker Engine on your Docker host, either through being granted sudo access or by having their user added to the Docker Linux group, has access to every Docker container that you are running. They can run new containers, they can stop existing containers, and can delete images as well. Be careful who you grant permission to access the Docker Engine on your hosts. They essentially hold the keys to the kingdom with respect to all your containers. Knowing this, it is recommended to use Docker hosts only for Docker; keep other services separate from your Docker hosts.

Image trust

If you are running virtual machines, you will most likely be setting them up from scratch yourself. While it is possible, it more than likely due to the size of the download and also the effort in launching it that you would not download a prebuilt machine image that some random person on the internet has created. Typically, if you were to do this, it would be a prebuilt virtual appliance from a trusted software vendor.

So, you will be aware of what is inside the virtual machine and what isn't as it is you that was responsible for building and maintaining it.

Part of the appeal of Docker is its ease of use; however, this ease of use can make it really easy to ignore quite a crucial security consideration: do you know what it is running inside your container?

We have already touched on image trust in earlier chapters. For example, we spoke about not publishing or downloading images that haven't been defined using Dockerfiles and not embedding custom code or secrets and so on directly into an image that you will be pushing to the Docker Hub.

While containers have the protection of namespaces, control groups, and network isolation, we discussed how a poorly judged image download can introduce security concerns and risk into your environment. For example, a perfectly legitimate container running an unpatched piece of software can introduce risk around the availability of your application and data.

Docker commands

Let's take a look at the Docker commands that can be used to help tighten up security as well as view information about the images you might be using. There are two commands that we are going to be focusing on.

The first will be the `docker container run` command, so you can see some of the items you can use to your advantage with this command. Second, we will take a look at the `docker container diff` command (that we went over in the previous chapter) that you can use to view what has been done with the image that you are planning to use.

Run

With respect to the `docker run` command, we will mainly focus on the option that allows you to set everything inside the container as read-only instead of a specified directory or volume. This helps limit the amount of damage that can be caused by malicious applications that also could hijack a vulnerable application by updating their binaries.

Let's take a look at an how to launch a read-only container and break down what it exactly does:

```
$ docker container run -d --name mysql --read-only -v /var/lib/mysql -v
/tmp -v /var/run/mysqld -e MYSQL_ROOT_PASSWORD=password mysql
```

Here, we are running a MySQL container and setting the entire container as read-only, except for the following folders:

- `/var/lib/mysql`
- `/var/run/mysqld`
- `/tmp`

These will all be created as three separate volumes and then mounted read/write. If you do not add these volumes then MySQL will not be able to start as it needs read/write access to be able to create the socket file in `/var/run/mysqld`, some temporary files in `/tmp`, and finally, the databases themselves in `/var/lib/mysql`.

Any other location inside the container won't allow you to write anything in it. If you try to run the following, it would fail:

```
$ docker container exec mysql touch /trying_to_write_a_file
```

Giving you the following message:

```
touch: cannot touch '/trying_to_write_a_file': Read-only file system
```

This can be extremely helpful if you want to control where the containers can write to or not write to. Be sure to use this wisely. Test thoroughly, as it could have consequences when the applications can't write to certain locations.

Similar to the previous command with `docker container run`, where we set everything to read-only except for a specified volume, we can now do the opposite and set just a single volume (or more if you use more -v switches) to read-only. The thing to remember about volumes is that when you use a volume and mount it into a container, it will mount as an empty volume over the top of that directory inside the container unless you use the `--volumes-from` switch or add data to the container in some other way after it has been launched:

```
$ docker container run -d -v /local/path/to/html/:/var/www/html/:ro nginx
```

This will mount `/local/path/to/html/` from the Docker host to `/var/www/html/` and set it to read-only. This can be useful if you don't want a running container to write to a volume to keep the data or configuration files intact.

Diff

Let's take another look at the `docker diff` command; since it relates to the security aspects of the containers, you may want to use the images that are hosted on Docker Hub or other related repositories.

Remember that whoever has access to your Docker host and the Docker daemon has access to all of your running Docker containers. This being said, if you don't have monitoring in place, someone could be executing commands against your containers and doing malicious things.

Let's take a look at the MySQL container we launched in the previous section:

```
$ docker container diff mysql
```

You will notice that no files are returned; why is that? Well, the `diff` command tells you the changes that have been made to the image since the container was launched. In the previous section, we launched the MySQL container with the image read-only and then mounted volumes to where we know MySQL would need to be able to read and write, meaning that there are no file differences between the image we downloaded and the container we are running.

Stop and remove the MySQL container by running:

```
$ docker container stop mysql
$ docker container rm mysql
```

Then launch the same container again, minus the read-only flag and volumes; this gives us a different story:

```
$ docker container run -d --name mysql -e MYSQL_ROOT_PASSWORD=password mysql
$ docker container exec mysql touch /trying_to_write_a_file
$ docker container diff mysql
```

As you can see, there are two folders created and several files added:

```
C /run/mysqld
A /run/mysqld/mysqld.pid
A /run/mysqld/mysqld.sock
A /run/mysqld/mysqld.sock.lock
C /tmp
A /trying_to_write_a_file
```

This is a great way to spot anything dodgy that may be going on.

Best practices

In this section, we will look at the best practices when it comes to Docker as well as the Center for Internet Security guide to properly secure all the aspects of your Docker environment.

Docker - best practices

Before we dive into the Center for Internet Security guide, let's go over some of the best practices to use Docker:

- **One application per container**: Spread out your applications to one per container. Docker was built for this and it makes everything easier at the end of the day. That isolation we talked about earlier is where this is key.
- **Only install what you need**: As we have already looked at in previous chapters, only install what you need in your container images. If you have to install more to support the one process your container should be running then I would recommend you review the reasons why. This not only keeps your images small and portable, it also reduces the potential attack surface.
- **Review who has access to your Docker hosts**: Remember that whoever has root or sudo access to your Docker hosts has access to manipulate all your images and containers on the host.
- **Use the latest version**: Always use the latest version of Docker. This will ensure that all security holes have been patched and you have the latest features as well. While fixing security issues, keeping up to date using the community version may possibly introduce problems caused by changes functionality or new features. If this is a concern for you then you might want to look at the LTS Enterprise versions available from Docker and also Red Hat.
- **Use the resources**: Use the resources available if you need help. The community within Docker is huge and immensely helpful. Use their website, documentation, and the Slack chat rooms to your advantage when planning your Docker environment and assessing platforms. For more information on how to access Slack and other parts of the community, see Chapter 13, *Next Steps with Docker*.

The Center for Internet Security benchmark

 The **Center for Internet Security (CIS)** is an independent non-profit organisation whose goal is to provide a secure online experience. They publish benchmarks and controls, which are considered best practices for all aspects of IT. For more information, visit their website at https://www.cisecurity.org/.

The CIS benchmark for Docker is available for download, for free, from `https://www.cisec urity.org/benchmark/docker/`. You should note that it is currently a 196-page PDF released under the Creative Commons license and covers Docker 1.13.0 and later.

You will be referring to this guide when you actually run the scan (in the next section of this chapter) and get results back to what needs to or should be fixed. The guide is broken down into the following sections:

- The host configuration
- The Docker daemon configuration
- The Docker daemon configuration files
- Container images/runtime
- Docker security operations

Host configuration

This part of the guide is about the configuration of your Docker hosts. This is that part of the Docker environment where all your containers run. Thus, keeping it secure is of the utmost importance. This is the first line of defense against attackers.

Docker daemon configuration

This part of the guide has the recommendations that secure the running Docker daemon. Everything you do to the Docker daemon configuration affects each and every container. These are the switches you can attach to the Docker daemon we saw previously, and to the items you will see in the next section when we run through the tool.

Docker daemon configuration files

This part of the guide deals with the files and directories that the Docker daemon uses. This ranges from permissions to ownerships. Sometimes, these areas may contain information you don't want others to know about that could be in plain text format.

Container images/runtime and build files

This part of the guide contains both the information for securing the container images as well as the build files.

The first part contains images, cover base images, and the build files that were used. As we covered previously, you need to be sure about the images you are using not only for your base images but for any aspect of your Docker experience. This section of the guide covers the items you should follow while creating your own base images.

Container runtime

This section was previously part of the later section but has been moved into its own section now in the CIS guide. The container runtime covers a lot of security-related items.

Be careful with the runtime variables you are using. In some cases, attackers can use them to their advantage, while you think you are using them to your own advantage. Exposing too much in your containers, such as exposing application secrets and database connections as environment variables, can compromise the security of not only your container but the Docker host and the other containers running on that host.

Docker security operations

This part of the guide covers the security areas that involve deployment; the items are more closely tied to Docker best practices. Because of this, it is best to follow these recommendations.

The Docker Bench Security application

In this section, we will cover the Docker Benchmark Security application that you can install and run. The tool will inspect:

- The host configuration
- The Docker daemon configuration
- The Docker daemon configuration files
- Container images and build files
- Container runtime
- The Docker security operations

Looks familiar? It should, as these are the same items that we reviewed in the previous section, only built into an application that will do a lot of the heavy lifting for you. It will show you what warnings arise with your configurations and provide information on other configuration items and even the items that have passed the test.

We will look at how to run the tool, a live example, and what the output of the process will mean.

Running on Docker for macOS and Docker for Windows

Running the tool is simple. It's already been packaged up for us inside a Docker container. While you can get the source code and customize the output or manipulate it in some way (say emailing the output), the default may be all you need.

The tool's GitHub project can be found at `https://github.com/docker/docker-bench-sec urity/`, and to run the tool on a macOS or Windows machine, you simply need copy and paste the following into your Terminal:

> The following command is missing the line needed to check `systemd` as Moby Linux, which is the underlying operating system for Docker for macOS and Docker for Windows, does not run `systemd`. We will look at a `systemd` based system shortly.

```
docker run -it --net host --pid host --cap-add audit_control \
    -e DOCKER_CONTENT_TRUST=$DOCKER_CONTENT_TRUST \
    -v /var/lib:/var/lib \
    -v /var/run/docker.sock:/var/run/docker.sock \
    -v /etc:/etc --label docker_bench_security \
    docker/docker-bench-security
```

Once the image has been downloaded, it will launch and immediately start to audit your Docker host, printing the results as it goes:

```
● ● ●                          1. russ (bash)
⚡ docker run -it --net host --pid host --cap-add audit_control \
→     -e DOCKER_CONTENT_TRUST=$DOCKER_CONTENT_TRUST \
→     -v /var/lib:/var/lib \
→     -v /var/run/docker.sock:/var/run/docker.sock \
→     -v /etc:/etc --label docker_bench_security \
→     docker/docker-bench-security
# ---------------------------------------------------------------
# Docker Bench for Security v1.3.2
#
# Docker, Inc. (c) 2015-
#
# Checks for dozens of common best-practices around deploying Docker containers in production.
# Inspired by the CIS Docker 1.13 Benchmark.
# ---------------------------------------------------------------

Initializing Mon Jul  3 13:43:22 UTC 2017

[INFO] 1 - Host Configuration
[WARN] 1.1  - Create a separate partition for containers
[NOTE] 1.2  - Harden the container host
[INFO] 1.3  - Keep Docker up to date
[INFO]       * Using 17.06.0, when 17.07.0 is current as of 2017-07-01
[INFO]       * Your operating system vendor may provide support and security maintenance for Docker
[INFO] 1.4  - Only allow trusted users to control Docker daemon
[INFO]       * docker:x:50:docker
[WARN] 1.5  - Audit docker daemon - /usr/bin/docker
[WARN] 1.6  - Audit Docker files and directories - /var/lib/docker
[WARN] 1.7  - Audit Docker files and directories - /etc/docker
[INFO] 1.8  - Audit Docker files and directories - docker.service
[INFO]       * File not found
[INFO] 1.9  - Audit Docker files and directories - docker.socket
[INFO]       * File not found
[INFO] 1.10 - Audit Docker files and directories - /etc/default/docker
[INFO]       * File not found
[WARN] 1.11 - Audit Docker files and directories - /etc/docker/daemon.json
[INFO] 1.12 - Audit Docker files and directories - /usr/bin/docker-containerd
[INFO]       * File not found
[INFO] 1.13 - Audit Docker files and directories - /usr/bin/docker-runc
[INFO]       * File not found
```

As you can see, there are a few warnings [WARN] given as well as notes as [NOTE] and information as [INFO]; however, as this host is managed by Docker, as you would expect, there is not too much to worry about.

Running on Ubuntu Linux

Before we look into the output of the audit in a little more detail, I am going to launch a vanilla Ubuntu 17.04 server and do a clean installation of Docker. Once installed, I will launch a few containers, all of which don't have very sensible settings.

I launched the following two containers from the Docker Hub:

```
$ docker container run -d --name root-nginx -v /:/mnt nginx
$ docker container run -d --name priv-nginx --privileged=true nginx
```

Then I built a customer image based on Ubuntu 16.04 that ran SSH and launched it using:

```
$ docker container run -d -P --name sshd eg_sshd
```

As you can see, in one image, we are mounting the root file system of our host with full read/write access in the `root-nginx` container. We are also running with extended privileges in `priv-nginx` and finally running SSH in `sshd`.

To start the audit on our Ubuntu Docker host, I ran the following:

```
docker run -it --net host --pid host --cap-add audit_control \
  -e DOCKER_CONTENT_TRUST=$DOCKER_CONTENT_TRUST \
  -v /var/lib:/var/lib \
  -v /var/run/docker.sock:/var/run/docker.sock \
  -v /usr/lib/systemd:/usr/lib/systemd \
  -v /etc:/etc --label docker_bench_security \
  docker/docker-bench-security
```

As we are running on an operating system that supports `systemd`, we are mounting `/usr/lib/systemd` so that we can audit it.

There is a lot of output and a lot to digest, but what does it all mean? Let's take a look and break down each section.

Understanding the output

There are three types of output that we will see:

- [PASS]: These items are solid and good to go. They don't need any attention but are good to read to make you feel warm inside. The more of these, the better!
- [WARN]: These are items that need to be fixed. These are the items we don't want to be seeing.
- [INFO]: These are items that you should review and fix if you feel they are pertinent to your setup and security needs.
- [NOTE]: These give best-practice advice.

There are six main sections that are covered in the audit:

- Host configuration
- Docker daemon configuration
- Docker daemon configuration files
- Container images and build files
- Container runtime
- Docker security operations

Let's take a look at what we are seeing in each section of the scan. These scan results are from a default Ubuntu Docker host with no tweaks made to the system at this point. We want to focus again on the [WARN] items in each section. Other warnings may come up when you run yours, but these will be the ones that come up most, if not for everyone, at first.

Host configuration

I had five items with a [WARN] status for my Host Configuration:

```
[WARN] 1.1 - Create a separate partition for containers
```

Be default, Docker uses /var/lib/docker on the host machine to store all of its files, including all images, containers, and volumes created by the default driver. This means that this folder may grow quickly. As my host machine is running a single partition, and depending on what your containers are doing, this could potentially fill the entire drive, which would render my host machine unusable.

```
[WARN] 1.5 - Audit docker daemon - /usr/bin/docker
[WARN] 1.6 - Audit Docker files and directories - /var/lib/docker
[WARN] 1.7 - Audit Docker files and directories - /etc/docker
[WARN] 1.10 - Audit Docker files and directories - /etc/default/docker
```

These warnings are being flagged because auditd is not installed and there are no audit rules for the Docker daemon and associated files; for more information on auditd, see the following blog post: https://www.linux.com/learn/customized-file-monitoring-auditd/.

Docker daemon configuration

My Docker daemon configuration flagged up seven [WARN] statuses:

[WARN] 2.1 - Restrict network traffic between containers

By default, Docker allows traffic to pass between containers unrestricted on the same host. It is possible to change this behavior; for more information on Docker networking, see `https://docs.docker.com/engine/userguide/networking/`.

[WARN] 2.8 - Enable user namespace support

By default, the user namespace is not remapped. Mapping them, while possible, can currently cause issues with several Docker features--see the following URL for more details on known restrictions: `https://docs.docker.com/engine/reference/commandline/dockerd/#user-namespace-known-restrictions`.

[WARN] 2.11 - Use authorization plugin

A default installation of Docker allows unrestricted access to the Docker daemon; you can limit access to authenticated users by enabling an authorization plugin. For more details, see `https://docs.docker.com/engine/extend/plugins_authorization/`.

[WARN] 2.12 - Configure centralized and remote logging

As I am only running a single host, I am not using a service such as `rsyslog` to ship my Docker host's logs to a central server, nor have I configured a log driver on my Docker daemon--see `https://docs.docker.com/engine/admin/logging/overview/` for more details.

[WARN] 2.13 - Disable operations on legacy registry (v1)

At the time of writing this, a `defaultDocker` installation is configured to interact with both the now legacy V1 Docker Registry API as well as the newer V2 Docker Registry API. For details on how to disable this, see `https://docs.docker.com/engine/reference/commandline/dockerd/#legacy-registries`.

[WARN] 2.14 - Enable live restore

The `--live-restore` flag enables full support of daemon-less containers in Docker; this means that rather than stopping containers on when the daemon shuts down, they continue to run and it properly reconnects to the containers when restarted. It is not enabled by default due to backward compatibility issues; for more details, see `https://docs.docker.com/engine/admin/live-restore/`.

[WARN] 2.18 - Disable Userland Proxy

There are two ways your containers can route to the outside world: either by using a hairpin NAT or a userland proxy. For most installations, the hairpin NAT mode is the preferred mode as it takes advantage of Iptables and has better performance. Where this is not available, Docker uses the userland proxy. Most Docker installations on modern operating systems will support hairpin NAT; for details on how to disable the userland proxy, see `https://docs.docker.com/engine/userguide/networking/default_network/binding/`.

Docker daemon configuration files

I had no `[WARN]` statuses in this section.

Container images and build files

I had three `[WARN]` statuses for container images and build files; you may notice that multiline warnings are prefixed with a * after the status:

```
[WARN] 4.1 - Create a user for the container
[WARN] * Running as root: sshd
[WARN] * Running as root: priv-nginx
[WARN] * Running as root: root-nginx
```

The processes in the containers I am running are all running as the root user; this is the default action of most containers. See the following article for more information: `https://docs.docker.com/engine/security/security/`.

```
[WARN] 4.5 - Enable Content trust for Docker
```

Enabling content trust for Docker ensures the provenance of the container images you are pulling as they are digitally signed when you push them; this means you are always running the images you intended to run. For more information on content trust, see `https://docs.docker.com/engine/security/trust/content_trust/`.

```
[WARN] 4.6 - Add HEALTHCHECK instruction to the container image
[WARN] * No Healthcheck found: [eg_sshd:latest]
[WARN] * No Healthcheck found: [nginx:latest]
[WARN] * No Healthcheck found: [ubuntu:16.04]
```

When building your image, it is possible to build in a `HEALTHCHECK`; this ensures that when a container launches from your image, Docker will periodically check the status of your container and if need be restart or relaunch it. More details can be found at `https://docs.docker.com/engine/reference/builder/#healthcheck`.

Container runtime

As we have been a little silly when launching our containers on the Docker Host we have audited, we know there should be a lot of vulnerabilities here, and there are: 11 of them altogether.

```
[WARN] 5.2 - Verify SELinux security options, if applicable
[WARN] * No SecurityOptions Found: sshd
[WARN] * No SecurityOptions Found: root-nginx
```

This one is false positive; we are not running SELinux as it is an Ubuntu machine and SELinux is only applicable to Red Hat-based machines; instead, 5.1 shows use the result, which is a [PASS], which we want:

```
[PASS] 5.1 - Do not disable AppArmor Profile
```

The next two [WARN] statuses are of our own making:

```
[WARN] 5.4 - Do not use privileged containers
[WARN] * Container running in Privileged mode: priv-nginx
```

As are these:

```
[WARN] 5.6 - Do not run ssh within containers
[WARN] * Container running sshd: sshd
```

They can safely be ignored; it should be very rare that you need to launch a container running in Privileged mode. It is only if your container needs to interact with the Docker Engine running on your Docker host, for example when you are running a GUI such as Portainer, which we covered in Chapter 8, *Portainer*.

We have also discussed that you should not be running SSH in your containers; there are a few use cases such as running a jump host within a certain network; however, these should be the exception.

The next two [WARN] statuses are flagged because by default on Docker, all running containers on your Docker hosts share the resources equally; setting limits on memory and the CPU priority for your containers will ensure that containers that you want to have a higher priority are not starved of resources by lower priority containers:

```
[WARN] 5.10 - Limit memory usage for container
[WARN] * Container running without memory restrictions: sshd
[WARN] * Container running without memory restrictions: priv-nginx
[WARN] * Container running without memory restrictions: root-nginx

[WARN] 5.11 - Set container CPU priority appropriately
```

```
[WARN] * Container running without CPU restrictions: sshd
[WARN] * Container running without CPU restrictions: priv-nginx
[WARN] * Container running without CPU restrictions: root-nginx
```

As we have already discussed earlier in the chapter, if possible, you should be launching your containers read-only and mounting volumes for where you know your process needs to write data to:

```
[WARN] 5.12 - Mount container's root filesystem as read only
[WARN] * Container running with root FS mounted R/W: sshd
[WARN] * Container running with root FS mounted R/W: priv-nginx
[WARN] * Container running with root FS mounted R/W: root-nginx
```

The reason the following flags are raised is that we are not telling Docker to bind our exposed port to a specific IP address on the Docker host:

```
[WARN] 5.13 - Bind incoming container traffic to a specific host interface
[WARN] * Port being bound to wildcard IP: 0.0.0.0 in sshd
```

As my test Docker host only has a single NIC, this isn't too much of a problem; however, if my Docker host had multiple interfaces, then this container would be exposed to all of the networks, which could be a problem if I had, for example, an external and internal network. See https://docs.docker.com/engine/userguide/networking/ for more details.

```
[WARN] 5.14 - Set the 'on-failure' container restart policy to 5
[WARN] * MaximumRetryCount is not set to 5: sshd
[WARN] * MaximumRetryCount is not set to 5: priv-nginx
[WARN] * MaximumRetryCount is not set to 5: root-nginx
```

Although I haven't launched my containers using the `--restart` flag, there is no default value for the `MaximumRetryCount`. This means that if a container failed over and over, it would quite happily sit there attempting to restart. This could have a negative effect on the Docker host; adding a `MaximumRetryCount` of 5 will mean the container will attempt to restart five times before giving up.

```
[WARN] 5.25 - Restrict container from acquiring additional privileges
[WARN] * Privileges not restricted: sshd
[WARN] * Privileges not restricted: priv-nginx
[WARN] * Privileges not restricted: root-nginx
```

By default, Docker does not put a restriction on a process or its child processes gaining new privileges via `suid` or `sgid` bits. To find out details on how you can stop this behavior, see `http://www.projectatomic.io/blog/2016/03/no-new-privs-docker/`.

```
[WARN] 5.26 - Check container health at runtime
[WARN] * Health check not set: sshd
[WARN] * Health check not set: priv-nginx
[WARN] * Health check not set: root-nginx
```

Again, we are not using any health checks, meaning that Docker will not periodically check the status of your containers. See the following GitHub issue for the pull request that introduced this feature: `https://github.com/moby/moby/pull/22719/`.

```
[WARN] 5.28 - Use PIDs cgroup limit
[WARN] * PIDs limit not set: sshd
[WARN] * PIDs limit not set: priv-nginx
[WARN] * PIDs limit not set: root-nginx
```

Potentially, an attacker could trigger a fork bomb with a single command inside your container. This has the potential to crash you Docker host and the only way to recover would be to reboot the host. You can protect against this by using the `--pids-limit` flag. For more information, see the following pull request: `https://github.com/moby/moby/pull/18697/`.

Docker security operations

This section is all `[INFO]` about best practices:

```
[INFO] 6.1 - Perform regular security audits of your host system and
containers
[INFO] 6.2 - Monitor Docker containers usage, performance and metering
[INFO] 6.3 - Backup container data
[INFO] 6.4 - Avoid image sprawl
[INFO] * There are currently: 4 images
[INFO] 6.5 - Avoid container sprawl
[INFO] * There are currently a total of 8 containers, with 4 of them
currently running
```

Summing up Docker Bench

As you have seen, running Docker Bench against your Docker host is a much better way of getting an understanding of how your Docker host stacks up against the CIS Docker Benchmark; it is certainly a lot more manageable than manually working through every single test in the 196-page document.

Docker security scanning

Both Docker Cloud and Docker Hub have an inbuilt feature that performs security scanning of your private images. At the time of writing this, this feature is available as a free preview for private repository subscribers; however, it is only for a limited time.

You can opt in and begin using the service from the **Plan** page of your Docker Hub account by ticking the following box:

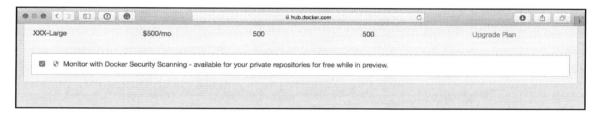

Once ticked, any push to a private repository will trigger a scan for the last three tags for your image. You can find the results of your scans in the **Repositories** section of Docker Cloud; as you can see, it is a little out of the way in its current free iteration.

An example of what a scan looks like is given here:

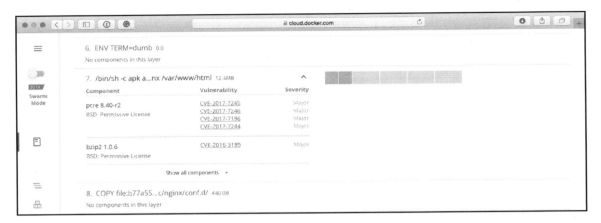

As you can see from the screenshot, my NGINX container needs an update as there are known issues with the versions of pcre and bzip2 that are installed.

It even gives the **Common Vulnerabilities and Exposures (CVE)** numbers and links so I can find out more information at the **National Vulnerability Database (NVD)**, which can be found at `http://cve.mitre.org/`, so I can see exactly what the vulnerability is and the possible impact it has on my application.

The functionality has been in free preview for about a year, and I must admit I am a little confused as to why it is hidden away as it is actually quite a good resource for providing a static analysis of your images. I hope that Docker will turn it into a more standalone service soon.

Static code analysis is a methodology of debugging code/binaries and is performed by examining the code/binaries without actually executing them. As nothing is ever executed, this makes it a perfect way of checking code/binaries for security related problems as any problematic code/binaries are never run to cause any issues on the host running the analysis. For more information, see `https://www.owasp.org/index.php /Static_Code_Analysis`.

Third-party security services

Before we finish this chapter, we are going to take a look at some of the third-party services available to help you with vulnerability assessments of your images.

Quay

Back in `Chapter 3`, *Storing and Distributing Images*, we looked at Quay, an image registry service by CoreOS. One thing we didn't touch upon is that Quay actually performs a security scan of each image after it is push/built.

You can see the results of the scan by viewing the **Repository Tags** for your chosen image; here you will see a column for **Security Scan**. As you can see from the following screenshot, in the example image we created, there are no problems:

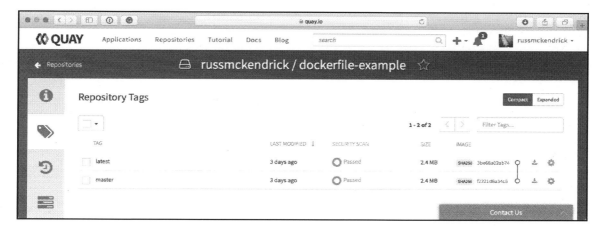

Clicking on where it says **Passed** will take you to a more detailed breakdown of any vulnerabilities that have been detected within the image. As there are no vulnerabilities at the moment (which is a good thing), this screen does not tell us much. However, clicking on the **Package** icon in the left-hand menu will present us with a list of the packages the scan has discovered. For our test image, it has found **13 packages with no vulnerabilities**, all of which are displayed here along with confirmation of the version of the package and how they were introduced to the image.

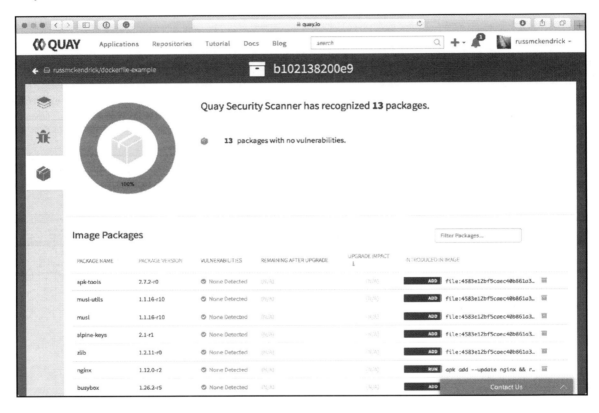

As you can also see, Quay is scanning our publicly available image, which is being hosted on the free-of-charge open source plan Quay offers. Security scanning comes as standard with all plans on Quay; like the Docker image scanning service, it uses static analysis.

For more information on Quay, see `https://quay.io/`.

Clair

Clair is an open source project from CoreOS. In essence, it is a service that provides the vulnerability static analysis functionality for both the hosted version of Quay as well as the commercially supported enterprise version.

It works by creating a local mirror of the following vulnerability databases:

- **Debian Security Bug Tracker**: https://security-tracker.debian.org/tracker/
- **Ubuntu CVE Tracker**: https://launchpad.net/ubuntu-cve-tracker/
- **Red Hat Security Data**: https://www.redhat.com/security/data/metrics/
- **Oracle Linux Security Data**: https://linux.oracle.com/security/
- **Alpine SecDB**: https://git.alpinelinux.org/cgit/alpine-secdb/
- **NIST NVD**: https://nvd.nist.gov/

Once it has mirrored the data sources, it mounts the image's filesystem and then performs a scan of the installed packages, comparing them to the signatures in the preceding data sources.

Clair is not a straightforward service; it only has an API-driven interface, there are no fancy web-based or command-line tools which ship with Clair by default. Documentation for the API can be found at https://coreos.com/clair/docs/latest/api_v1.html.

Installation instructions can be found at the project's GitHub page at https://github.com/coreos/clair/. Also, you can find a list of tools that support Clair on its integration page, https://coreos.com/clair/docs/latest/integrations.html.

Summary

In this chapter, we covered some aspects of Docker security. First, we took a look at some of the things you need to consider when running containers versus typical virtual machines with regard to security. We looked at the advantages, your Docker host, and spoke about image trust. We then took a look at what Docker commands we can use for security purposes.

We launched a read-only container so that we can minimize any potential damage any potential intruder can do within our running containers. As not all applications lend themselves well to running in read-only containers, we then looked at how we can track changes that have been made to the image since launching. It is always useful to be able to easily find out any changes made on the filesystem at runtime when trying to look into any problems.

Next, we discussed the Center for Internet Security guidelines for Docker. This guide will assist you in setting up multiple aspects of your Docker environment. Lastly, we took a look at the Docker Bench for Security. We looked at how to get it up and running and ran through an example of what the output would look like once it has been run. We then took a look at the said output to see what all it meant. Remember the six items that the application covered: the host configuration, Docker daemon configuration, Docker daemon configuration files, container images and build files, container runtime, and Docker security operations.

In the next chapter, we are going to take a look at how Docker can fit into your existing workflows as well as some new ways to approach working with containers.

12
Docker Workflows

In this chapter, we will be looking at Docker and various workflows for Docker. We'll put all the pieces together so you can start using Docker in your production environments and feel comfortable doing so. Let's take a peek at what we will be covering in this chapter:

- Docker for development
- Monitoring Docker
- Extending to external platforms
- What does production look like?

Docker for development

We are going to start our look at workflows by discussing how Docker can be used to aid developers. Right back at the start of `Chapter 1`, *Docker Overview*, one of the first things we discussed in the *Understanding Docker* section was developers and the *works on my machine* problem. So far, we have not really fully addressed this, so let's do that now.

For this section, we are going to look at how a developer could develop their WordPress project on their local machine using Docker for macOS or Docker for Windows along with Docker Compose.

The aim of this is for us to launch a WordPress installation, which is what you will do with the following steps:

1. Download and install WordPress.
2. Allow access to the WordPress files from desktop editors, such as Atom (https ://atom.io/), Visual Studio Code (https://code.visualstudio.com/), or Sublime Text (https://www.sublimetext.com/) on your local machine.
3. Configure and manage WordPress using WP-CLI (http://wp-cli.org/).
4. Allow you to stop, start, and even remove containers without losing your work.

Before we launch our WordPress installation, let's take a look at the Docker Compose file and what services we have running:

> The following files are available in the https://github.com/russmckendr ick/mastering-dockerGitHub repository in the /chapter12/docker-wordpress folder.

```
version: "3"

services:

  web:
    image: nginx:alpine
    ports:
      - "8080:80"
    volumes:
      - "./wordpress/web:/var/www/html"
      -
  "./wordpress/nginx.conf:/etc/nginx/conf.d/default.conf"
    depends_on:
      - wordpress

  wordpress:
    image: wordpress:php7.1-fpm-alpine
    volumes:
      - "./wordpress/web:/var/www/html"
    depends_on:
      - mysql

  mysql:
    image: mysql:8
    environment:
      MYSQL_ROOT_PASSWORD: "wordpress"
      MYSQL_USER: "wordpress"
```

```
      MYSQL_PASSWORD: "wordpress"
      MYSQL_DATABASE: "wordpress"
    volumes:
      - "./wordpress/mysql:/var/lib/mysql"

wp:
  image: wordpress:cli-php7.1
  volumes:
    - "./wordpress/web:/var/www/html"
    - "./wordpress/export:/export"
```

We can visualize the Docker Compose file using `docker-compose-viz` (`https://github.com/pmsipilot/docker-compose-viz`) from PMSIpilot. To do this, run the following command in the same folder as the `docker-compose.yml` file:

```
$ docker run --rm -it --name dcv -v $(pwd):/input pmsipilot/docker-compose-viz render -m image docker-compose.yml
```

This will output a file called `docker-compose.png`, and you should get something that looks like this:

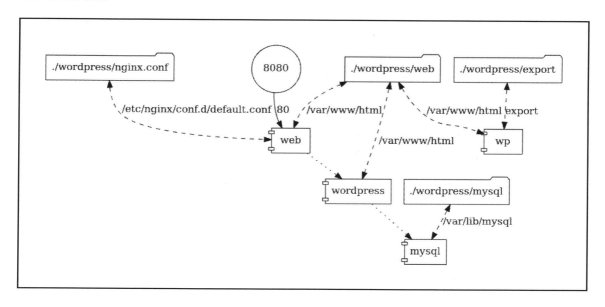

You can use `docker-compose-viz` to give yourself a visual representation of any Docker Compose file. As you can see from ours, we have four services defined:

The first is called `web`; this service is the only one of the four that is exposed to the host network, and it acts as a frontend to our WordPress installation. It runs the official NGINX image from `https://store.docker.com/images/nginx/`, and it performs two roles.

Take a look at the following NGINX configuration:

```
server {
  server_name _;
  listen 80 default_server;

  root /var/www/html;
  index index.php index.html;

  access_log /dev/stdout;
  error_log /dev/stdout info;

   location / {
     try_files $uri $uri/ /index.php?$args;
   }

  location ~ .php$ {
    include fastcgi_params;
    fastcgi_pass wordpress:9000;
    fastcgi_index index.php;
    fastcgi_param SCRIPT_FILENAME
   $document_root$fastcgi_script_name;
    fastcgi_buffers 16 16k;
    fastcgi_buffer_size 32k;
   }
  }
```

You can see that we are serving all content, apart from PHP, using NGINX from `/var/www/html/`, which we are mounting from our host machine using NGINX, and all requests for PHP files are being proxied to our second service, which is called `wordpress`, on port `9000`. The NGINX configuration itself is being mounted from our host machine to `/etc/nginx/conf.d/default.conf`.

The second service is `wordpress`; this is the official WordPress image from `https://store.docker.com/images/wordpress`, and I am using the `php7.1-fpm-alpine` tag. This gives us a WordPress installation running on PHP 7.1 using PHP-FPM built on top of an Alpine Linux base.

FastCGI Process Manager (PHP-FPM) is a PHP FastCGI implementation with some great features. For us, it allows PHP to run as a service that we can bind to a port and pass requests to; this fits in with the Docker approach of running a single service on each container. For more information on PHP-FPM, go to `https://php-fpm.org/`.

We are mounting the same web root as we are doing for the web service, which on the host machine is `wordpress/web` and on the service is `/var/www/html/`. To start off with, the folder on our host machine will be empty; however, once the `wordpress` service starts, it will detect that there isn't any core WordPress installation and copy one to that location, effectively bootstrapping our WordPress installation and copying it to our host machine, ready for us to start work on.

The next service is `mysql`, which uses the official MySQL image (`https://store.docker.com/images/mysql/`) and is the only image out of the four we are using that doesn't use Alpine Linux (come on MySQL, pull your finger out and publish an Alpine Linux-based image!). We are passing a few environment variables so that a database, username, and password are all created when the container first runs; the password is something you should change if you ever use this as a base for one of your projects.

Like the `web` and `wordpress` containers, we are mounting a folder from our host machine. In this case, it is `wordpress/mysql`, and we are mounting it to `/var/lib/mysql/`, which is the default folder where MySQL stores its databases and associated files.

You will notice that when the container starts, `wordpress/mysql` is populated with a few files; I do not recommend editing them using your local IDE.

The final service is simply called `wp`. It differs from the other three services: this service will immediately exit when run, because there is no long-running process within the container. Instead of a long-running process, it provides access to the WordPress command-line tool in an environment that exactly matches our main `wordpress` container.

You will notice that we are mounting the web root as we have done on `web` and `wordpress` as well as a second mount called `/export`; we will look at this in more detail once we have WordPress configured.

To start WordPress, we just need to run the following two commands:

```
$ docker-compose pull
$ docker-compose up -d
$ docker-compose ps
```

This will pull the images and start the `web`, `wordpress`, and `mysql` services as well as readying the `wp` service. Before the services start, our `wordpress` folder looks like this:

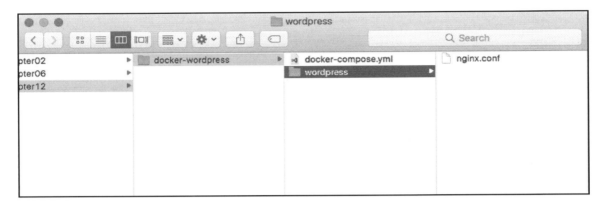

As you can see, we only have `nginx.conf` in there, which is part of the Git repository. Launch the service:

```
⚡ docker-compose up -d
Creating network "dockerwordpress_default" with the default driver
Creating dockerwordpress_wp_1 ...
Creating dockerwordpress_mysql_1 ...
Creating dockerwordpress_wp_1
Creating dockerwordpress_mysql_1 ... done
Creating dockerwordpress_wordpress_1 ...
Creating dockerwordpress_wordpress_1 ... done
Creating dockerwordpress_web_1 ...
Creating dockerwordpress_web_1 ... done
russ in ~/Documents/Code/mastering-docker/chapter12/docker-wordpress on master*
⚡ docker-compose ps
            Name                    Command              State          Ports
-----------------------------------------------------------------------------------------
dockerwordpress_mysql_1      docker-entrypoint.sh mysqld    Up      3306/tcp
dockerwordpress_web_1        nginx -g daemon off;           Up      0.0.0.0:8080->80/tcp
dockerwordpress_wordpress_1  docker-entrypoint.sh php-fpm   Up      9000/tcp
dockerwordpress_wp_1         docker-entrypoint.sh wp shell  Exit 1
russ in ~/Documents/Code/mastering-docker/chapter12/docker-wordpress on master*
⚡ ▯
```

You should see that three folders have been created in the `wordpress` folder: `export`, `mysql`, and `web`. Also, remember that we are expecting `dockerwordpress_wp_1` to have an exit state.

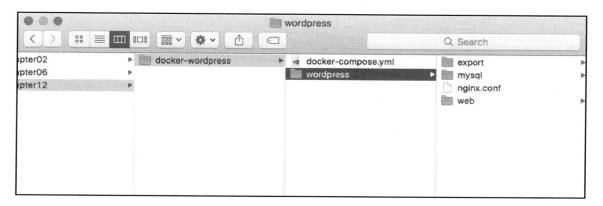

Opening a browser and going to `http://localhost:8080/` should show you the standard WordPress pre-installation welcome page, where you can select the language you wish to use for your installation:

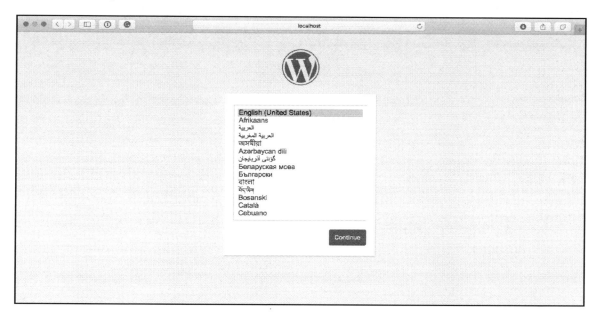

Do not click on **Continue**, as it will take you to the next screen of the GUI-based installation. Instead, return to your terminal.

Rather than using the GUI to complete the installation, we are going to use WP-CLI. There are two steps to this. The first step is to create a `wp-config.php` file; to do this, run the following command:

```
$ docker-compose run wp core config --dbname=wordpress --dbuser=wordpress --dbpass=wordpress --dbhost=mysql --dbprefix=wp_
```

As you will see in the following Terminal output, before I ran the command, I just had the `wp-config-sample.php` file, which ships with core WordPress. Then, after running the command, I had my own `wp-config.php` file:

```
russ in ~/Documents/Code/mastering-docker/chapter12/docker-wordpress on master*
⚡ ls -lhat wordpress/web/ | grep wp-config
-rw-r--r--@  1 russ  staff  2.8K 16 Dec  2015 wp-config-sample.php
russ in ~/Documents/Code/mastering-docker/chapter12/docker-wordpress on master*
⚡ docker-compose run wp core config --dbname=wordpress --dbuser=wordpress --dbpass=wordpress --dbho
st=mysql --dbprefix=wp_
Success: Generated 'wp-config.php' file.
russ in ~/Documents/Code/mastering-docker/chapter12/docker-wordpress on master*
⚡ ls -lhat wordpress/web/ | grep wp-config
-rw-r--r--   1 russ  staff  2.5K  8 Jul 13:20 wp-config.php
-rw-r--r--@  1 russ  staff  2.8K 16 Dec  2015 wp-config-sample.php
russ in ~/Documents/Code/mastering-docker/chapter12/docker-wordpress on master*
⚡ 
```

You will notice that in the command, we are passing the database details we defined in the Docker Compose file and telling WordPress that it can connect to the database service at the address `mysql`.

Now that we have configured database connection details, we need to configure our WordPress site as well a create an admin user and set a password. To do this, run the following:

```
$ docker-compose run wp core install --url="http://localhost:8080" -- --admin_user="admin" --admin_password="password" --admin_email="email@domain.com"
```

Running this command will produce an error about the email service; do not worry about that message as this is only a local development environment. We are not too worried about emails leaving our WordPress installation:

```
●  ●  ●                        1. docker-wordpress (bash)
russ in ~/Documents/Code/mastering-docker/chapter12/docker-wordpress on master*
⚡ docker-compose run wp core install --url="http://localhost:8080" --title="Blog Title" --admin_use
r="admin" --admin_password="password" --admin_email="email@domain.com"
sendmail: can't connect to remote host (127.0.0.1): Connection refused
Success: WordPress installed successfully.
russ in ~/Documents/Code/mastering-docker/chapter12/docker-wordpress on master*
⚡ 
```

We have used WP-CLI to configure the following in WordPress:

- Our URL is `http://localhost:8080`
- Our site title should be `Blog Title`
- Our admin username is `admin` and password is `password`, and the user has an email of `email@domain.com`

Going back to your browser and entering `http://localhost:8080/` should present you with a vanilla WordPress site:

Before we do anything further, let's customize our installation a little, first by installing and enabling the *JetPack* (`https://en-gb.wordpress.org/plugins/jetpack/`) plugin:

```
$ docker-compose run wp plugin install jetpack --activate
```

The output of the command is given here:

```
● ● ●                      1. docker-wordpress (bash)
russ in ~/Documents/Code/mastering-docker/chapter12/docker-wordpress on master*
⚡ docker-compose run wp plugin install jetpack --activate
Installing Jetpack by WordPress.com (5.1)
Downloading install package from https://downloads.wordpress.org/plugin/jetpack.5.1.zip...
Unpacking the package...
Installing the plugin...
Plugin installed successfully.
Activating 'jetpack'...
Plugin 'jetpack' activated.
Success: Installed 1 of 1 plugins.
russ in ~/Documents/Code/mastering-docker/chapter12/docker-wordpress on master*
```

Then, install and enable the *Customizr* (`https://en-gb.wordpress.org/themes/customizr/`) theme:

```
$ docker-compose run wp theme install customizr --activate
```

The output of the command is given here:

```
● ● ●                      1. docker-wordpress (bash)
russ in ~/Documents/Code/mastering-docker/chapter12/docker-wordpress on master*
⚡ docker-compose run wp theme install customizr --activate
Installing Customizr (3.5.17)
Downloading install package from https://downloads.wordpress.org/theme/customizr.3.5.17.zip...
Unpacking the package...
Installing the theme...
Theme installed successfully.
Activating 'customizr'...
Success: Switched to 'Customizr' theme.
Success: Installed 1 of 1 themes.
russ in ~/Documents/Code/mastering-docker/chapter12/docker-wordpress on master*
```

Refreshing our WordPress page at `http://localhost:8080/` should show something like the following:

Before we open our IDE, let's destroy the containers running our WordPress installation using the following command:

```
$ docker-compose down
```

The output of the command is given here:

As our entire WordPress installation, including all of the files and database, is stored on our local machine, we should be able to run the following to return to our WordPress site where we left it:

```
$ docker-compose up -d
```

Once you have confirmed it is up and running as expected by going to `http://localhost:8080/`, open the `docker-wordpress` folder in your desktop editor. I used Microsoft Visual Studio Code.

In your editor, open the file `wordpress/web/wp-blog-header.php` and add the following line to the opening PHP statement and save it:

```
echo "Testing editing in the IDE";
```

The output of the command is given here:

Once saved, refresh your browser and you should see the message `Testing editing in the IDE` at the very bottom of the page (the following screen is zoomed; it may be more difficult to spot if you are following along as the text is is quite small):

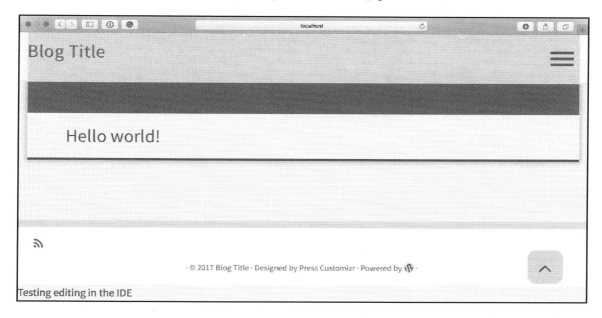

The final thing we are going to look at is why we had the `wordpress/export` folder mounted on the `wp` container.

As already mentioned earlier in the chapter, you shouldn't be really touching the contents of the `wordpress/mysql` folder; this also includes sharing it. While it would probably work if you were to zip up your project folder and pass it to a colleague, it is not considered best practice. Because of this, we have mounted the export folder to allow us to use WP-CLI to make a database dump and import it.

To do this, run the following:

```
$ docker-compose run wp db export --add-drop-table /export/wordpress.sql
```

The following Terminal output shows the export and also the contents of
`wordpress/export` before and after, and finally, the top few lines of the MySQL dump:

```
● ● ●                          1. docker-wordpress (bash)
russ in ~/Documents/Code/mastering-docker/chapter12/docker-wordpress on master*
⚡ ls -lht wordpress/export/
russ in ~/Documents/Code/mastering-docker/chapter12/docker-wordpress on master*
⚡ docker-compose run wp db export --add-drop-table /export/wordpress.sql
Success: Exported to '/export/wordpress.sql'.
russ in ~/Documents/Code/mastering-docker/chapter12/docker-wordpress on master*
⚡ ls -lht wordpress/export/
total 992
-rw-r--r--  1 russ  staff  496K  8 Jul 14:54 wordpress.sql
russ in ~/Documents/Code/mastering-docker/chapter12/docker-wordpress on master*
⚡ head -5 wordpress/export/wordpress.sql
-- MySQL dump 10.16  Distrib 10.1.22-MariaDB, for Linux (x86_64)
--
-- Host: mysql    Database: wordpress
-- ------------------------------------------------------
-- Server version       8.0.1-dmr
russ in ~/Documents/Code/mastering-docker/chapter12/docker-wordpress on master*
⚡ 
```

If I needed to--because, say, I had made a mistake during development--I could roll back to
that version of the database by running the following:

```
$ docker-compose run wp db import /export/wordpress.sql
```

The output of the command is given here:

```
● ● ●                          1. docker-wordpress (bash)
russ in ~/Documents/Code/mastering-docker/chapter12/docker-wordpress on master*
⚡ docker-compose run wp db import /export/wordpress.sql
Success: Imported from '/export/wordpress.sql'.
russ in ~/Documents/Code/mastering-docker/chapter12/docker-wordpress on master*
⚡ 
```

As you have seen, we have installed WordPress, interacted with it both using WP-CLI and
the browser, edited the code, and also backed up and restored the database, all without
having to install or configure NGINX, PHP, MySQL, or WP-CLI. Nor did we have to log in
to a container; by mounting volumes from our host machine, our content was safe when we
tore our WordPress containers down and we didn't lose any work.

Also, if needed, we could have easily passed a copy of our project folder to a colleague who
has Docker installed, and with a single command, they could be working on our code,
knowing it is running in the exact environment as our own installation.

Finally, as we're using official images from the Docker Store, we know we can safely ask to have them deployed into production as they have been built with Docker's best practices in mind.

 Don't forget to stop and remove your WordPress containers by running `docker-compose down`.

Monitoring

Next, we are going to take a look at monitoring our containers and also Docker hosts. In `Chapter 4`, *Managing Containers,* we discussed the `docker container top` and `docker container stats` commands; you may recall that both of these commands show real-time information only; there is no historical data kept.

While this is great if you are trying to debug a problem as it is running or want to quickly get an idea of what is going on inside your containers, it is not too helpful if you need to look back at a problem: maybe you have configured your containers to restart if they have become unresponsive. While that will help with the availability of your application, it isn't much of a help if you need to look at why your container became unresponsive.

We are going to be looking at quite a complex setup. There are alternatives to this configuration, and also, there is ongoing development within the Docker community to make the configuration that we are going to be looking at more straightforward over the next few releases of Docker Engine, but more on that later.

In the GitHub repository at `https://github.com/russmckendrick/mastering-docker` in the `/chapter12` folder, there is a folder called `prometheus` in which there is a Docker Compose file that launches four different containers. All of these containers launch services that we need to monitor not only our containers but also our Docker hosts.

Rather than looking at the Docker Compose file, itself let's take a look at the visualization:

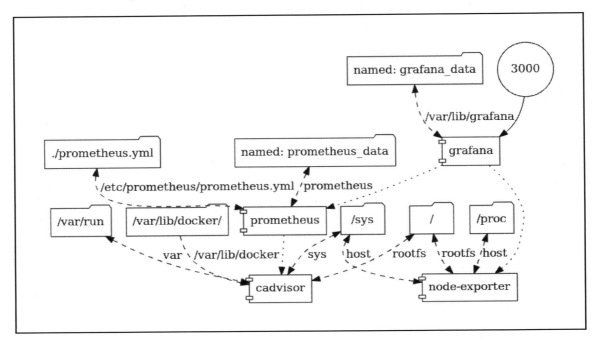

As you can see, there is a lot going on; the four services we are running are:

- cadvisor: https://github.com/google/cadvisor/
- node-exporter: https://github.com/prometheus/node_exporter/
- prometheus: https://prometheus.io/
- grafana: https://grafana.com/

Before we launch and configure our Docker Compose services, we should talk about why each one is needed, starting with cadvisor.

As you may have noticed from the URL, cadvisor is a project released by Google. The service section in the Docker Compose file looks like the following:

```
cadvisor:
  image: google/cadvisor:latest
  container_name: cadvisor
  volumes:
    - /:/rootfs:ro
    - /var/run:/var/run:rw
    - /sys:/sys:ro
```

```
  - /var/lib/docker/:/var/lib/docker:ro
restart: unless-stopped
expose:
  - 8080
```

As you can see, we are mounting the various parts of our host's filesystem to allow `cadvisor` access to our Docker installation in much the same way as we did in Chapter 8, *Portainer*. The reason for this is that in our case, we are going to be using `cadvisor` to collect stats on our containers. While it can be used as a standalone container-monitoring service, we do not want to publicly expose the `cadvisor` container; instead, we are just making it available to other containers within our Docker Compose stack.

While `cadvisor` is a self-contained web frontend to the `docker container stat` command, displaying graphs and allowing you to drill down from your Docker host into your containers from an easy-to-use interface, it doesn't keep more than 5 minutes' worth of metrics. As we are attempting to record metrics that can be available hours or even days later, having no more than 5 minutes of metrics means that we are going to have to use additional tools to record the metrics it processes.

`cadvisor` exposes the information we want to record about our containers as structured data at the following endpoint: `http://cadvisor:8080/metrics/`. We will look at why this is important in a moment.

The next service we are launching is `node-exporter`. Its service definition in the Docker Compose file looks like the following:

```
node-exporter:
  container_name: node-exporter
  image: prom/node-exporter
  volumes:
    - /proc:/host/proc:ro
    - /sys:/host/sys:ro
    - /:/rootfs:ro
  command: '-collector.procfs=/host/proc -collector.sysfs=/host/sys -
collector.filesystem.ignored-mount-
points="^(/rootfs|/host|)/(sys|proc|dev|host|etc)($$|/)"
collector.filesystem.ignored-fs-
types="^(sys|proc|auto|cgroup|devpts|ns|au|fuse\.lxc|mqueue)(fs|)$$"'
  expose:
    - 9100
```

Again, we are mounting various parts of the Docker host's filesystem but this time you will notice that we are not mounting `/var/lib/docker/` as we are not using `node-exporter` to monitor our containers and we only need information about the CPU, RAM and Disk utilization of our host machine. The command also dynamically configures `node-exporter` as the process starts rather than us having to bake or mount our configuration file into the container itself.

Again, we are only exposing the `node-exporter` port to our Docker Compose services; this is because like `cadvisor`, it is acting as nothing more than an endpoint, which is `http://node-exporter:9100/metrics/`, to expose the stats from our Docker host.

Both the `cadvisor` and `node-exporter` endpoints are being scraped automatically by our next service, `prometheus`. This is where most of the heavy lifting happens: **Prometheus** is a monitoring tool written and open sourced by SoundCloud (`https://soundcloud.com/`).

```
prometheus:
  image: prom/prometheus
  container_name: prometheus
  volumes:
    - ./prometheus.yml:/etc/prometheus/prometheus.yml
    - prometheus_data:/prometheus
  restart: unless-stopped
  expose:
    - 9090
  depends_on:
    - cadvisor
    - node-exporter
```

As you can see from the preceding service definition, we are mounting a configuration file and also have a volume called `prometheus_data`. The configuration file contains information about the sources we want to scrape, as you can see from the following configuration:

```
global:
  scrape_interval: 15s
  evaluation_interval: 15s
  external_labels:
    monitor: 'monitoring'

rule_files:

scrape_configs:

  - job_name: 'prometheus'
    static_configs:
      - targets: ['localhost:9090']
```

```
- job_name: 'cadvisor'
  static_configs:
    - targets: ['cadvisor:8080']

- job_name: 'node-exporter'
  static_configs:
    - targets: ['node-exporter:9100']
```

We are instructing Prometheus to scrape data from our endpoints every 15 seconds. The endpoints are defined in the `scrape_configs` section, and as you can see, we have `cadvisor` and `node-exporter` in there as well as Prometheus itself defined. The reason we are creating and mounting the `prometheus_data` volume is that `prometheus` is going to be storing all of our metrics, so we need to keep it safe.

At its core, Prometheus is a time-series database. It takes the data is has scraped, processes it to find the metric name and value, and then stores it along with a timestamp.

 For more information on the data model used by Prometheus, visit `https://prometheus.io/docs/concepts/data_model/`.

Prometheus also comes with a powerful query engine and API, making it the perfect database for this kind of data. While it does come with basic graphing capabilities, it is recommended that you use Grafana, which is our final service and also the only one to be exposed publicly.

Grafana is an open source tool for displaying monitoring graphs and metric analytics, which allows you to create dashboards using time-series databases such as Graphite (`https://graphiteapp.org`), InfluxDB (`https://www.influxdata.com`), and also Prometheus. There are also further backend database options that are available as plugins.

The Docker Compose definition for `grafana` follows a similar pattern to our other services:

```
grafana:
  image: grafana/grafana
  container_name: grafana
  volumes:
    - grafana_data:/var/lib/grafana
  env_file:
    - grafana.config
  restart: unless-stopped
  ports:
    - 3000:3000
  depends_on:
    - prometheus
```

We are using the `grafana_data` volume to store Grafana's own internal configuration database, and rather than storing the environment variables in the Docker Compose file, we are loading them from an external file called `grafana.config`.

The variables are as follows:

```
GF_SECURITY_ADMIN_USER=admin
GF_SECURITY_ADMIN_PASSWORD=password
GF_USERS_ALLOW_SIGN_UP=false
```

As you can see, we are setting the username and password here, so having them in an external file means that you can change these values without editing the core Docker Compose file.

Now that we know the role each of the four services fulfills, let's launch them. To do this, simply run the following command from the `/chapter12/prometheus/` folder:

```
$ docker-compose up -d
```

This will create a network and the volumes and pull the images from the Docker Hub. It will then go about launching the four services:

```
● ● ●                           1. prometheus (bash)
russ in ~/Documents/Code/mastering-docker/chapter12/prometheus on master*
⚡ docker-compose up -d
Creating network "prometheus_default" with the default driver
Creating volume "prometheus_prometheus_data" with default driver
Creating volume "prometheus_grafana_data" with default driver
Creating cadvisor ...
Creating node-exporter ...
Creating cadvisor
Creating cadvisor ... done
Creating prometheus ...
Creating prometheus ... done
Creating grafana ...
Creating grafana ... done
russ in ~/Documents/Code/mastering-docker/chapter12/prometheus on master*
⚡ []
```

You may be tempted to go immediately to `http://localhost:3000/`; if you did, you would not see anything, as Grafana takes a few minutes to initialize itself. You can follow its progress by following the logs:

```
$ docker-compose logs -f grafana
```

The output of the command is given here:

```
●  ●  ●                          1. prometheus (docker-compose)
"Set dashboard version to 1 where 0"
grafana         | t=2017-07-09T09:59:38+0000 lvl=info msg="Executing migration" logger=migrator id=
"save existing dashboard data in dashboard_version table v1"
grafana         | t=2017-07-09T09:59:39+0000 lvl=info msg="Created default admin user: admin"
grafana         | t=2017-07-09T09:59:39+0000 lvl=info msg="Starting plugin search" logger=plugins
grafana         | t=2017-07-09T09:59:39+0000 lvl=warn msg="Plugin dir does not exist" logger=plugin
s dir=/var/lib/grafana/plugins
grafana         | t=2017-07-09T09:59:39+0000 lvl=info msg="Plugin dir created" logger=plugins dir=/
var/lib/grafana/plugins
grafana         | t=2017-07-09T09:59:39+0000 lvl=info msg="Initializing Alerting" logger=alerting.e
ngine
grafana         | t=2017-07-09T09:59:39+0000 lvl=info msg="Initializing CleanUpService" logger=clea
nup
grafana         | t=2017-07-09T09:59:39+0000 lvl=info msg="Initializing Stream Manager"
grafana         | t=2017-07-09T09:59:39+0000 lvl=info msg="Initializing HTTP Server" logger=http.se
rver address=0.0.0.0:3000 protocol=http subUrl= socket=
```

Once you see the `"Initializing HTTP Server"` message, Grafana will be available.
There is, however, one more thing we need to do before we access Grafana, and that is to
configure our data source. We can do this by running the following command, which is for
macOS and Linux only, to set up the data source using the API:

```
$ curl 'http://admin:password@localhost:3000/api/datasources' -X POST -H
'Content-Type: application/json;charset=UTF-8' --data-binary
'{"name":"Prometheus","type":"prometheus","url":"http://prometheus:9090","a
ccess":"proxy","isDefault":true}'
```

The preceding command is available in the repository in the README.md
file, so you don't have to type it out; you can copy and paste.

```
●  ●  ●                          1. prometheus (bash)
russ in ~/Documents/Code/mastering-docker/chapter12/prometheus on master*
⚡ curl 'http://admin:password@localhost:3000/api/datasources' -X POST -H 'Content-Type: application
/json;charset=UTF-8' --data-binary '{"name":"Prometheus","type":"prometheus","url":"http://prometheu
s:9090","access":"proxy","isDefault":true}'
{"id":1,"message":"Datasource added","name":"Prometheus"}russ in ~/Documents/Code/mastering-docker/c
hapter12/prometheus on master*
⚡
```

If you are unable to configure the data source using the API, then don't worry; Grafana will help you add one when you log in, which is what we are now going to do. Open your browser and enter `http://localhost:3000/`, and you should be greeted with a login screen:

Enter the **User** admin and the **Password** password. Once logged in, if you have configured the data source, you should see the following page:

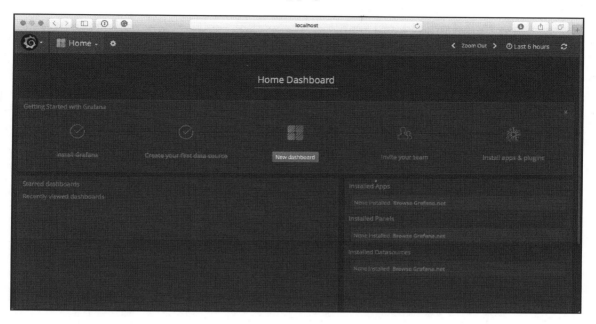

If you haven't entered the data source, you will be prompted to; follow the onscreen instructions. You can use the information from the curl command further up; once you enter it, you will be taken to the **New Dashboard** screen.

Click on **Home** in the top left and you will be shown a menu. On the right-hand side is an **Import Dashboard** button; click on it to be taken to a page that will ask you to **Upload .json File**, enter a **Grafana.com Dashboard** or **paste JSON**. Enter the number 893 into the **Grafana.com Dashboard** box and click on the **Load** button. You will be taken to the import options:

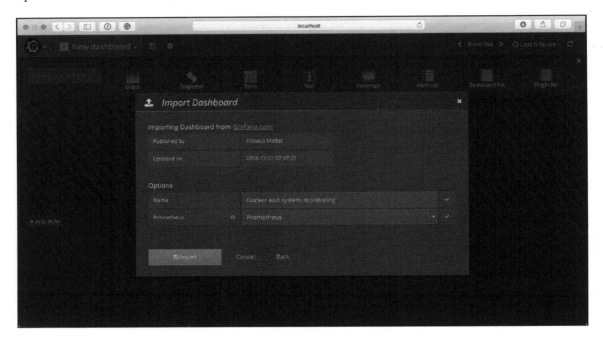

Leave everything at its default options and select your data source, which should be Prometheus, the last option. Once this is complete, click on the **Import** button.

This will import the prepared **Docker and system monitoring** by *Thibaut Mottet*. This has been built with `cadvisor`, `node-exporter`, and `Prometheus` in mind; once imported, you should see something similar to the following:

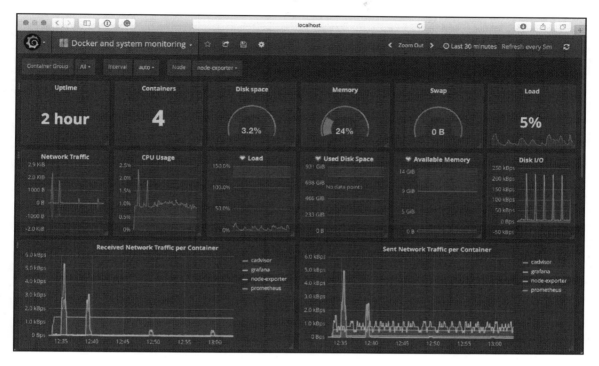

As you can see, I have over 2 hours of metrics stored, which I can explore by clicking on the various graphs as well as the display options in the top right of the screen. For more information on the Grafana dashboard, go to the dashboards project page at `https://grafa na.com/dashboards/893/`.

I have already mentioned that this is a complex solution; eventually, Docker will expand the recently released built-in endpoint, which presently only exposes information about the Docker Engine and not the containers themselves. For more information on the built-in endpoint, check out the official Docker documentation, which can be found at `https://doc s.docker.com/engine/admin/prometheus/`.

There are other monitoring solutions out there; most of them take the form of third-party Software as a Service productions:

- **Sysdig Cloud**: https://sysdig.com/
- **Datadog**: http://docs.datadoghq.com/integrations/docker/
- **CoScale**: http://www.coscale.com/docker-monitoring/
- **Dynatrace**: https://www.dynatrace.com/capabilities/microservices-and-container-monitoring/
- **SignalFx**: https://signalfx.com/docker-monitoring/
- **New Relic**: https://newrelic.com/partner/docker
- **Sematext**: https://sematext.com/docker/

There are also other self-hosted options, such as:

- **Elastic Beats**: https://www.elastic.co/products/beats
- **Sysdig**: https://www.sysdig.org
- **Zabbix**: https://github.com/monitoringartist/zabbix-docker-monitoring

As you can see, there are a few well-established monitoring solutions listed; in fact, you may already be using them, so it would be easy for you when expanding your configuration to take into account your monitoring your containers.

Once you have finished exploring your Prometheus installation, don't forget to remove it by running:

```
$ docker-compose down --volumes --rmi all
```

This removes all of the containers, volumes, images, and network.

Extending to external platforms

We have looked at how we can extend to some other external platforms using tools such as Docker Machine, Docker Swarm, Docker for Amazon Web Services, and Rancher to launch Docker hosts and clusters into public cloud services such as Amazon Web Services, Microsoft Azure, and DigitalOcean.

In this section, we are going to take a quick look at three other container platforms, starting with Kubernetes using Tectonic.

Tectonic

Tectonic by CoreOS is a fully managed Kubernetes installer; it is great for bootstrapping and managing large Kubernetes clusters from a central, easy-to-use interface. While it is a commercial offering, it is free to launch clusters of up to 10 nodes. To sign up, go to the product page at `https://coreos.com/tectonic/` and follow the on-screen instructions.

Once you have signed up and downloaded Tectonic, you will be asked to run the installer, which creates a local web service:

It takes you to the guided installer:

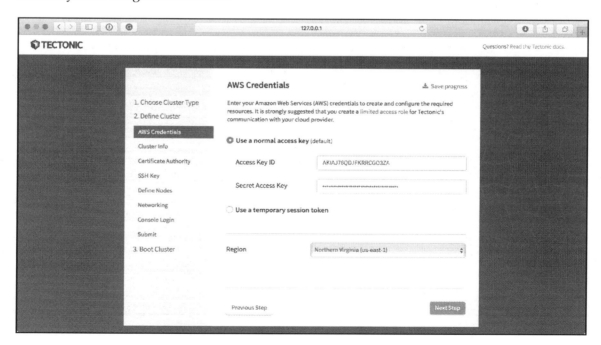

As you can see from the preceding screen, the installer walks you through every step of defining your Kubernetes cluster. There are some very sensible defaults, so I recommend using those for your first installation.

Once you have provided the Tectonic installer with your public cloud credentials, details about the cluster size, your networking and DNS preferences, SSH keys, and so on, it will produce a Terraform configuration and then execute it for you.

Terraform is an open source orchestration tool written by HashiCorp; its one goal is to allow you to define your infrastructure as code. It works with most common public cloud providers and has quite a large coverage of each of their APIs, meaning you don't lose out on features by using the tool. For more information, see `https://www.terraform.io/`.

You get the option of downloading the Terraform code, along with other assets created by the Tectonic installer. I strongly recommend downloading them and keeping them safe as you will need them to tear down your cluster.

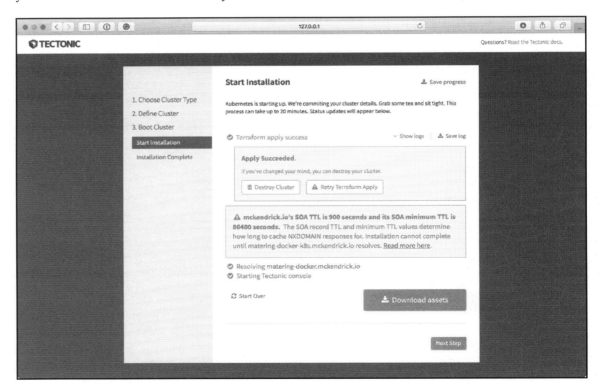

Once the installation has completed--it will take around 15 minutes--you will be given the option to access the **Tectonic Console**:

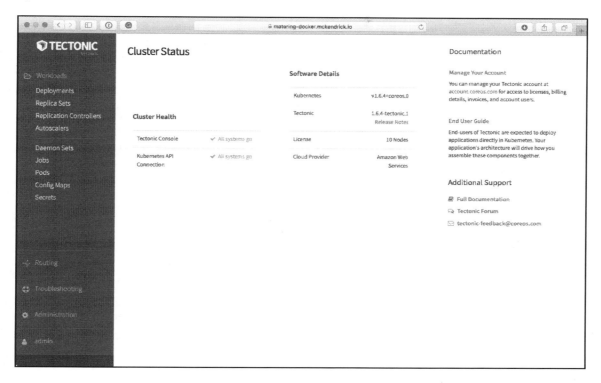

From here, you can manage your Kubernetes installation and download a `kubectl` configuration file so that you can interact with your Kubernetes cluster from the command line, as you would do with any other Kubernetes cluster:

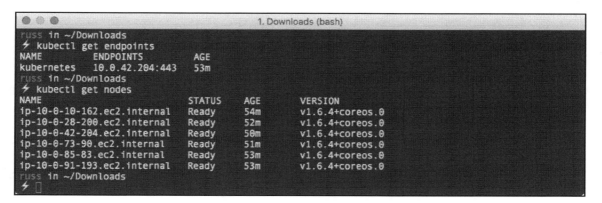

Going forward, you have a fully functional Kubernetes cluster you can use like any other. I recommend following the tutorial on deploying your first application at `https://coreos.com/tectonic/docs/latest/tutorials/first-app.html`.

For full details on how to deploy your own Kubernetes cluster using Tectonic, check out their excellent installation guides at `https://coreos.com/tectonic/docs/latest/`, which cover Amazon Web Services, Microsoft Azure, OpenStack, and bare metal deployments.

Kubernetes is extremely complex to configure and maintain. While it can be straightforward to get a basic cluster up and running, configuring auto-scaling nodes and performing in-place upgrades can be very troublesome. Using Tectonic takes the hard work of performing these tasks away from you in a way where you can see exactly what it is doing, by downloading the Terraform assets. Also, it does it in a way that applies current Kubernetes best practices.

I would recommend that if you have an interest in Kubernetes, you check out Tectonic.

Heroku

Heroku is a little different than the other cloud services, as it is a considered a **Platform as a Service (PaaS)**. Instead of deploying containers on it, you link your containers to that Heroku platform, from which it will be running a service, such as PHP, Java, Node.js, or Python. So you can run your Rails application on Heroku and then attach your Docker container to that platform.

The way you can use Docker and Heroku together is to create your application on the Heroku platform, and then in your code, you will have something similar to the following:

```
{
  "name": "Application Name",
  "description": "Application to run code in a Docker
  container",
  "image": "<docker_image>:<tag>",
  "addons": [ "heroku-postgresql" ]
}
```

To take a step back, we first need to install the plugin to be able to get this functionality working. Simply run the following:

```
$ heroku plugins:install heroku-docker
```

Now, if you are wondering what image you can or should be using from the Docker Hub, Heroku maintains a lot of images you can use in the preceding code:

- `heroku/nodejs`
- `heroku/ruby`
- `heroku/jruby`
- `heroku/python`
- `heroku/scala`
- `heroku/clojure`
- `heroku/gradle`
- `heroku/java`
- `heroku/go`
- `heroku/go-gb`

Amazon Elastic Container Service

Amazon has their own container offering built on top of Docker, called **Amazon Elastic Container Service**, or **Amazon ECS**. Like most AWS services, it really comes into its own when used alongside other AWS services.

The service itself is free to use; you just pay for the underlying resources consumed by the containers you launch. Services include the following:

- **Amazon Elastic Compute Cloud (EC2)**: This service provides the compute power (RAM, CPU, and network) for your ECS hosts. Without it, you don't have anywhere to launch your containers.
- **Amazon Elastic Block Storage (EBS)**: EBS provides persistent block-level storage for your compute resources and containers.
- **Elastic Load Balancing (ELB)**: These are Amazon-managed load balancers that span multiple availability zones (data centers) within your chosen region.
- **Auto Scaling**: This service allows you to scale your ECS cluster up and down, based on a number of user-defined alarms, such as the number of ECS hosts, CPU load, and the number of connections to an ELB, to name but a few.
- **Virtual Private Cloud (VPC)**: This service allows you to create your own private networking with AWS to run all of your services in, giving you an extremely high level of control of the routing of your traffic within your VPC and also externally by letting you configure route tables, network ACLS, and security groups.

All of these services combined with Amazon's own container scheduler allow you to quickly create both highly scalable and also highly redundant container clusters that can be managed through the Amazon ECS web interface, the AWS command-line tools, or Amazon's powerful API.

For more information on Amazon ECS, visit the product page at `https://aws.amazon.com/ecs/`.

What does production look like?

For the final section of this chapter, we are going to discuss what production should look like. This section isn't going to be as long as you think it will be; this is due to the sheer number of options that are available, so it would be impossible to cover them all. Also, you should already have a good idea based on the previous sections and chapters on what would work best for you.

Instead, we are going to be looking at some questions you should be asking yourself with planning your environments.

Docker hosts

Docker hosts are the key component of your environment. Without these, you won't have anywhere to run your containers. As we have already seen in previous chapters, there are a few considerations when it comes to running your Docker hosts. The first thing you need to take into account is that your hosts, if they are running Docker, should not run any other services.

Mixing of processes

You should resist the temptation of quickly installing Docker on an existing host and launching a container. This might not only have a security implication with you having a mixture of isolated and non-isolated processes on a single host, it can also cause performance issues as you are not able to add resource limits to your non-containerized applications, meaning that potentially, they can have a negative impact on your running containers.

Multiple isolated Docker hosts

If you have a few more Docker hosts, how are you going to manage them? Running a tool such as Portainer is great, but it can get troublesome when attempting to manage more than a few hosts. Also, if you are running multiple isolated Docker hosts, you do not have the option of moving containers between hosts.

Sure, you can use tools such as Weave Net to span the container network across multiple individual Docker hosts. Depending on your hosting environment, you may also have the option of creating volumes on external storage and presenting them to Docker hosts as needed, but you are very much creating a manual process to manage the migration of containers between hosts.

Routing to your containers

You need to consider how are you going to route requests among your containers if you have multiple hosts.

For example, if you have an external load balancer, such as an ELB in AWS or a dedicated device in front of an on-premise cluster, do you have the ability to dynamically add routes for traffic hitting port x on your load balancer to port y on your Docker hosts, at which point the traffic is then routed through to your container?

If you have multiple containers that all need to be accessible on the same external port, how are you going handle that?

Do you need to install a proxy such as **Traefik** (`https://traefik.io/`), **HAProxy** (`http://www.haproxy.org/`), or **NGINX** (`https://nginx.org/`) to accept and then route your requests based on virtual hosts based on domains or subdomains, rather than just using port-based routeing?

For example, you could use just ports for a website, everything on ports `80` and `443` to the container that is configured by Docker to accept traffic on those ports. Using virtual host routing means that you can route `domain-a.com` to `container a` and then `domain-b.com` to `container b` and that both `domain-a.com` and `domain-b.com` can point toward the same IP address and port.

Clustering

A lot of what we have discussed in the previous chapter can be solved by introducing clustering tools such as Docker Swarm, Kubernetes, or Cattle, to name a few.

Compatibility

Even though an application works fine on a developer's local Docker installation, you need to be able to guarantee that if you take the application and deploy it to, for example, a Kubernetes cluster, it works in the same way.

Nine out of ten times you will not have a problem, but you do need to consider how the application is communicating internally with other containers within the same application set.

Reference architectures

Are there reference architectures available for your chosen clustering technology? It is always best to check when deploying a cluster; there are best-practice guides that are close to or match your proposed environment; after all, no one wants to create one big single point of failure.

Also, what are the recommended resources? There is no point in deploying a cluster with five management nodes and a single Docker host, just like there is little point in deploying five Docker hosts and single management server as you have quite a large single point of failure.

What supporting technologies does your cluster technology support, for example, remote storage, load balancers, and firewalls?

Cluster communication

What are the requirements when it comes to the cluster communicating with either management or Docker hosts? Do you need an internal or separate network to isolate the cluster traffic?

Can you easily lock a cluster member down to only your cluster? Is the cluster communication encrypted; what information about your cluster could be exposed; does this make it a target for hackers?

What external access does the cluster need to APIs, such as your public cloud providers? How securely are any API/access credentials stored?

Image registries

How is your application packaged? Have you baked the code into the image? If so, do you need to host a private local image registry, or are you okay with using an external service such as Docker Hub, **Docker Trusted Registry (DTR)**, or Quay?

If you need to host your own private registry, where in your environment should it sit? Who has or needs access? Can it hook into your directory provider, such as an Active Directory installation?

Summary

In this chapter, we looked at a few different workflows for Docker along with how to get some monitoring for your containers and Docker hosts up and running.

We looked at three external platforms and worked through some questions you should be asking yourself when defining what your production environments look like. As mentioned in the chapter, there is no real right answer for this; you know your own requirements, which may be different to mine or anyone else reading this.

The best thing you can do when it comes to your own environment is building a proof of concept and trying as hard as you can to cover every disaster scenario you can think of. You can get a head start by using a service such as Tectonic or Amazon ECS or by looking for a good reference architecture, which should all limit your trial and error.

In the next chapter, we are going to take a look at how you move service discovery from the container level to the application as well as looking at what your next step in the world of containers could be.

13
Next Steps with Docker

We've made it to the last chapter and you've stuck with it until the end! In this chapter, we will look at how your applications can better run in a containerized environment by discussing discovery services. We will also look at where Docker is going and also how you can contribute to its future as well as to the community.

Service discovery

So far, the applications we have been launching don't really have to know about the environment they are running in as we have been doing all of our routing at the network level. What if our application itself needed to be aware of where other containers are within our environment?

Consul

One of the more popular options for discovery services, not only with Docker but also outside of the world of containers, is Consul. Consul is an open source service discovery engine by Hashicorp (`https://www.hashicorp.com`). Its four main features are:

- Service discovery
- Key/value storage
- Health checking
- Multi-data center awareness

We are going to be looking at just service discovery in detail; however, we will also touch on how the other Consul services could be used.

Running Consul

The first thing we need to do is launch Consul. To do this, we will be using the official Consul image from the Docker Hub. It should be pointed out at this stage that this is not going to be a highly available Consul installation, though Consul does support highly available clustered configurations.

To launch our single Consul container, we should first create a network and then launch the container. To do that run the following commands:

```
$ docker network create consul
$ docker container run -d --name=consul --network=consul -p 8500:8500 -p
8600:8600/udp consul
```

As you can see, we have a network named `consul` and container with ports `8500` and `8600` open. We will look at port `8600` later in this section. For now, open your browser and go to `http://localhost:8500/`. This will open the Consul web GUI which is running on port `8500`. You should be able to see something like the following:

As you can see, there is not much going on; we have a single service registered, which is Consul itself.

Running Registrator

Out of the box, Consul has no visibility or knowledge of your containers, so we have to find a way of making an HTTP request to Consul each time a container launches. There is a service called **Registrator** by *Glider Labs* (`http://gliderlabs.com/registrator/`) which does exactly this, so let's look at launching a container running Registrator:

```
$ docker container run -d \
  --name=registrator --network=consul \
  --volume=/var/run/docker.sock:/tmp/docker.sock \
  gliderlabs/registrator:latest consul://consul:8500
```

As you can see from the preceding command, our Registrator container has our Docker Engine's socket file mounted. This means that it has direct access to the Docker Engine running on our host and that it will be aware of all changes, such as launching new containers. The other thing you may notice is that Registrator was executed with the following: `consul://consul:8500`. This is all of the configuration we have to do. It tells Registrator to use Consul and also the URL that Consul can be accessed on. In our case, as we launched our Registrator container on the same network as the Consul container, all requests will be routed through to the name and port of target container, which in this case is Consul and port `8500`.

Going back to our browser, you should be able to see that two additional services are now being displayed:

Because we called our Consul container `consul` and we exposed ports `8500` and `8600`, Registrator has added these to Consul. Now that our new containers are being registered with Consul, we can launch a test container. Like other chapters, we will use the Cluster application, though this time we won't be too worried about being able to access the application itself.

Querying Consul

To launch the application container, run the following command:

```
$ docker container run -d -p 80 -l "SERVICE_NAME=cluster" -l
"SERVICE_TAGS=app,web" russmckendrick/cluster
```

As you can see from the command, we have added two labels using the -l flag; these pass metadata to the Registrator service which then, in turn, sends the data to Consul. The two labels we added are:

- SERVICE_NAME: This names our services, allowing containers to be grouped together
- SERVICE_TAGS: This adds tags to our containers, useful when trying to identify a service

You should now notice a service called cluster in your browser; selecting it should give you some more information on the service itself:

You can see the tags we defined and we have 1 passing check in the service. We can also check the service using the API that is built into Consul. To do this, run the following command:

```
$ curl http://localhost:8500/v1/catalog/service/cluster/
```

This will return a JSON array containing information about the service, for example:

```
[
  {
    "ID": "c6aeffbb-a64d-1d54-e335-f339e692dc71",
    "Node": "230667de6b6c",
    "Address": "127.0.0.1",
    "Datacenter": "dc1",
    "TaggedAddresses": {
    "lan": "127.0.0.1",
    "wan": "127.0.0.1"
  },
    "NodeMeta": {},
    "ServiceID": "fd2a45346a81:peaceful_shirley:80",
    "ServiceName": "cluster",
    "ServiceTags": [
    "app",
    "web"
  ],
    "ServiceAddress": "",
    "ServicePort": 32790,
    "ServiceEnableTagOverride": false,
    "CreateIndex": 184,
    "ModifyIndex": 184
  }
]
```

As you can see from the preceding example there are a few bits of important information about our running service.

We can see:

- The IP address of the host the container is running on (`Address`)
- The container UUID, name, and also which port is open on the container (`ServiceID`)
- The name of the service (`ServiceName`)
- The tags we defined (`ServiceTags`)

We can also find out details on the service itself, like which port is exposed on the host (`ServicePort`).

As well as the web-based API, Consul allows you to query its database using DNS.

We can query Consul's built-in DNS service on port 8600, which was opened up on the UDP protocol when we launched the Consul container; to do this, run the following command:

```
$ dig @127.0.0.1 -p8600 cluster.service.consul
```

You should see something like the following returned:

```
; <<>> DiG 9.8.3-P1 <<>> @127.0.0.1 -p8600 cluster.service.consul
; (1 server found)
;; global options: +cmd
;; Got answer:
;; ->>HEADER<<- opcode: QUERY, status: NOERROR, id: 43651
;; flags: qr aa rd; QUERY: 1, ANSWER: 1, AUTHORITY: 0, ADDITIONAL: 0
;; WARNING: recursion requested but not available

;; QUESTION SECTION:
;cluster.service.consul.         IN

;; ANSWER SECTION:
cluster.service.consul. 0 IN A 127.0.0.1

;; Query time: 1 msec
;; SERVER: 127.0.0.1#8600(127.0.0.1)
;; WHEN: Mon May 29 18:21:23 2017
;; MSG SIZE rcvd: 56
```

As our example is configured to use localhost / 127.0.0.1, the output isn't very interesting; however, we can get a little more detail by running:

```
$ dig @127.0.0.1 -p8600 cluster.service.consul SRV
```

As you can see from the following example, adding SRV to the end of the command has returned the SRV record, which gives more details on the ports being used (which in my case is port 32790):

```
; <<>> DiG 9.8.3-P1 <<>> @127.0.0.1 -p8600 cluster.service.consul SRV
; (1 server found)
;; global options: +cmd
;; Got answer:
;; ->>HEADER<<- opcode: QUERY, status: NOERROR, id: 21185
;; flags: qr aa rd; QUERY: 1, ANSWER: 1, AUTHORITY: 0, ADDITIONAL: 1
;; WARNING: recursion requested but not available

;; QUESTION SECTION:
;cluster.service.consul.         IN SRV

;; ANSWER SECTION:
```

```
cluster.service.consul. 0 IN SRV 1 1 32790 230667de6b6c.node.dc1.consul.

;; ADDITIONAL SECTION:
230667de6b6c.node.dc1.consul. 0 IN A 127.0.0.1

;; Query time: 1 msec
;; SERVER: 127.0.0.1#8600(127.0.0.1)
;; WHEN: Mon May 29 18:25:44 2017
;; MSG SIZE rcvd: 98
```

Launch two more containers by running the following command twice:

```
$ docker container run -d -p 80 -l "SERVICE_NAME=cluster" -l
"SERVICE_TAGS=app,web" russmckendrick/cluster
```

This changes the results to:

```
; <<>> DiG 9.8.3-P1 <<>> @127.0.0.1 -p8600 cluster.service.consul SRV
; (1 server found)
;; global options: +cmd
;; Got answer:
;; ->>HEADER<<- opcode: QUERY, status: NOERROR, id: 51192
;; flags: qr aa rd; QUERY: 1, ANSWER: 3, AUTHORITY: 0, ADDITIONAL: 3
;; WARNING: recursion requested but not available

;; QUESTION SECTION:
;cluster.service.consul. IN SRV

;; ANSWER SECTION:
cluster.service.consul. 0 IN SRV 1 1 32792 230667de6b6c.node.dc1.consul.
cluster.service.consul. 0 IN SRV 1 1 32790 230667de6b6c.node.dc1.consul.
cluster.service.consul. 0 IN SRV 1 1 32791 230667de6b6c.node.dc1.consul.

;; ADDITIONAL SECTION:
230667de6b6c.node.dc1.consul. 0 IN A 127.0.0.1
230667de6b6c.node.dc1.consul. 0 IN A 127.0.0.1
230667de6b6c.node.dc1.consul. 0 IN A 127.0.0.1

;; Query time: 1 msec
;; SERVER: 127.0.0.1#8600(127.0.0.1)
;; WHEN: Mon May 29 18:28:54 2017
;; MSG SIZE rcvd: 170
```

As you can see, we are now getting details on all three running containers that have been launched into the `cluster` service. This is also reflected in the web interface where we can now also see the three containers:

You can also filter on tags. For example, let's launch a fourth container but this time replace the `app` tag with `dev` by running:

```
$ docker container run -d -p 80 -l "SERVICE_NAME=cluster" -l
"SERVICE_TAGS=dev,web" russmckendrick/cluster
```

We can then filter just the `dev` tag by running:

```
$ curl http://localhost:8500/v1/catalog/service/cluster?tag=dev
```

This should only return a single result, as should doing a dig on `dev.cluster.service.consul` by running:

```
$ dig @127.0.0.1 -p8600 dev.cluster.service.consul SRV
```

So far we have been using the Consul built-in API and DNS service to discover information about our containers. If you are hooking your own application into Consul then it is more than likely you will be using the API to find out information about the containers running on your host.

However, what if you just want to find out information about your containers to update a simple configuration file? Odds are you do not want to do a lot of work to write your own code to process data that is accessible in Consul.

Consul template

Hashicorp has also developed a supporting tool that allows you connect to a Consul installation and then parse a template, populating it with the results it finds. The tool is called Consul Template; if you are running macOS with a Homebrew installation, you can install `consul-template` by running:

```
brew install consul-template
```

If you don't have Homebrew, then installation instructions can be found on the project's GitHub page which you can find at `https://github.com/hashicorp/consul-template/`.

Let's create a simple template that puts the **Address** and **Port** of each of the containers in our **cluster** service into a really basic configuration file. We will save the template to `/tmp/consul.ctmpl`:

```
$ echo $'{{range service "cluster"}}server {{.Address}}:{{.Port}}\n{{end}}'
> /tmp/consul.ctmpl
```

 Consul Template uses the Go Template format; for more information on this format, see `https://golang.org/pkg/text/template/`.

As you can see from the example, we are querying the service called **cluster** using `{{range service "cluster"}}`. By not having the word `server` in curly braces, we are displaying it rather than a value from Consul. We are then getting the value for the IP address using `{{.Address}}` and the same for the port by using `{{.Port}}`. Note that we are also adding a : and a line break `\n`. Finally, we are telling the query that we have all of the information we need and it should move on to the next result, or finish, by adding `{{end}}`.

Now that we have our template, we can run the following command to run the query and output the file with the details on our service called cluster to a file called `/tmp/consul.result`:

```
$ consul-template -once -consul-addr 127.0.0.1:8500 -template
/tmp/consul.ctmpl:/tmp/consul.result
```

Opening the output file should show you something similar to mine:

```
server 127.0.0.1:32792
server 127.0.0.1:32790
server 127.0.0.1:32791
server 127.0.0.1:32793
```

If you noticed, the command we ran to generate the template had the -once flag in it; this told consul-template to run once and then quit. If we omitted this flag, consul-template would continue to run and every time a change was made to our cluster service, the template file would be regenerated. Using -exec we could execute a command each time the configuration file was rewritten. For example, run something like the following command:

```
$ consul-template -consul-addr 127.0.0.1:8500 \
  -template /tmp/nginx.ctmpl:/etc/nginx/conf.d/default.conf \
  -exec "systemctl nginx reload"
```

This would generate an NGINX config file and reload the service each time a container was added or removed from our service.

Add to that information you could get from the key/value store, which could be useful for storing configuration such as entries we would use in our NGINX configuration:

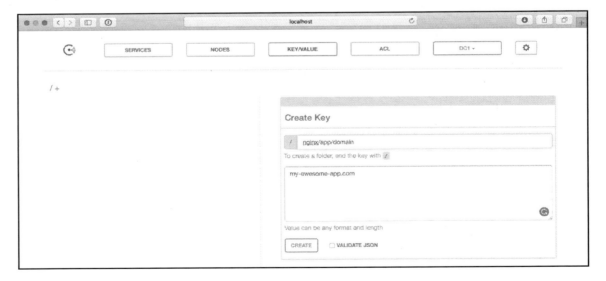

Think of a key/value store as a database for environment variables. For example, when we are launching containers, we can set something like DOMAIN_NAME = www.domain.com. In this example, the key would be DOMAIN_NAME and the value www.domain.com.

The advantage of using the key/value store in Consul is that the information available in the API at:

```
$ curl http://localhost:8500/v1/kv/nginx/app/domain?raw
```

It is also available in consul-template:

```
$ echo $'{{range service "cluster"}}{{ key "nginx/app/domain" }}
{{.Address}}:{{.Port}}\n{{end}}' > /tmp/consul.ctmpl
$ consul-template —consul-addr 127.0.0.1:8500 —template
/tmp/consul.ctmpl:/tmp/consul.result
```

The command gives the following result:

```
my-awesome-app.com 127.0.0.1:32792
my-awesome-app.com 127.0.0.1:32790
my-awesome-app.com 127.0.0.1:32791
my-awesome-app.com 127.0.0.1:32793
```

Highly available Consul

As already mentioned at the start of this section, I would not recommend running Consul in a single-node configuration. One of the key features of Consul is its ability to run in a highly available cluster. For more information on running a highly available Consul cluster, see the Consul agent in the **Client Mode** section of the Consul images, the Docker Store page at https://store.docker.com/images/consul/, or the Consul *Getting Started* guide at https://www.consul.io/intro/getting-started/install.html.

etcd

An alternative to Consul is etcd. If you are going extremely lightweight with your host environments and using CoreOS, then you should already be very familiar with etcd as it is the default service discovery service for CoreOS. It uses a dynamic configuration registry to do discovery. When etcd is configured on each CoreOS host, they can do key/value distribution and replication, which allows them to discover each other as well as new etcd hosts.

To find out more about etcd, refer to `https://en.wikipedia.org/wiki/CoreOS#ETCD`. You can also visit `https://github.com/coreos/etcd`, which contains information not just about what etcd can do, but also the ways you can get support for it, roadmap, mailing list, and reported bugs. You can also refer to `https://coreos.com/etcd/`.

Registrator also supports etcd as a backend service, meaning that if you already have etcd up and running as part of your CoreOS or Kubernetes installation, it will be easy to hook your own services in.

Docker API

There is nothing stopping you from also using the Docker API; however, it is quite complicated and very easy to overwhelm yourself with information. For example, let's look at launching a simple, single container by running:

```
$ docker container run -d -p 80 russmckendrick/cluster
```

That is the only running container on my host. Running the following command will query the Docker API, listing all of the running containers as a JSON array:

```
$ curl --unix-socket /var/run/docker.sock "http:/v1.27/containers/json" |
python -m json.tool
```

This returns the following information:

```
[
  {
    "Command": "supervisord -c /etc/supervisord.conf",
    "Created": 1496083791,
    "HostConfig": {
      "NetworkMode": "default"
    },
    "Id":
"a4c2c76ace78e25e1c42833967447042f8607c453c14f443b730f605f2e6_5039",
    "Image": "russmckendrick/cluster",
    "ImageID":
"sha256:53b0bf5f7c7cd98bb2e1d259cb93d222a7612002b761aed511fc6978a49335c2",
    "Labels": {},
    "Mounts": [],
    "Names": [
      "/relaxed_cori"
    ],
    "NetworkSettings": {
      "Networks": {
        "bridge": {
```

```
        "Aliases": null,
        "EndpointID":
"2707504775f366e46995017d74feacc748fd42e31f8d96bb38dc00d9bc68535f",
        "Gateway": "172.17.0.1",
        "GlobalIPv6Address": "",
        "GlobalIPv6PrefixLen": 0,
        "IPAMConfig": null,
        "IPAddress": "172.17.0.2",
        "IPPrefixLen": 16,
        "IPv6Gateway": "",
        "Links": null,
        "MacAddress": "02:42:ac:11:00:02",
        "NetworkID":
"a42aafd143a718fec2d790615dce9edcd03b84ed3176c270193e0fcb4ff945c4"
            }
        }
    },
    "Ports": [
        {
            "IP": "0.0.0.0",
            "PrivatePort": 80,
            "PublicPort": 32794,
          "Type": "tcp"
        }
    ],
    "State": "running",
    "Status": "Up 34 seconds"
    }
    ]
```

As you can see, that is basically the same information that the Docker client returns when you run:

```
$ docker container ls
```

You can then find out more information on the running container by running the following, ensuring you replace the long container ID with that of your own:

```
$ curl --unix-socket /var/run/docker.sock
"http:/v1.27/containers/a4c2c76ace78e25e1c42833967447042f8607c453c14f443b73
0f605f2e65039/json" | python -m json.tool
```

There is way too much information returned to display here, just short of 200 lines of information to be exact. Also, the information returned is a more verbose version of what you would see if you were to run:

```
$ docker container inspect container_name
```

While it is possible to use the Docker API for service discovery, I would not recommend it due to the steep learning curve and because there are much more suitable applications such as Consul and etcd available. You can find out more information on the API including its full definition at the following URL: `https://docs.docker.com/engine/api/v1.29/`.

The Moby Project

One of the announcements made at DockerCon 2017 was the **Moby Project**. When this project was announced, I had a few questions about what the project is from work colleagues, because on the face of it, Docker have appeared to have released another container system.

So how did I answer? After a few days of getting puzzled looks, I settled on the following answer:

> *Moby Project is the collective name for an open source project that collects together several libraries used to build container-based systems. The project comes with its own framework for combining these libraries into a usable system and also a reference system called Moby Origin; think of this as a "hello world" that allows you to build and even customize your own Docker.*

One of two things happened after I gave the answer; typically the response was "but what does that actually mean?" I responded by saying:

> *Moby Project is the open source playground for Docker (the company) and anyone else who wishes to contribute to the project to develop new and extend existing features to the libraries and frameworks that go to make up container-based systems in a public forum. One output of this is the bleeding-edge container system called Moby Origin and the other is Docker (the product), which is delivered as the open source community edition or the commercially supported enterprise edition.*

For anyone who asks for an example of a similar project that combines a bleeding-edge version, a stable open source release, and an enterprise supported version, I explain what Red Hat do with Red Hat Enterprise Linux:

> *Think of it like the approach Red Hat have taken with Red Hat Enterprise Linux. You have Fedora, which is the bleeding edge version development playground for Red Hat's operating system developers to introduce new packages, features, and also to remove old outdated components. Typically, Fedora is a year or two ahead of the features found in Red Hat Enterprise Linux, which is the commercially supported long-term release based on the work done in the Fedora project; as well as this release, you also have the community support version in the form of CentOS.*

You may be thinking to yourself, *why has this only been mentioned right at the very end of the book?* Well, at the time of writing this, the project is still very much in its infancy. In fact, work is still ongoing to transition all of the components required for Moby Project from the main Docker projects.

The only real usable component of the project as I write this is `LinuxKit`, which is the framework that pulls together all of the libraries and outputs a bootable system that is capable of running containers.

Due the extremely fast pace of the project, I am not going to give any examples on how to use `LinuxKit` or go into any more detail about Moby Project as it is likely to change by the time you read this; instead, I would recommend bookmarking the following pages to keep up to date with this exciting development:

- The project's main website at `https://mobyproject.org/`
- `Moby Project GitHub pages at https://github.com/moby/`
- The Moby Project Twitter account, a good source of news and links to how-to's at `https://twitter.com/moby/`
- The home of LinuxKit, which contains examples and instructions on how to get started at `https://github.com/linuxkit/`

Contributing to Docker

So you want to help contribute to Docker? Do you have a great idea that you would like to see in Docker or one of its components? Let's get you the information and tools that you need to do that. If you aren't a programmer-type person, there are other ways you can help contribute as well. Docker has a very massive audience and another way you can help contribute is to help with supporting other users with their services. Let's learn how you can do that as well.

Contributing to the code

One of the biggest ways you can contribute to Docker is helping with the Docker code. Since Docker is all open source, you can download the code to your local machine and work on new features and present them as pull requests back to Docker. They will then get reviewed on a regular basis and if they feel what you have contributed should be in the service, they will approve the pull request. This can be very humbling when it comes to knowing that something you have written has been accepted.

You first need to know how you can get set up to contribute: pretty much everything at the Docker (`https://github.com/docker/`) and Moby Project, which we spoke about in the previous section. But how do we go about getting set up to help contribute? The best place to start is by following the guide that can be found on the official Docker documentation at `https://docs.docker.com/project/who-written-for/`.

As you may have already guessed, you do not need much to get a development environment up and running as a lot of development is done within containers. For example, other than having a GitHub account, Docker list the following three pieces of software as the bare minimum:

- **Git**: `https://git-scm.com/`
- **Make**: `https://www.gnu.org/software/make/D`
- **Docker**: if you made it this far you shouldn't need a link

You can find more details on how to prepare your own Docker development for Mac and Linux at `https://docs.docker.com/opensource/project/software-required/` and for Windows users at `https://docs.docker.com/opensource/project/software-req-win/`.

To be a successful open source project, there have to be some community guidelines. I recommend reading through the excellent quickstart guide which can be found at `https://docs.docker.com/opensource/code/` as well the more detailed contribution workflow documentation at `https://docs.docker.com/opensource/workflow/make-a-contribution/`.

Docker are currently in the process of adopting a formal code of conduct; until that is in place, they ask that all contributors follow the contributor covenant, which is as follows:

> *As contributors and maintainers of this project, we pledge to respect all people who contribute through reporting issues, posting feature requests, updating documentation, submitting pull requests or patches, and other activities. We are committed to making participation in this project a harassment-free experience for everyone, regardless of level of experience, gender, gender identity and expression, sexual orientation, disability, personal appearance, body size, race, ethnicity, age, or religion.*

> *Examples of unacceptable behavior by participants include the use of sexual language or imagery, derogatory comments or personal attacks, trolling, public or private harassment, insults, or other unprofessional conduct. Project maintainers have the right and responsibility to remove, edit, or reject comments, commits, code, wiki edits, issues, and other contributions that are not aligned to this Code of Conduct. Project maintainers who do not follow the Code of Conduct may be removed from the project team.*

> *Instances of abusive, harassing, or otherwise unacceptable behavior may be reported by opening an issue or contacting one or more of the project maintainers. This Code of Conduct is adapted from the Contributor Covenant, version 1.0.0, available from* `http ://contributor-covenant.org/version/1/0/0/`.

Offering Docker support

You can also contribute to Docker by other means beyond contributing to the Docker code or feature sets. You can help by using the knowledge you have obtained to help others in their support channels. The community is very open and someone is always willing to help. I have found it of great help when I run into something that I come across and am found scratching my head. It's also nice to get help but also to contribute back to others then; a nice give and take. It also is a great place to harvest ideas for you to use. You can see what questions others are asking based on their setups and it could spur ideas that you may want to think about using in your environment.

You can also follow the GitHub issues that are brought up about the services. These could be feature requests and how Docker may implement them or they could be issues that have cropped up through the usage of services. You can help test out the issues that others are experiencing to see whether you can replicate the issue or whether you find a possible solution to their issue.

Docker has a very active community which can be found at `https://community.docker.com/`; here you will not only be able to see the latest community news and events, you will also be able to chat with Docker users and developers in their Slack channels. At the time of writing, there are over 80 channels covering all sorts of topics such as Docker for Mac, Docker for Windows, Alpine Linux, Swarm, Storage, and Network to name but a few, with hundreds of active users at any one time.

Finally, there are also the Docker forums, which can be found at `https://forums.docker.com/`. These are a good source if you want to search for topics/problems or keywords.

Other contributions

There are other ways to contribute to Docker as well. You can do things such as promoting the service and gathering interest at your institution. You can start the communication through your own organisation's means of communications, whether that be email distribution lists, group discussions, IT round tables, or regularly scheduled meetings. You can also schedule meetups within your organisation to get people talking. These meetups are designed to not only include your organisation but the city or town members that your organisation is in to get more widespread communication and promotion of the services. You can search whether there are already meetups in your area by visiting `https://www.docker.com/community/meetup-groups`.

Summary

In this chapter, we looked at how you can extend your application's awareness on the environment it is running by using service discovery tools.

For the most part, you may not need to go to this level of integration with your hosting platform. However, to truly ensure that your application has the least number of single points of failure, combining service discovery with technologies we discussed in previous chapters such as Docker Swarm should ensure that you are deploying your application on a highly available, self-healing, and production-ready platform.

We also took a brief look at how you can contribute to both Docker and Moby Projects either by contributing code, support, or just spreading the word on containerization.

Index